This book is for you are any of these:

- **bodybuilder**
- **fitness trainee**
- **strength trainee**
- **powerlifter**

The emphasis you place on weight training will vary according to your specific interest, and the degree of size and strength you desire. But the pool of the most effective exercises you can select from is universal to almost everyone who lifts weights.

When you lift weights, the bottom line is exactly the same no matter who you are, what your goals are, or where you train:

If you want your training to be successful, and not cause injuries, you must use excellent exercise form.

- Without excellent exercise technique, your physique, strength or fitness goals can never be achieved.

- Properly done, all weight-training activities are safe and hugely satisfying. But too few people experience the rewards of weight training—and largely because they use poor exercise form.

- The use of excellent exercise form is the exception in nearly all gyms, not the rule. Do not expect to learn first-class exercise technique from a gym.

In step-by-step detail this book will teach you precisely how to use excellent exercise technique.

visit us online at www.**hardgainer.com**

What others are saying...

Here are some excerpts from a review by Dr. Gregory Steiner in the March 1999 issue of CONTACT, the Professional Journal of the British Chiropractic Association. Dr. Steiner was specifically addressing chiropractors, but because the book is strongly recommended for chiropractors and their patients, it is also strongly recommend for *anyone* who lifts weights. In fact, by following the advice of this book, you should *never* sustain a serious training-related injury, and thus never need to be treated for one.

"Here is a book for any chiropractor or patient who ever touches a barbell — and wants to train injury-free for his or her entire life. The focus of the well-written, safety-first THE INSIDER'S TELL-ALL HANDBOOK ON WEIGHT-TRAINING TECHNIQUE *is to contribute to the booming world of fitness by clearly explaining to the weight trainee how and why to perform useful, effective exercises in a cartilage, ligament and tendon friendly way. The author does all of this in a motivating style.*

"As a clinician for eight years, and exercise fanatic for twenty, I have been pleased to come across this book, and have recommended it in the strongest terms to my patients who train with weights. The book has added value because it reads well for beginners and even for experienced trainers who need fine-tuning in performance form.

"All major exercises are detailed, and even more importantly, techniques for training the rotator cuff, neck, wrists and fingers are included, along with the 'reverse back extension' for the glutes and paravertebrals.

"According to McRobert, when referring to exercise technique: 'Make no compromises, ever!'"

———

And here is just one comment from the great many received from readers of the first edition of this book. This comment is very typical, and reflects what thousands of people have discovered.

"I've been lifting weights for most of my life now. I'm no novice. So I was blown away when I realized, after reading your book, how much I DIDN'T *know about proper exercise form. I can't recommend this book enough."*

– John Leschinski, Connell, Washington

The Insider's Tell-All Handbook On
Weight-Training Technique

244 PHOTOS

THE ILLUSTRATED STEP-BY-STEP GUIDE TO PERFECTING YOUR EXERCISE FORM FOR INJURY-FREE MAXIMUM GAINS

2ND EDITION

CS PUBLISHING LTD
NICOSIA, CYPRUS

Stuart McRobert

COMMON SENSE PUBLISHING

Published by CS Publishing Ltd., P.O. Box 20390, CY-2151 Nicosia, Cyprus
tel + 357-233-3069   fax + 357-233-2018   e-mail: cspubltd@spidernet.com.cy
web site: www.hardgainer.com

US office: CS Publishing Ltd., P.O. Box 1002, Connell, WA 99326
tel 509-234-0362   fax 509-234-0601   web site: www.hardgainer.com

Photography by Mike Christofides at Gold's Gym, Nicosia, Cyprus
Cover illustration by Stephen Wedan copyright © 1998
Cover design by Mike Adamou Designs, and Nicholas Zavallis

Printed and bound by J. G. Cassoulides & Son Ltd., Nicosia, Cyprus
Second edition reprinted in 2001 and 2002 (with revisions), and 2003

Publisher's Cataloging-in-Publication
(Provided by Quality Books, Inc.)
McRobert, Stuart.
    The insider's tell-all handbook on
weight-training technique / Stuart McRobert. --
2nd ed.
    p. cm.
    Includes index.
    ISBN: 9963-616-09-7

    1. Weight training--Handbooks, manuals, etc.   I. Title

GV546.M37 1999   796.41
                                        QBI99-600

Contents

Preface to the Second Edition

Over the years following the publication of the first edition of this book, the stress I have placed on the use of safe exercises and impeccable exercise form has strengthened *even more*. The more experienced I become, and the more feedback I get from others, the more I emphasize appropriate and responsible exercise selection, and the use of perfect form.

The need for the instruction given in this book is, however, *even greater today* than it was when the first edition was published. Though weight training is even more popular today, the myths and harmful practices of conventional gym folklore are still reeking havoc and destroying the training aspirations of millions of trainees worldwide. Use this book to gain the knowledge you need in order to take charge over your exercise form. Without excellent form, and staying free of injuries, you will never be able to achieve your physique, strength and fitness goals.

Acknowledgments

What we have in the training world today we owe to the past. Nothing new is claimed in this book because it has all been done and taught before. But the fact that the information contained in this book has been around for decades is of no use to the training public of today if there is no ready access to that knowledge. The presentation of a wealth of detailed guidance on exercise technique in a single volume is what makes this book unique.

It is impossible to attribute specific technique tips to individuals because most of the tips, if not all of them, have long been practiced in some quarters. Even the people who today claim to be the originators of "new" tips are usually ignorant of the fact that men long-since dead came up with the original ideas ages ago.

Without the publicity arising from being published in newsstand bodybuilding magazines, the interchange with authors of HARDGAINER, and feedback from readers of my writing, this book could not exist. To all the publishers and editors, HARDGAINER authors, and countless readers, thank you very much.

I specifically want to thank John Christy, John Leschinski and Dave Maurice for providing valuable feedback during the writing of this book.

Special thanks are owed to Mike Christofides and Constantinos Demetriou for the photographs, and to Aris Hadjipanayi for making Gold's Gym in Nicosia available for the photography. These three men were cooperative and patient almost to a fault.

A debt of gratitude is owed to the workmanship of our printer, J. G. Cassoulides & Son, Ltd., to Mike Adamou and Nicholas Zavallis for the design of the cover and assistance with the presentation of the book, to Mangoian Brothers for printing the photographs, to the software of QuarkXPress® and WordPerfect®, to Carolyn Weaver for the index, and to John Leschinski for his guidance on product creation and business savvy.

Trademarks

Attention, please!
This second revised edition has all-new material starting on page 199, in addition to the many revisions, corrections and additions found throughout the rest of the book.

Introduction

Thank you for buying THE INSIDER'S TELL-ALL HANDBOOK ON WEIGHT-TRAINING TECHNIQUE. This book can save your training life and help you to build a superbly-muscled, strong and fit physique. Educate yourself with this book, apply what you learn, *do not overtrain*, and then you can look forward to being free of training-related injuries for your entire life. This is no advertising hype, and this book will prove it to you.

Successful bodybuilding, or any other type of weight training, is one of the most satisfying activities around. Transforming your body is a thrilling journey. But done *improperly*, training will damage your body. Training-related injuries are universal.

The same basic pool of exercises applies whether you are a bodybuilder, fitness enthusiast, strength trainee, or powerlifter. But to benefit from training you must be able to work out consistently and progressively. You cannot do this if you repeatedly suffer from injuries. Abuse yourself with poor exercise technique for long enough and you will be frustrated with one injury after another, and eventually do so much damage that you will put an end to your days of hard training.

Do not be discouraged by any of this. Take comfort from knowing that, properly done, weight training is very safe. This book will show you how to train safely.

Excellent exercise technique is needed not just to avoid training injuries. The use of first-class exercise form is one of the pivotal requirements for stimulating the fastest rate of muscular development and strength gains.

While there are many books around that attempt to give instruction on exercise technique, most of them place too much emphasis upon isolation exercises. When they do cover the major exercises there is often focus on distorting the safe forms in favor of potentially dangerous variations. And when the safest forms of the best exercises are covered, the treatment is so skimpy that critical information is left out.

This book will teach you the conservative forms of the most productive exercises. Without a conservative approach you will be racked with so many injuries that you will be unable to train consistently enough to achieve your goals. A few people have unusually strong joints and are able to get away with poor exercise technique. But for each trainee who gets away with poor technique there are hundreds who do not. Because this book only concerns itself with the conservative approach, you will not find descriptions in it of every exercise under the sun.

Some people's advice for how to deal with exercises that are irritating is to drop poundage and do much higher reps. While increasing rep count and reducing poundage is sometimes a desirable action, it is usually a mere salve because the root of the problem—poor exercise technique—has not been corrected. If flawed technique is being used, then once the poundages are built up and intensive work is delivered, the original problem that drove you to using high reps will resurface.

Any exercise performed at any number of reps will hurt you if you use poor technique and train intensively. But if you always use very good technique, then *all* rep counts should be safe. The critical qualification is that your body is accustomed to the rep count you are using *before* you start to push yourself very hard. This especially applies to singles (one-rep sets) and very low rep work (sets of 2–4 reps). Singles and very low reps have more potential for causing injuries than have higher reps. This is because the per-rep stress on joints, muscles and connective tissues is much greater from singles and very low rep work. Comparing the *same* degree of form error, if you get out of the ideal groove during a maximum single you are more likely to hurt yourself than if you get out of the groove during a hard set of medium or high reps. But this does not mean that high reps with reduced weights are guaranteed to be safe. Even with high reps and reduced weights, if you use poor technique and train intensively you will hurt yourself.

The education needed to write this book came from many sources. My own training experiences and a life consumed by weight training make up only a part of the education. The publishing and editing of HARDGAINER magazine since its inception in 1989 has given me a deep insight into weight training. The education was bolstered by feedback from readers of my books BRAWN and BEYOND BRAWN, a lot of writing for newsstand bodybuilding magazines, answering countless questions, providing many hours of personal hands-on coaching, and extensive studying of training in general. The gathering and dissemination of information about weight training is my full-time employment. This has put me in a privileged position. Much of the accumulated understanding of exercise technique was distilled for inclusion in this book.

This book can save you years if not decades of wasted training toil. You can learn a wealth of useful information from just a few days of serious study. You no longer have to learn the hard way—through pain and frustration—about what constitutes good exercise form and its central importance in your training.

This book is your constant reference on exercise technique. But it does not cover program design. I have covered program design in the book BEYOND BRAWN; and it is also covered in HARDGAINER magazine—from a multitude of view points.

To your training success,

Stuart McRobert
cspubltd@spidernet.com.cy
www.hardgainer.com

> **Properly done, weight training is safe and enormously satisfying. This book will show you how to train safely. It will make you the master of exercise technique, and take you a giant step towards achieving your physique, strength and fitness goals.**

Do not assume that, because you have been performing an exercise for a long time, you know its proper technique. Please study all of this book no matter how experienced you are.

Please do not treat this book as a one-time read. There is far more information in it than can be absorbed from a single reading. Repeatedly refer to the book throughout your training life. Then you will give yourself the opportunity to apply excellent exercise technique on a consistent basis.

Use this instruction manual like a workbook, e.g., highlight parts you want to stand out, and make notes in the margins. But only do this if the book is yours. If you borrowed this copy, order your own from the publisher.

Part 1
Building a secure foundation

Exercise selection

In short, and with few exceptions, the exercises that are excluded from this book are either dangerous, only of marginal value or no value, require machinery that is not commonly available, or are technically so demanding that expert *hands-on* coaching is needed to ensure good form. An area of exception is grip training. There are many fine exercises for training the grip but only a handful of the best ones have been included in this book.

If you cannot achieve your physique, strength or fitness goals by using the exercises described in this book, then using any other weight-training exercises will not improve your situation. In such a case it would not be the exercises that would be limiting you, but what you are doing with them, i.e., the program design, level of effort, and progression scheme you are using. There are no "magic" exercises that can yield benefits which the exercises described in this book cannot.

Do not try to include all the exercises from this book in a single training program. This book provides the *pool* of exercises from which you *select* in order to compose each training program you use.

Here are the major factors that were involved in the process of selecting the exercises to be detailed in this book.

Equipment considerations

Though a well-equipped gym was used for the photography that illustrates this book, such a gym is *not* a necessity for implementing the exercises. In a home-gym that has a barbell, plates, dumbbell handles, heavy-duty adjustable bench, and power rack, most of the exercises described in this book can be performed. It is not the equipment per se that counts, but what you *do* with it. If you know what you are doing,

a home-gym is an excellent place to train. It can even be superior to a commercial gym.

Exercises can be done with free weights (primarily long-bar barbells and short-bar dumbbells), or machines. The former are the traditional and most versatile way of training. When used properly they *are* safe, but require more skill than machines do.

Machines are good drawing cards for gyms, and convenient because they reduce the need for instruction. They also reduce the chance of acute injury because it is harder to lose control with a machine than free weights. The quality of machines varies greatly. Some are valuable if used properly, and a few are outstanding. Some are poor, and even dangerous, because they lock the user into a pathway that may not fit individual parameters such as height and limb lengths. Though the risk of acute injury is usually reduced in machine exercises, there's still a considerable chance of chronic injuries and irritations. (Of course, the same can be said of free-weight exercises if they aren't performed safely.) For home-gym trainees, machines are usually prohibitively expensive *and* require more space than is available.

A distinction needs to be made between machines that lock you into a fixed groove, and those which use cables that allow freedom of movement. A lat machine that uses a cable and an overhead pulley, for example, allows a lot of individual freedom of motion and positioning, but a pullover machine offers much less.

If you have machines at hand that can be excellent for many if not most users, e.g., Cybex®, Hammer Strength®, MedX®, Nautilus® and the Tru-Squat®, experiment with them. Few people have that sort of gear available, hence why the focus in this book is on exercises that use free weights.

Equipment other than the basics usually serves to divert attention from where most application should be given. When presented with many different pieces of gear, trainees nearly always get confused and lose sight of training priorities.

The advantage of a well-equipped gym is that it is likely to have a power rack, squat rack and other important basic items, and maybe some of the better pieces of machinery. Ironically, the well-equipped gym with its many sources of potential distraction and confusion may be your best bet for equipment because in amongst its abundance of gear is what you really need.

Some outstanding but relatively inexpensive equipment is promoted in this book, e.g., Trap Bar, cambered bar, thick bars, parallel-grip shoulder-width bar for the pulldown and cable row, little discs, grip machine and some other specific items for training the grip. This gear is rarely found, even in well-equipped gyms. Try to persuade the management of where you train to invest in this equipment, or buy some it yourself and trade it for membership fees, or consider investing in your own home-gym. A few suppliers of some of this gear are listed in *Resources*, on page 209. You can even get the more simple of these pieces of equipment made by a local metal worker, even one who has no prior experience of making exercise gear.

No mania for isolation exercises

Never forget the central aim of body*building* and strength training: progressive poundages in good form for plenty of reps. This applies to all exercises, but especially the big multi-joint ones. Generally speaking, if you are not getting stronger in the multi-joint exercises, your training is not working well.

Even fitness trainees should employ compound exercises as the spine of their programs. The multi-joint exercises deliver the biggest payback per training minute.

A few trainees gain well despite including *many* popular isolation (i.e., single-joint) exercises such as leg extensions, leg curls, laterals, pec deck work, triceps kickbacks, and cable crossovers. (Of these, the leg curl is the most valuable, though not included in this book.) Unless you are one of their number and are gaining well without any joint irritation, do not copy their example. But even these easy gainers would probably progress quicker if they dropped much of the isolation work and focused more on the big compound movements.

A lot of isolation work usually is needed by competition-level bodybuilders who are *already* very big and strong, and who want to add "spit and polish" to their physiques. But what is needed by fewer than 1% of those who lift weights should be of no concern to the other 99+%. Countless trainees like to think they are more advanced than they really are, to try to justify imitating the routines of the top competitive bodybuilders. But they are fooling themselves, and as a result experience minimal or zero progress.

An emphasis on specific isolation work is often needed during rehabilitation following an injury or accident. This book does not, however, deal with the specific needs of rehabilitation work.

Though the multi-joint/compound exercises occupy the most space in this book, important isolation exercises have been included too. These are needed to develop the balanced muscular strength necessary to help keep you injury free and able to benefit from the big compound exercises. *The BEST approach for most people for most of the time is a prudent mixture of both multi- AND single-joint movements, using PERFECT form for both groups.*

Groups of excluded exercises

Here are three specific groups of exercises that are not included in this book:

❑ Exercises that are technically very difficult to perform and which require expert *hands-on* coaching, e.g., Olympic weightlifting, power clean, and old-time lifts. Some of these exercises, even if performed with good technique, can eventually cause serious injuries.

❑ Traditional bodybuilding exercises that are potentially very dangerous for most people, e.g., barbell row, T-bar row, press behind neck, machine hack squat, upright row, good morning, "sissy" squat, Smith machine squat, "French" press variations for the triceps, lunges, and many machine movements. Exercises in this category are usually tied in with the "dangerous training dogma" described below.

❑ "Special" exercises (or variants) touted by some people but which yield benefits only for a very limited number of trainees. While beneficial for a few people, some "special" exercises have the potential to cripple everyone else. You will not find those exercises in this book.

Dangerous training dogma

One of the most dangerous principles behind modern bodybuilding in particular, and the training world in general, is the strategy of trying to build a physique as a collection of many small individual parts; not just specific body parts, but specific aspects of each part. Because this strategy causes so much frustration and injury, it has not been subscribed to in this book.

The "lots of pieces" approach does work for the small minority of people who have very responsive bodies and unusually robust joints, but it does not work for the great majority of trainees. This book is targeted at all weight trainees, not just a small minority of them. Very young adults may appear to be able to perform many hostile exercises without apparent damage, but the joint trauma accumulates and in time will take its toll.

Of course there are many body parts that make up the whole physique, and at least some of them do need to be worked individually; but to break up these parts into sub parts and get overly concerned with specifically training them bit by bit, is what leads to so much trouble.

In the "lots of pieces" approach, many exercises are distorted from their orthodox safe forms into dangerous forms. For example, the squat done in good form is a safe exercise for most people. But many people do it with a board under their heels in order to try to focus more of the stress onto the lower part of their thighs, instead of directing the stress evenly over the whole involved musculature. The price of this distortion is increased stress on the knees. Sooner or later this causes knee problems for most people. A similar negative comment can be made for "sissy" squats, and squats using the hack machine and Smith machine.

Another example is doing bench presses to the upper chest. Even if this did work the pectorals more than in a conventional bench press pathway, it would do it at a cost of greatly increased shoulder stress. This will cause shoulder problems.

A further example is performing the barbell curl with different width grips. Wide and close grips are thought to have different developmental effects on the biceps. Even if there is something to this, you will soon cause so much trauma to your elbow joints that you will be unable to do any form of curl without elbow discomfort or pain.

While the specificity of focus of different interpretations of the same exercise may be achieved to some extent, at least in some exercises, it is at the cost of the involved joint(s). If you damage your joints you will be unable to use the safe forms of exercises, let alone the hostile ones.

But much of the specificity of different interpretations of the same exercise, for targeting individual aspects of a given muscle group, is bodybuilding hokum—it either does not deliver what the gym rhetoric says it will, or the effect is only very minimal. Thus you get increased joint stress but for little or no benefit.

Stick to the safe forms of exercises as given in this book, protect your joints, and then you will be able to train consistently over the long term. Being able to train consistently over the long term should be your priority, because without being able to do so you will never achieve your physique, strength or fitness goals. Damaging one or more of your joints will not help you. Understand this *before* you actually damage your body. Do not learn the hard way.

There is another major shortcoming of the "lots of pieces" approach to weight training. It necessitates the inclusion of a lot of isolation exercises in a training program in order to work all the "pieces." Such a volume of training is beyond the limits of most trainees' recovery abilities. The result of this is overtraining, perhaps *along with* excessive stress on the joints. So, for most users, not only does the "lots of pieces" approach not deliver the expected physique, it will eventually damage the body and thus seriously threaten any type of serious training thereafter.

Need for individualization

One person's selection of a safe, enjoyable and productive core group of exercises may be different from another's. This is why many exercises and variations are described in this book. Do not get locked into a group of exercises just because it is the group that

you hear about most often. There is much more to a core of good exercises than, for example, the barbell squat, bench press and deadlift, though these exercises produce fine returns for people who *do them properly*. EITHER DO THEM PROPERLY, OR NOT AT ALL.

Whichever exercises you choose, you must perform them *safely* and enjoy them despite the demands of hard work. If you do not enjoy the exercises you do, you are unlikely to give your all to them.

Not everyone can perform each major exercise safely, even when using textbook safe form. While you should learn as much as possible about orthodox safe form, there comes a time, at least for most people some of the time, when ideals cannot be realized in practice. In these cases you *must* modify and personalize an exercise to ensure that it is safe for you. If you cannot do that, you need to find an alternative exercise. *How to individualize exercise performance is an important feature of this book.*

Back "rounding" and "arching"
When the back is rounded, the shoulders slump forward, the lower back is flattened, and the natural and strong inward curve is lost. When the inward curve in the lower back is restored—through MODERATE arching of the back—the shoulders are pulled to the rear, the back is no longer rounded, and a strong lower back is preserved. But DO NOT exaggerate the inward curve.

Exercise technique needs to be covered in detail if you are to grasp what good form is. A mere few bullet-headed points will not do. Exercise technique is too serious a matter to be treated skimpily.

Exercise form and injuries

Training injuries come from at least three main sources—bad exercises, overtraining, and good exercises done in poor form. Descriptions of the bad exercises have been excluded from this book, and overtraining comes from poor program design. Program design is not in the scope of this book. This book's concern is with teaching you how to do the good exercises in perfect form.

Once you have studied the book you will realize how universal poor exercise form is. Then you will quickly see why injuries are so widespread.

For example, consider the shoulders. From reading this book you will come across many technique flaws that put excessive stress on the shoulders, e.g., the wrong bar pathway for the bench press, excessively deep dips, pulldowns to the rear of the neck, presses behind the neck, not keeping tight shoulders at the arms-extended position in back work, and slamming into lockouts of pressing movements. All these flaws are probably common practices in all gyms of the world. These flaws alone are enough to give anyone shoulder problems, sooner or later.

And when you add the bad exercises that are also commonly done, e.g., close-grip upright row, and the deep pec fly, then a bad situation becomes even worse. Then factor in gross overtraining of the shoulders, and it should be no surprise that almost every weight trainee of experience has shoulder problems.

Once you have studied this book you will be able to compile a list of common form defects that contributes to each of the other universal training-related problem areas—the knees, lower back and elbows.

Stick to the safe forms of exercises as given in this book, protect your joints, and then you will be able to train consistently over the long term. Being able to train over the long term should be your priority, because without being able to do so you will never achieve your physique, strength or fitness goals.

Rep speed

Elite bodybuilders, lifters and athletes can tolerate and even prosper on explosive training *because they have the required robustness of joints and connective tissue*. But even they often pay a heavy price in terms of injuries, *eventually*. There is absolutely no need to take any risk with explosive training. A slower and controlled rep tempo is so much safer, and by far the best option for typical trainees. Why seriously risk pushing your body beyond its structural limits, and possibly suffering permanent injuries, when there is a safer way to train that is super productive?

Rather than try to find the "ideal" rep speed, focus on keeping each rep *smooth*, and totally free of explosive or sudden movements. In practice, however, "smooth" reps take about 3 seconds for each negative phase, and 2–3 seconds for each positive phase—and perhaps even longer for the positive phase at the end of a set when the reps grind to a near halt. "Long stroke" exercises require more time than "short stroke" ones.

Critical general factors

In alphabetical order, here are sixteen critical points that apply to all exercises:

1. Adapting to exercises

Never move directly into intensive training on an exercise you are not used to. Take at least 4–6 weeks to learn the form and build up the weights before you start to train that exercise intensively.

If you have a lot of experience with an exercise but have not included it in your program for a few months, take a few weeks to refamiliarize yourself with it before you go full bore at it.

Successful weight training is about *progressive resistance*. That means increasing poundage and intensity in *gradual* steps which you can adapt to. Especially when you are training intensively, the use of very small weight plates—those lighter than 2.5 lbs or 1.25 kgs—is vital for ensuring that progressive resistance occurs gradually.

2. Breathing

Holding your breath during the hard (or positive) stage of a rep in a big exercise may cause blackouts, especially if you are not used to intensive training. Even if just for a split second, a loss of consciousness could cause a calamity if you were bench pressing, squatting, or pressing. Though you may never suffer blackouts or dizziness, headaches are a common result of breath holding during intensive training.

Especially in the big exercises, exhale during the positive phase of each rep. It does not have to be an explosive expulsion, but exhaling in an explosive way can help to get the bar through a sticking point. *Keeping your mouth open stops breath holding.*

During demanding exercise you will not be able to get enough air through your nose alone. Breathe through your mouth.

3. Concentration

Be 100% focused while you train—always. Never be casual. And never talk during a set, or pay attention to what anyone is saying other than a spotter who may be giving you technique reminders. Training is a serious matter. Even a slight loss of focus leads to a loss of form, and risks injury.

Many injuries occur because the subject has ignored his better judgement and given in to bravado. Do not try something you know you are not ready for, and do not try another rep when your form has already started to break down. Never go heavy in an exercise you are not familiar with or have not done for a long time. Do not adopt the attitude, "It won't happen to me," because, sooner or later, it will. Ignore people who encourage you to try something that you know is risky. They will not have to live with the consequences of a moment of foolishness, but you will.

4. Control

Lift the weight, do not throw it; and lower the bar, do not drop it. Most people lift and lower too fast. When doing the exercises described in this book you should be able to stop each at any point, hold the weight briefly, and then continue. In an intensive set you will probably not be able to pause *and* get your target reps, depending on which rep you paused. The idea is that you *could* pause as a demonstration of control. Perform the "pause test" every week in each exercise, to check your control.

The more difficult it is to perform a rep, the more critical it is that you pay attention to the negative (or lowering) portion of the rep. If you lower the bar slightly out of the groove, you will be out of the groove on the positive (or lifting) portion too, and risk missing the rep and/or hurting yourself.

5. Equipment safety

Do not use equipment that may let you down. Check that bolts are tight, cables are not frayed, cable connections are secure, collars are locked in place, rack pins are securely in position, adjustable weight saddles are rigidly fixed in place, locking pin(s) for adjustable benches are secure, and benches are stable and strong.

6. Flexibility

While most exercises do not call for anything other than an average level of flexibility, a few exercises call for better-than-average flexibility. Perhaps the most striking examples are the squat and deadlift. If you have tight Achilles tendons, hamstrings, thigh adductor muscles, and glutes, it will be impossible for you to squat or deadlift in good form.

In the squat, if you are inflexible in your hamstrings, thigh adductors, and glutes, you will round your lower back as you descend, lean forward excessively, and be in danger of toppling over. Back injuries will be inevitable as soon as you squat with some effort. If your Achilles tendons are tight, your heels will not stay flat on the floor. And if you are inflexible in your shoulders and pectorals you will have trouble holding the bar over your shoulders with clenched hands. No matter how good or bad your leverages are for squatting, a flexible body will go a long way to improve your squatting form.

Stretching is not advocated here as a response to a fad. Developing and then maintaining a flexible body matters a great deal. It should become a lifetime habit. The older you become, the more important stretching becomes.

If currently you are tight and inflexible, especially in your lower body, a careful, progressive and systematic stretching routine on alternate days is needed for 4–6 weeks, to loosen you up. Only then will you be able to adopt the proper form in those exercises that demand a better-than-average degree of flexibility. A program of stretches is given in this book.

7. Footwear

Shoes with thick and spongy soles and heels may be fine for some activities, but not for weight training. A spongy base will not keep your feet solidly in position in your shoes. Especially when you are squatting, deadlifting or overhead pressing, if your feet move just a little, then the rest of your body will move too. It does not have to be much movement to throw you out of the correct exercise groove.

Function comes first in the gym. Get yourself a solid and sturdy pair of shoes with a good grip, arch support and no more than the standard height of heel. Worn shoes can lead to deviations in exercise form, so discard shoes that have unevenly or excessively worn soles or heels. And when you train, always keep your laces tied tightly.

Please also see the box on page 23.

8. Head and eye control

An important factor behind symmetrical lifting is the maintenance of a fixed face-forward head position, and keeping your eyes riveted on one spot during a set. Except for some neck exercises, avoid lateral movement of your head when you train with weights.

9. Pain avoidance

Never do an exercise that hurts you. Muscular discomfort and systemic fatigue from an exercise done intensively and in good form is desirable, but pain is another matter. Some people have been led to believe that they "must" do certain exercises even if those exercises hurt. The macho maxim "No pain, no gain" has done untold damage in the training world. But if it is poor form that is responsible for the pain—and it usually is—then learn about good form, apply it, and there should be no further pain.

> **Do not include all the exercises from this book in a single training program. This book provides the pool of exercises from which you SELECT in order to compose each training program you use.**

10. Preparation for each set

Check that the poundage you have loaded is what you actually want—consult your training log. Then add up the total of the plates and bar to check that you have actually loaded what you think you have. It is quite easy to load a barbell, dumbbell or machine incorrectly. Leave no room for errors that could ruin a set.

If you do not use calibrated weight plates, set some time aside soon to weigh all the plates you use. They may not actually weigh what they are supposed to.

Before a set, review the correct exercise technique that you need to use. Then when you get in position for a set, pay attention to ensure that you adopt the right grip, stance and body position. Do not charge into a set, grab the bar and then realize after the first rep that you took an imbalanced grip, the wrong stance, or are lopsided while on a bench. Take the necessary time, be conscientious, and get positioned correctly for every set you do. Mentally go through a few reps and establish that everything is in perfect order before you take the bar and start the set.

11. Range of motion

While making an exercise harder usually makes it better, there are many exceptions. Increasing the depth of squatting and

deadlifting, for example, makes those exercises harder, but for some people that "harder" means harmful, if not ruinous. Use as full a range of motion as possible, so long as it does not hurt you.

12. Spotting

Spotting, i.e., help from one or more assistants, can come from a training partner or from anyone who is in the gym at the time and who is willing and able to spot you. While trainees working out solo at home are not going to have a spotter, everyone training at a public gym can usually get a spotter when needed.

Good spotting helps your training in three important ways:

❑ To assist you with lifting the weight when you can lift it no further, e.g., when the bar stalls during a bench press ascent.

❑ To provide the minimum assistance to ensure that the last rep of a set is done in good form. In this case, you probably could get the rep out under your own power but your form would break down. Consider the last rep of a set of bench presses when one hand gets slightly above the other, and you feel like increasing the arch in your back in order to get that rep out. This is a dangerous situation. A spotter can make the difference between safety and injury.

❑ During a set you may forget a key point of form. A spotter can alert you to key form pointers while ensuring that you put forth maximum effort. You need excellent exercise form *and* intensity of effort.

The spotter must have an alert eye and be ready at all times of a set. He should spot with an arched lower back, not a rounded back—the spotter must be safety conscious and use good lifting form himself. He should be particularly alert when the lifter begins to struggle and good form starts to break down. An alert, serious and strong spotter should especially be present for squatting, bench pressing, and pressing, including all dumbbell pressing.

For effective spotting, the help must be applied with two hands in a balanced way. For example, spotting the bench press by putting one hand under the center of the bar will lead to the bar tipping, as will using two hands but not applying them to the bar symmetrically.

After an assisted rep, the trainee is going to be very fatigued. The spotter must help the lifter to return the bar to the weight saddles at the end of a set.

If two spotters are involved, there must be excellent communication. Take the squat as an example. If there is not excellent communication, one spotter could take one end before the other spotter grabs his end of the bar. If one spotter shouts "Take it!" then the other must respond even if he thinks the assistance could have been delayed a little.

13. Surface to train on

Lifting on a wooden or rubber surface, preferably one that does not have concrete directly underneath it, is much better than training directly on concrete. Wood and rubber "give" whereas concrete does not. Wood and rubber reduce the amount of "giving" that your joints and connective tissues have to tolerate.

Before starting any set of any exercise you must have your feet planted securely. Wherever you place your feet be sure it is on a non-slip surface. Having a foot slip out of position as you train can be dangerous. Wearing shoes that have a good grip is critical.

14. Symmetrical lifting

Other than for one-sided exercises such as side bends and one-legged calf raises, you must focus on symmetrical form. Losing the groove and making an exercise even just slightly asymmetrical greatly increases the risk of injury, e.g., taking more of the stress on one side of your body than the other during the squat or bench press.

Do not let the bar slope to one side during barbell work. Keep it level at all times. Both hands must move in perfect unison, in both the horizontal *and* vertical planes. For example, in barbell pressing, one hand should neither be above nor in front of the other. For standing and seated exercises, the use of a mirror will help you to find and correct asymmetrical form.

A critical factor behind symmetrical lifting is perfect hand and foot positioning. If one hand is placed farther from the center of the bar than the other hand, or if one foot is positioned differently to the other, you will have set yourself up for asymmetrical lifting.

Before any set, as noted earlier, check that you have loaded the bar correctly. If you loaded one end of the bar with more weight than the other, you will inevitably lift asymmetrically. A substantial weight difference will be noticeable during the first rep of a set. Then the bar can be set down or racked, and the loading corrected. A bar that is only slightly lopsided may not be detectable as such and will lead to asymmetrical lifting and perhaps injury.

If you lift on a surface that is not perfectly horizontal, it is certain you will lift asymmetrically. Train on a level floor.

15. Warming up, keeping warm

Before any intensive training, you need a general low-intensity warmup for about 5 minutes that breaks you into a sweat, e.g., stationary cycling. And before intensive work on any individual weight-training

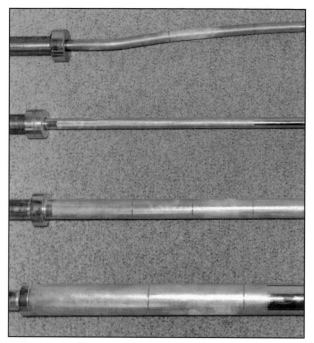

A comparison of four different long bars referred to in the course of this book. From the top: cambered squat bar, standard Olympic bar, 2"-diameter bar, and 3"-diameter bar.

exercise, do 1–3 sets of warmup work. The heavier the exercise, the more warmup sets you should do. Performing the "pause test" (see *Control*, page 17) during each warmup set will remind you of good control.

Unless the temperature is high, keep yourself well covered as you train, especially between sets, and avoid drafts.

16. Weight selection

Most trainees use more weight than they can handle correctly. This leads to "cheating" and a loss of control. When learning how to use good form you must use comfortable weights, not demanding ones. But once you can apply perfect form, use a weight for a given work set that lets you *just* squeeze out your target reps in good form. (Work sets are the intensive non-warmup sets in your program.) For warmup sets, use lighter weights.

Initially you will almost certainly need to reduce the weights you use in your work sets, relative to the poundages you were employing prior to the change to using perfect form. But by using good form, and training intensively, you will deliver the primary requirements needed for building the strength to take you way beyond where you were when you used inferior form.

Special note on hands

Your hands have a big strength potential. But few people get even close to achieving the strength potential of their hands and forearms because they rely on grip crutches and fail to train their hands properly.

Do not use gloves, wrist straps, or hooks that attach you to a bar. If you use grip supports you will eventually end up with underdeveloped hands on a well-developed body. You cannot lengthen your hands, but you can thicken them. As your grip strength increases, so will the muscle and connective tissue of your hands.

Appreciate the skin-on-metal contact of weight training, and the increased mental focus it provides. Toughen your hands with support-free training and use chalk as your only gripping aid.

Train your hands with the grip and forearm work described in this book. Be persistent and you will develop a pair of very strong hands. If you get any *excessive* build up of calluses, control it by weekly use of a pumice stone after a shower.

Physical self-knowledge

Many common and not-so-common conditions can greatly influence how well you will tolerate certain exercises or specific variations of them. What may be safe for most people may be unsafe for you. Knowing your body well will help you to train with safety uppermost in your mind. Always remember that you cannot make any gains in the gym if you are injured and unable to train hard.

Many people go through life knowing little or nothing about their physical irregularities, until they get injured. Conditions including scoliosis, arms or legs that are different in length, excessive lordosis, postural problems, spondylolysis, and flexion imbalances between one side of the body and the other, can all influence the exercises you select or avoid in the gym, and how specifically you perform them. Some physical irregularities may be correctable, or at least treatable so that their negative effects can be lessened.

Get a thorough understanding of your physical structure and biomechanics, especially as it influences training. Do this *before* you get an injury that may force you to discover your physical irregularities. To do this, locate a chiropractor, ideally one who specializes in sports injuries. Look for the Certified Chiropractic Sports Physician qualification (CCSP). Some experienced osteopaths and physiotherapists can also provide excellent service. To try to ensure that the person you consult is competent, check that he is registered with your country's appropriate national association.

In addition, consult a foot specialist such as a podiatrist. Foot problems such as flat feet or bunions can seriously affect squatting and deadlifting form. A foot specialist may be able to help you to reduce if not eliminate the negative impact of a foot problem on your exercise form.

The emphasis is upon getting advice from an expert in biomechanics and manipulative therapy who is familiar with weight training, or at least sympathetic to it. Ideally, the professional you consult should be a trainee himself and know the weight-training movements, or at least he should be willing to learn them from you. He should then be able to help you to determine the exercises or specific variations of them that are not well suited to your individual structure, and which need to be used with special caution, or perhaps even avoided.

Of course, any skilled physical therapist should be able to help you with most injuries, and greatly speed up recovery time should you get injured. For example, skilled chiropractic adjustment, used appropriately, may make you believe in miracles. But recovering from injury is not enough. You need to make the right decisions about exercise selection and technique to prevent the injuries from recurring. This is why you need to know your own body very well, *and* use excellent exercise technique.

Within practical constraints, seek the best possible sports-minded expert in biomechanics, manipulative therapy, and injuries. You may need more than one person to cover all these areas. By doing this you will add life to your training years, and years to your training life.

Body parts

Exercises target specific body parts, or muscle groups. In a simplified format, here are the main body parts:

- ❑ calves—gastrocnemius and soleus

- ❑ thighs—quads or quadriceps on the front, hams or hamstrings on the rear, and the thigh adductors

- ❑ buttocks or glutes—glutei muscles of the hips

- ❑ abdominals (abs) and obliques—muscles on the front and sides of the midsection

- ❑ erectors of the back—columns of muscle on either side of the spine

- ❑ lats—latissimus dorsi muscles on the back under the arms

- ❑ upper back—small muscles around the shoulder blades, and the large kite-shaped trapezius which covers much of the upper back and slopes into the neck

- ❑ shoulders—deltoids, or delts

- ❑ neck

- ❑ chest—pectorals, or pecs

- ❑ triceps—rear of the upper arm

- ❑ biceps and brachialis—front of the upper arm

- ❑ forearms

The following anatomy charts show the muscles of the body in detail. The muscle groups have been divided into their constituent parts.

Problems from training with bare feet

I used to train bare foot—in my own home gym—*but no longer*. I did it because I wanted to squat without any heel elevation, and couldn't find suitable shoes—e.g., see page 204.

Feet are *highly* complex structures. Foot defects are very common, and a defect affects how stresses placed on the feet are borne by the feet *and* the rest of the body. When forces on the feet are exaggerated by high-load activities such as heavy weight training, and running, the defects are magnified. While foot defects might not be the whole story behind foot, ankle, knee or back problems, they are contributing factors, perhaps major ones.

I recommend high quality shoes with molded internal soles, to compensate for any structural or postural instability in the feet, *or*, in the case of defect-free feet, to *maintain* that existing good condition over the *long term*. While orthopedic shoes with *custom-made* molded internal soles are the ideal, off-the-shelf shoes with molded internal soles are, in most cases, light years ahead of no support. You can get molded internal soles that can be slipped inside your regular footwear (but you may need to remove some of the existing soles to make room).

A change in footwear, or the insertion of high-quality molded soles into your existing footwear, will help greatly to keep you lifting intensively, heavily and free of injuries.

I recommend you consult a podiatrist, preferably a sports podiatrist, or a chiropractor with training in orthotics, to get your feet checked out.

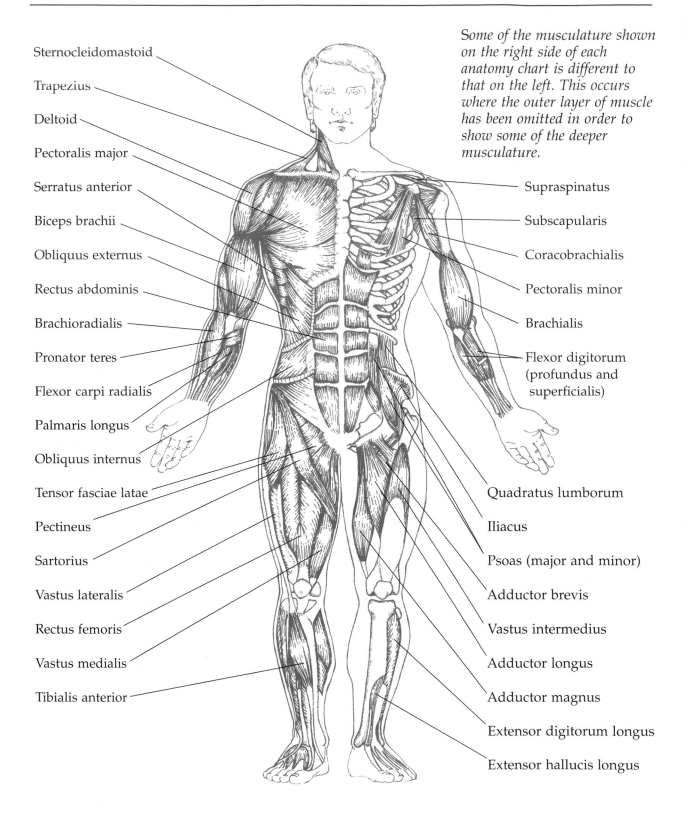

Some of the musculature shown on the right side of each anatomy chart is different to that on the left. This occurs where the outer layer of muscle has been omitted in order to show some of the deeper musculature.

Sternocleidomastoid

Trapezius

Deltoid

Pectoralis major

Serratus anterior

Biceps brachii

Obliquus externus

Rectus abdominis

Brachioradialis

Pronator teres

Flexor carpi radialis

Palmaris longus

Obliquus internus

Tensor fasciae latae

Pectineus

Sartorius

Vastus lateralis

Rectus femoris

Vastus medialis

Tibialis anterior

Supraspinatus

Subscapularis

Coracobrachialis

Pectoralis minor

Brachialis

Flexor digitorum (profundus and superficialis)

Quadratus lumborum

Iliacus

Psoas (major and minor)

Adductor brevis

Vastus intermedius

Adductor longus

Adductor magnus

Extensor digitorum longus

Extensor hallucis longus

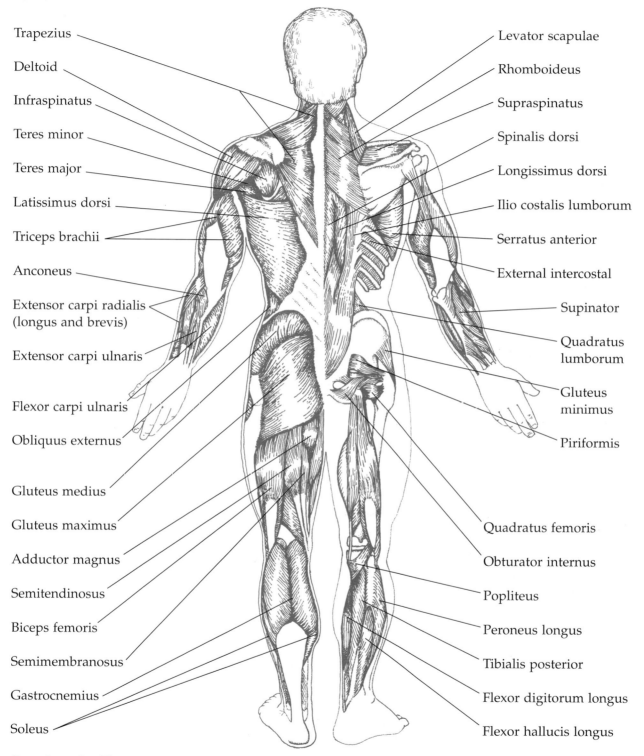

Trapezius

Deltoid

Infraspinatus

Teres minor

Teres major

Latissimus dorsi

Triceps brachii

Anconeus

Extensor carpi radialis
(longus and brevis)

Extensor carpi ulnaris

Flexor carpi ulnaris

Obliquus externus

Gluteus medius

Gluteus maximus

Adductor magnus

Semitendinosus

Biceps femoris

Semimembranosus

Gastrocnemius

Soleus

Levator scapulae

Rhomboideus

Supraspinatus

Spinalis dorsi

Longissimus dorsi

Ilio costalis lumborum

Serratus anterior

External intercostal

Supinator

Quadratus
lumborum

Gluteus
minimus

Piriformis

Quadratus femoris

Obturator internus

Popliteus

Peroneus longus

Tibialis posterior

Flexor digitorum longus

Flexor hallucis longus

Drawings by Eleni Lambrou based on the complex ones of Chartex Products, England.

Adapting to superior form

It is impossible to learn improved form at a stroke and immediately apply it to your usual working poundages. You must first practice the improved form using light weights for several workouts, and then progressively build your poundages back to where they used to be. How much time you will need to do this largely depends on how many bad habits you have to "unlearn." If your current form is in a mess, then you will need to reduce your weights substantially and take several months to build the poundages back.

Be patient. Most people who learn of improved form immediately want to apply it to their usual weights. Then because they cannot maintain the new form with those weights they immediately return to their old inferior form. To implement an overhaul of your exercise form, take a temporary break from full-bore training. Start a new training cycle, reduce all your poundages, practice the new form with light weights, and then gradually build the weights back. *Be religiously uncompromising about using perfect form.*

Once you have built your weights back to your best inferior-form level, but while now using perfect form, you will probably have to settle for a slower rate of progression. Use *small* weight increments and *only* when you have truly earned them. This is one of the most important rules for safe and effective weight training. If you rush to add weight, like most people do, you will ruin your exercise form.

If, once you know what good form is, you apply it without exception to every rep of each set you do, then you will use good form indefinitely. But if you relax just a bit here and just a bit there, then before you know it you will be back to where you started, with all the accompanying aches, pains, injuries and frustration. *Make no compromises, ever!*

> **Resolving to learn and then apply good exercise technique may be the most important decision you ever make in your training.**

Some general tips for handling weights

Even strong trainees can easily injure themselves while handling weights when getting into position for an exercise, or returning the weights after an exercise. If, for example, you lift a barbell loaded with small diameter plates from off the floor, or heavy dumbbells from off the floor, the increased range of motion relative to what you are conditioned for, together with perhaps not keeping a flat back, can injure you. Instead, for example, take dumbbells from a rack or stand; and return dumbbells to a stand/rack after an exercise rather than put them on the floor. Lifting with a rounded back can cause injury even when light weights are involved.

Always apply good lifting mechanics that preserve a flat back, in and out of the gym, and don't be shy about getting help to move a heavy or awkward object.

Avoid carrying a single heavy dumbbell in one hand, as that produces skewed and asymmetrical stress that can easily trigger injury.

Prelude to the exercises

The exercises are presented in alphabetical order. Those that are the most technically demanding are covered in the most detail. The other exercises are simpler to perform and thus need much less description.

The squat, deadlift and bench press are covered in extensive detail. This is not because they are the three powerlifts, but because they have the potential to be wonderfully productive exercises for most people. But for any exercise to do you good and no harm, it must be consistently performed with good technique.

Exercise technique is not a simple matter. There is much to learn and practice before you can master the "groove" of each exercise. You need to invest a lot of time.

Chalk

The chalk that is used in the gym is magnesium carbonate. Properly used, it helps a lot to ensure a secure grip.

Use chalk everywhere you need the help, especially in back exercises, upper-body pressing movements, and specialized grip work. Where it is especially needed, the use of chalk will be stressed in the exercise descriptions that follow.

Get some chalk from an outdoor goods store that sells mountaineering gear, or from a general sporting goods store. To use chalk, firmly rub a piece on your fingers and palms, including the inside area of your thumb and index finger. Rub your hands together and then blow off the excess, if there is any. Be careful where you blow any excess chalk. Keep it away from your face or else the dust may impair your breathing or get in your eyes.

Clean the knurled parts of your bar(s) with a stiff brush every few weeks, depending on use, to prevent clogging of the knurling.

Different grips
Please see page 81 for illustrations and explanations of the different grips referred to in this book—pronated, supinated, parallel and mixed/reverse.

Critical note
Photos alone cannot explain good exercise form. Please do not skip any of the text. Study it all very carefully.

Trap bar and shrug bar
Where the trap bar is referred to in this book, you may also read "shrug bar." The shrug bar came onto the market several years after the initial writing of this book. The two bars are produced by different manufacturers. Both are excellent training tools, with the shrug bar having a hexagonal shape as against the trap bar's rhombus. The shrug bar provides more knee room. See page 209 for suppliers.

The standard spacing for the gripping sites, on either the shrug bar or trap bar, may not suit you. Discuss your needs with the manufacturer before ordering a bar.

Collars
Always use collars. Without tight collars, plates can move out of position, mar balance and form, and cause injury.

Genetic realities

The model used to illustrate this book— Constantinos Demetriou—is not genetically typical. He is a competitive bodybuilder. From his German mother and Cypriot father he inherited an exceptional ability to build big and strong muscles, and the aesthetic qualities needed for success as a competitive bodybuilder. Those very rare gifts, and eight years of dedication to bodybuilding, produced the physique that you will see in this book. The weights he used were intentionally very light, for demonstration purposes only.

As inspirational as you may find Constantinos' physique to be, what should matter the most to you is making the most of *your* potential.

Whatever genetic potpourri you have been dealt is all that you are going to get. Rather than spending time complaining about your genetic fate, or comparing yourself with the very few who have phenomenal natural talent, pour your energy into achieving your own genetic potential. For example, even a less-than-average potential for bodybuilding, *if achieved*, is stunning to most people. If you train intelligently for long enough you may achieve far more than what you used to think was realistic and possible.

Learn what good exercise form is, apply it to a good training program, invest years of hard work, eat well and get plenty of rest, and then you will do what will satisfy you most of all as far as training goes— *actually achieve your own full potential.* But it is not just the end result that is satisfying. The process of getting there is great fun.

Though lean at the time, Constantinos was not in contest condition when he posed for the photographs used in this book. On page 208 you will find a factual and illuminative analysis of his physique.

Part 2
Step-by-step exercise technique

1

Back extension

Main muscles worked
glutes, lower back structure, hamstrings, thigh adductors

Capsule description
lying face down, lift your torso while keeping your legs fixed, or vice versa

Introduction
The regular back extension, often called a hyperextension, has your legs fixed and your torso moving into line with them. In the reverse back extension your torso is fixed and your legs move into line with it.

Back extensions work the glutes, hamstrings, thigh adductors, and the musculature, tendons and ligaments of the lower back differently to variations of the deadlift. This is why back extensions provide protection against back injuries, and are so valuable. Perform an intensive set or two of one or both back extensions once a week. Back extensions are *not*, however, a substitute for deadlifts and stiff-legged deadlifts (unless you are unable to do any form of deadlift).

The primary use of back extensions is as *assistance* work, to help keep your back in the robust condition needed to exploit the huge potential benefits from deadlift variations, and the squat. Back extensions can also be excellent therapy movements if you suffer from a lower-back injury. If available, a hip-and-back machine can be used as an alternative to back extensions.

Regular back extension
A purpose-built glute/ham apparatus, or a type of "Roman-chair" device, is available in some gyms for this exercise. Because the knees can bend when using some versions of these apparatuses, the involvement of the rear thighs may be increased a little relative to the conventional back extension.

To do the conventional back extension, lie face down on a high or elevated bench, with your torso hanging off one end. With your hands on the floor, find the position so that the edge of the bench does not hurt your groin area. You may need to place some padding over the edge of the bench. Have your legs strapped to the bench, or have someone hold you down. But be sure that the bench will not topple over.

Fold your arms on your chest and raise your torso in a controlled fashion to where it is parallel to the floor. *Never jerk into the contracted position.* If you are very careful, and move *slowly* at the top, you can and even should go into a higher contraction. But do not do this if you have a history of intervertebral disc problems.

Do not round your back. Keep it flat or slightly arched. This exercise is usually done with arms behind the head, or with a plate held behind the head. Both positions encourage rounding the back, as well as placing excessive strain on the back of the neck, and the cervical vertebrae. This is why it is best to keep your arms folded on your chest, and to hold a plate to your chest when extra resistance is needed.

The parallel position of the orthodox back extension, using an improvised setup in a power rack. This setup does not involve a partner.

Breathe between reps, at the bottom position. Take your last breath, and then exhale during the ascent.

Manual resistance can be applied to your shoulders, as an alternative to holding weight. Weight is easier to monitor because you can control it precisely, and increase it by a small increment when required. With manual resistance you have no way of ensuring progressive resistance. But properly done, manual resistance can be effective. It can be applied while you come up. Perhaps an easier and more effective application is to come up by yourself and then be pushed down—resist hard, to keep the descent slow. A few hard reps like that will wipe you out and you will find coming up to be very difficult. After adapting to the exercise over a few weeks, with increasing intensity, take each set to failure, i.e., until you cannot come up.

If you are held down at your ankles while lying on a flat bench, this will produce tension on your knees. And if you are held down too near your knees, the force pressing down on those joints can be uncomfortable. Find a comfortable position from which to be held down.

If where you train has a formal setup for the conventional back extension, try it. It may make the exercise more practical.

The 45° back extension

The 45° back extension is an alternative to the regular back extension, if the setup is available. Exercise the same control and care as in the regular back extension, and the same method of holding resistance. To bring your torso into line with your legs in the 45° back extension, your back has to come up above parallel to the floor. Generally speaking, the regular back extension is the superior movement, so long as you have the required strength.

Reverse back extension

This variation, also called the reverse hyperextension, puts less strain on your knees. There are two interpretations. The first can be done by almost anyone. But the second needs purpose-built apparatus.

To perform the first interpretation, lie face down on an elevated horizontal bench, with your legs off the end. If need be, place some padding under the part of your groin area that contacts the edge of the bench. You may be able to find the right position so that no artificial padding is needed. Tightly hold the bench in front of your head. Keep your head facing forward and do not turn it during the exercise.

Slowly raise your legs as high as you can. *Never* jerk into the top position. And never jerk your head back as you lift your legs. Keep your head steady and inhale on the descent, and exhale on the ascent.

For resistance, have someone stand behind you and apply manual resistance to your ankles. Your helper should bow forward (pushing against your ankles) as you lower your legs, and then straighten up as you raise your legs. Following warmup reps he should apply enough resistance to make you work. More resistance should be provided while you lower your legs than while you raise them. Alternatively, strap weight to your ankles.

The second interpretation of the reverse back extension needs special apparatus. With it, resistance can easily be applied in small increments, and no partner is needed. The result is a face-down and straight-legged version of a hip-and-back machine. Following David Crocco's example in HARDGAINER issue #41, use a setup in a power rack. You will need an attachment that can be "locked" into position in a power rack using one of the rack's pins. Use dimensions that are appropriate to your rack's width and pin thickness. A strap is fixed to the bottom of the device, to

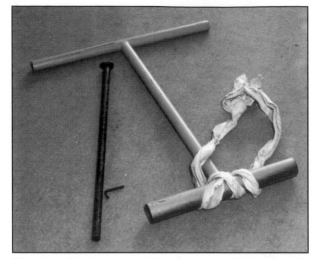

Device for reverse back extensions, and rack pin for locking the device in place.

place around your ankles. Above is the device I had made by a local metal worker in 1995, for about $35.00.

The top piece of pipe is 24" long, the bottom piece is 16" long and a little less than 2" thick (for loading Olympic plates), and the connecting piece is 26" long. When placed in the power rack I use, it is a good fit for most adult leg lengths.

By varying the length of the strap and the position of the device relative to the bench, it can accommodate different leg lengths. Ideally, the distance from the bench to where the strap is attached to the metal device, should approximately match leg length. Experiment to find the best strap length and bench position to suit you and your device. A longer strap will let you place your feet wider than will a shorter strap. To be able to use the wider spacing you need to have sufficient room between the rack's uprights. If you have the choice between a wide and a close spacing of your feet, alternate them from set to set, or workout to workout. Otherwise use just the close spacing.

I position the rotating part of the device as close as possible to the board I lie on. If the rotating part of the device you use is well away from the board or bench you lie on, it may obstruct your thighs if you use a short strap and an extended range of motion in the bottom phase.

The poundage potential of your setup will be influenced by factors that include the distance between the axis of rotation and your hips, the length of the device, your leg length, and length of the strap.

Be sure that the bench or board you use is centered on the pins of your power rack,

and that it cannot slip out of position. For example, and as shown in the photograph below, have a strip of wood fixed at each end on the underside of a padded board so that it can be "locked" between the pins.

Hold the bench or board in front of your head. Keep your head facing forward and do not turn it during the exercise. Slowly raise your legs to parallel to the floor. *Never* jerk into the top position. Lower the resistance under control. Inhale on the descent, and exhale on the ascent.

The reverse back extension in action.

The "locking" setup on a board used for the reverse back extension. See text.

2

Bench press

Main muscles worked
pectorals, deltoids, triceps

Capsule description
lie on your back, bar at arm's length, lower it to your chest, then push it up

Introduction

This exercise, the standard bench press, is done supine, i.e., lying on your back on a horizontal bench. A barbell is held at arm's length above your chest, lowered to your chest, and then pressed back to arm's length. Alternatively, a barbell rests on bars set at chest height, and is then pressed from and lowered to those bars.

Touch-and-go bench pressing means that the bar touches your chest and is immediately driven back to lockout. In competition-style bench pressing you must briefly pause at your chest until you receive the command to press.

Rack bench pressing is done inside a power rack, with the bar resting on the rack's pins prior to being pressed. Each rep is done from a dead stop. The pins are usually set at chest height.

Setup and positioning

Bench press inside a four-post power rack with pins and saddles correctly and securely in place. The pins are the bars that are placed horizontally between the rack's uprights. The pins are locked in place in the rack's uprights using small locking pins. Alternatively, bench press between sturdy and stable squat stands together with spotter bars or racks, or use a half rack, or use a combination bench-and-weight-stands unit together with spotter racks. Some bench-and-stands units have built-in adjustable safety bars. If you use one of those units, set the safety bars at the appropriate height, and position yourself on the bench so that you will not miss the bars if you need to set the barbell on them.

The barbell tends to roll or slide when placed on a power rack's pins. To reduce this tendency, slip over each pin a piece of garden hose sliced down its length. This also reduces the clanging of metal against metal, and the vibrations that result. But if you are controlling the bar properly you should not be making much noise.

If there is no setup available to stop the bar getting stuck on your chest if you fail on a rep, you *must* have an alert and strong spotter in attendance.

Center a sturdy and stable bench between the weight supports. In a power rack, if possible, mark where the bench should be to be centered. Use a tape measure to ensure perfect centering.

Do not bench press with naked skin against the bench. Wear a top that covers all of your torso.

If you are doing regular touch-and-go bench presses starting from the top, set the rack's pins, or whatever safety bars you use, at an inch below the height of your inflated chest. If you fail on a rep, lower

A four-post power rack and its "accessories": two adjustable bar saddles (on the rear uprights), four pins, four small locking pins (on the base), and two lengths of hose.

the bar, exhale, and set the bar on the supports.

The spacing between the pin settings of the rack you use may not give you the precise height you need. For example, perhaps you need to raise the bar's height by an inch, but your rack only has pin holes every couple of inches. What you can do then is raise the bar a couple of inches in the rack *and* raise the height of the bench by an inch. Do this by placing rubber matting or thin boards under the bench. Then you will end up with a net increase of one inch in the height of the bar relative to your chest.

If the setting at your chest causes you shoulder discomfort, move the bar position up a couple of inches. Then, shoulders permitting, gradually move to the full range of motion over a couple of months.

Position yourself on the bench so that you do not hit the uprights of the rack or stands during the ascent.

If you bench press in the regular from-the-top style, have the bar saddles correctly positioned. Have them neither too high nor too low. Have a spotter or training partner give you a handoff at the start of each set. And get a helping hand to guide you to put the bar back in the weight saddles at the end of a set.

Because of the horizontal movement involved in the ascent of the bench press,

When doing rack bench presses that start from the bottom position at your chest, use a slightly different setup to that used for touch-and-go bench pressing. Set your pins at the exact height so that the bar just grazes your inflated chest when the bar rests across the pins.

the bar can hit the uprights which hold the saddles. If, however, you are positioned the right distance from the saddles' uprights so that you cannot strike them on the ascent, you will have trouble getting the bar out of the saddles for your first rep.

If you do not have a spotter to give you a handoff, then train the bench press from the bottom position and do away with the need to use saddles. If you bench press in the rack from the bottom position, then no handoff or guided return is necessary.

Pins set at chest height for rack bench pressing from the bottom. For touch-and-go benching, the pins would be set an inch or so below chest height.

Plant yourself on the bench with your feet, hips, back and head all solidly in position. To remove dangerous stress from your lower spine, minimize the space between your lower back and the bench. Bench press with a platform under your feet. Do not, however, place your feet on the bench because that would seriously reduce your stability. The height of the platform depends on leg length and bench height. Try one about 4" high if you are of average height. Use a single wide platform, or two small platforms (or blocks), so that your feet can be well spaced for stability. (Powerlifters should, during the few weeks prior to a meet, carefully ease into using a competition arch, but minimize the arch.)

While the bar is at the line of your lower pecs, take a hand spacing that puts your forearms in a vertical position when viewed (by an assistant) from the side *and* from your feet. Your elbows should be directly under your wrists. Adult men can use a grip with 21" between their index fingers *as a starting point.* Women can use a grip 4" narrower. Fine-tune from there to find the grip that gives you the proper forearm and elbow positioning. Once you find your optimum grip, have someone measure the distance between your index fingers, and make a written record of it.

Do not use a thumbless grip because it reduces your control over the bar. Grip with your hands equally distanced from the bar's center. Take your grip carefully and be sure you are not even a fraction of an inch off center. Before a set, know precisely where your hands should be. Use a tape measure if need be. If you train at home, you could even mark the spacing on your bench press bar (perhaps with tape).

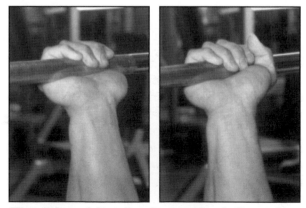

The "thumbless" grip on the left, and the correct grip on the right.

Performance of the bench press

After having had a handoff to help you get the bar out of the saddles, pause until the bar is steady at arm's length above your chest. Now retract your shoulder blades, i.e., try to pinch them together, and then immediately lower the bar, under control. Take about two seconds for the descent. A perfect descent is critical for the correct positioning from which to start the ascent.

Lower the bar to a point below your nipples, at the bottom line of your pectoral muscles. This will probably mean lowering the bar position on your chest relative to your former style. Find the precise point on your chest that is best for you. As noted earlier, when the bar is on your chest, your forearms should be vertical when viewed from the side *and* the front (or rear, depending on where the viewer is). If they are not, your hand spacing is incorrect.

Never bounce the bar off your chest or the pins. Either touch your chest and then press immediately, or pause very briefly on your chest (or on the pins if pressing from the bottom in a rack) before driving the bar up. In either case, squeeze the bar, tighten up further, spread your lats and press.

See the drawing for an approximation of the pathway options for the bench press ascent, considering that your head is on the right. It also considers that you have correctly lowered the bar to a point at or very near to the bottom line of your pectoral muscles, and that your elbows are directly below your wrists. Experiment with both pathways, or even one somewhere in between, to see which one works best for you.

The first few inches of the ascent should be vertical, or very near to vertical, but *never* moving away towards your feet. To be sure that the bar does not move even slightly towards your feet, move it up and *slightly* back towards your face rather than perfectly vertical.

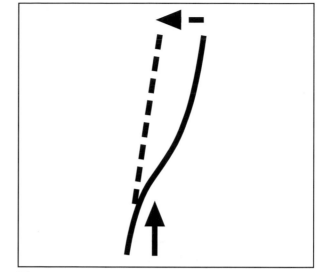

Two approximations of the pathway of the bar during the bench press ascent, considering that your head is on the right. See text for explanation.

Check yourself on a video recording, or have someone watch you from the side. What you may think is an initial vertical movement may actually be slightly towards your feet. Or what you may think is slightly towards your face may actually be perfectly vertical. Find out what you are really doing, and then determine, through trial and error, which precise pathway for the first few inches is best for you.

There are two options for the rest of the ascent. First, continue the bar in a straight line directly following the first phase just described. Thus the bar goes almost vertically up from your lower pec line, only very slightly slanting towards your head. The second option, following the common first phase already described, is to move the bar towards your clavicles in a steep diagonal line, prior to the final near-vertical phase either above your upper chest or, in the most exaggerated case, above your clavicles. Keep your forearms as vertical as possible during the ascent. Do this by keeping your elbows directly beneath your wrists.

In the first printing of this book a much more exaggerated horizontal movement was described. But because this can produce shoulder discomfort for some people, the conservative pathways promoted in this printing are safer and thus more productive.

The ascent, just like the descent, should be symmetrical. The bar should not be held off center, the bar should not tip to one side, both hands should move in unison, and you should not take more weight on one side of your body than on the other. It is very important that you keep the stress distributed symmetrically.

After locking out the bar, pause briefly. Do not allow the bar to drift towards your face. Keep it where it was at the top of the ascent, i.e., somewhere between about the middle of your pecs, and your clavicles.

Keep your arms locked out during the pause between reps. While keeping your arms locked out, move the bar forward slightly until it is directly above your lower pecs. Pause briefly until the bar is perfectly stationary, retract your shoulder blades, and then lower the bar slowly to the correct position on your lower chest.

Inhale while the bar is overhead, hold the breath during the descent, and exhale during the ascent. If you are doing rack bench presses from the bottom, inhale while the bar rests across the pins, or even take a few quick breaths in that position.

Other tips for the bench press

Use chalk on your hands to improve your grip on the bar, and keep the knurling clean. Then your hands will not slide outwards during a set.

Never turn your head while you are lifting or lowering the bar. If you do, the bar will tip slightly, your groove will be ruined, and you could hurt yourself.

Prior to each rep when doing rack bench presses from the bottom, be sure that the bar is centered over the pins, and that the distance between the bar and the uprights is the same on both sides. A spotter can make any necessary corrections during the pause between reps. But with practice, and very careful descents, you will be able to lower the bar to the correct position on the pins every time.

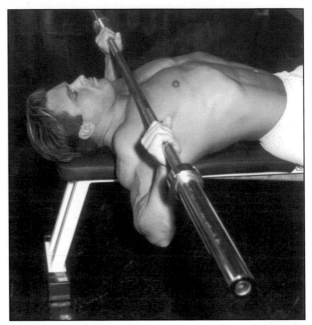

An illustration of bench pressing to the upper chest. NEVER DO THIS. It has permanently damaged the shoulders of countless trainees.

Using half your usual poundage for the reps concerned, perform several sets of 10 reps, comparing the two ascent pathways. Decide which one feels the most natural and powerful. You will probably need more than one workout to make your mind up. Then take a few weeks to return to your best working poundages, and perhaps longer if your recent form was very different to that described here. Only *then* can you go into new personal best weights and start to build muscle. The improved form will *increase* your bench press potential and *reduce* your chances of getting injured. But if you rush to build your poundages back, you will destroy the new form and start injuring yourself.

Once you know and can apply good technique in the bench press, drill yourself on a fixed setup and approach-to-the-bar procedure. With the bar already loaded, approach and get positioned on the bench in an orderly, focused, serious and consistent manner.

As seen from the side view of your bench press, get feedback from a training partner or assistant, or record yourself with a video camera. This is critical because the form you think you use is almost certainly not what you actually use.

When applying chalk, cover each hand well, including the area on the inside of your thumb and index finger.

Once you have mastered the new bench pressing technique, you must still give 100% attention to ensure that you deliver perfect form on every rep you do. Never become overconfident and think that you

can deliver good technique even if your attention is not 100%. Even a slight slip of concentration can lead to lowering the bar slightly out of position, or having one hand out of step with the other. Either of these will ruin your groove. This will make the weight feel heavier, make your reps harder, cause frustration, and risk injury.

Spotting

A handoff to get the bar out of the saddles to commence the set is the first valuable function of a spotter. During a set, as soon as the bar stalls or tips, one hand gets forward of the other, or the bencher starts to arch or tries to lift one shoulder, then the spotter must act to prevent the rep deteriorating further and causing injury.

> **To demonstrate exercise form clearly, the model did not wear a shirt, and weight stands and safety bars were often not used. This was only for illustration purposes. When you train, wear a shirt and always take proper safety measures—for all exercises.**

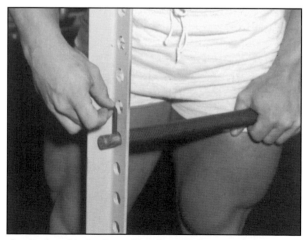

A rack pin being "locked" in so that it cannot come out of position during use.

One spotter is adequate for general training. For maximum single attempts, three spotters—one at each end and one in the center—is the ideal number. In this situation, all spotters must act together. If one spotter calls, then all must respond.

Multiple spotters are there in case they need to *take* the bar. With more than one person involved, balanced help cannot be provided. With multiple spotters, assisted reps should be avoided because otherwise there is a high chance of the bencher losing the groove and sustaining injury.

A single spotter must use both hands and provide sufficient assistance to keep the bar horizontal and moving perfectly centered above the lifter.

Even if the spotter does not need to assist during a rep, he should guide the bar back into the weight saddles after the final rep. At the end of a hard set of bench presses you will be very tired. Without a guiding pair of hands on the bar from a spotter you may miss getting the bar into the weight saddles.

If you are bench pressing in a rack from the bottom position, you will not be using saddles. A spotter will not be needed to help you get the bar to and from the saddles. But a spotter will be invaluable for repositioning the bar on the pins if it has been set down slightly out of position.

Dumbbell bench press

The bench press can also be done with dumbbells. Once the 'bells are in pressing position, the technique is similar to the barbell version.

There are some striking advantages of the dumbbell version. First, it is a rarely performed exercise whereas the barbell bench press could be the most popular weight-training exercise around. The rarity of the dumbbell version means, assuming there are suitable dumbbells available, that in a busy gym you can probably dumbbell bench press whenever you want to, and spare yourself having to wait your turn at the barbell bench press station. Second, the dumbbell bench press does not require a power rack or other safety setup, and a spotter is not compulsory (though it is strongly recommended). Third, the 'bells provide more potential than a barbell does for accommodating individual adjustment for physical irregularities.

The disadvantages of the dumbbell bench press are several. First, getting two heavy dumbbells into and out of position is difficult unless you have at least one competent assistant. There is scope for injuring yourself. Second, there is a greater chance of overstretching than with a barbell. Third, if control is lost over one or both dumbbells during a set, serious injury could occur, in addition to damage to the floor and equipment. But, of course, the barbell bench press can be very dangerous unless done inside a power rack with pins properly positioned. Plenty of ribs and shoulders have been badly damaged as a result of losing control of a long bar. Some people have even been killed under a bench press barbell.

Used with caution, and after having taken the time to develop good control before working hard on progressive poundages, the dumbbell bench press can be a valuable exercise. Keep in mind, though, that the dumbbell bench press is not the only alternative to barbell bench pressing. If the barbell bench press station is too busy where you work out, and you cannot train at a quieter time, then you could substitute the parallel bar dip. This assumes that where you train has a suitable dip stand, and you are strong enough to do dips. Done with good form, the dip may be safer and more manageable than the dumbbell bench press, depending on the individual. Alternatively you could use the low-incline barbell bench press.

To get into position for dumbbell bench pressing, have a spotter hand you the 'bells one at a time while you are in place on a bench. Alternatively you could get them into position by yourself. Sit on the end of a bench with the 'bells held vertically on your thighs near your torso. Be sure that your hands are centered on the handles. Keeping your arms bent, chin on your chest, and with a push on the 'bells from your legs, roll back onto the bench. With your forearms vertical, immediately begin pressing. While pressing, your feet must be stable and elevated on a platform, like in the barbell bench press.

Press in a similar pathway as in the barbell version—same bottom position but perhaps with less horizontal movement, if that gives you better control. Keep the 'bells moving in tandem. Do not let them drift out, or let one get ahead of the other.

With dumbbells you do not have to hold your hands as if holding a barbell. You could use a parallel grip, or one somewhere in between that and the barbell style grip. You can even change your wrist positioning during the course of each rep. This flexibility of wrist positioning is one of the big benefits of using dumbbells.

Do not seek an exaggerated range of motion in the dumbbell bench press. Keep your hands near to the spacing that was recommended for the barbell bench press. Do not use a wider grip so that you can get your hands lower at the bottom of the exercise. Go no deeper than you would on a barbell bench press.

Use light dumbbells for a few workouts and do not push any set hard. Wait until you have developed good control before you start to train this exercise intensively. Your control may be very poor to begin with. But with practice you will develop good control over the dumbbells.

A spotter should kneel behind your head, and place his hands under your elbows. Then he would be ready to provide assistance. But do not push this exercise to failure. Stop one rep short so that you do not risk losing control. Losing control could cost you an injury, perhaps a serious one. Even an alert spotter might not be able to prevent loss of control of both dumbbells if you push a set too hard.

A spotter, or better still two spotters, can take the dumbbells off you at the end of a set. Alternatively you can get off the bench while holding the dumbbells. Lower the 'bells to your lower torso, keep your arms, shoulders and chest tight, and lift your knees as high as you can with bent legs. With the 'bells touching your thighs, and your chin on your chest, immediately "throw" your legs forward and *roll* into a seated position. This is especially easy to do if a spotter places his hands under your shoulders and helps you to roll up.

Fixed-weight 'bells usually increase in increments of 5 lbs (or 2.5 kgs). Going up in dumbbells usually means a *total* increase of 10 lbs, which is a big single increment. Stick with a pair of dumbbells until you can comfortably do several reps more than your target count, before going up in weight the next time you dumbbell bench press. Using wrist weights may not be a good idea, though, to work up from the weight of one pair of 'bells to the next. The wrist weights could spoil your balance.

If you use adjustable dumbbells, you can use smaller increments than 5 lbs, assuming you have very small discs. Even if you use fixed-weight dumbbells you can attach a couple of small discs to each dumbbell. Use strong adhesive tape and be sure that the discs are *securely* attached. Over time, build up to the poundage of the next pair of fixed-weight dumbbells. To ensure proper balance, be sure to attach the small discs in pairs to each dumbbell, one at each end. An alternative is to use small plates that are magnetic.

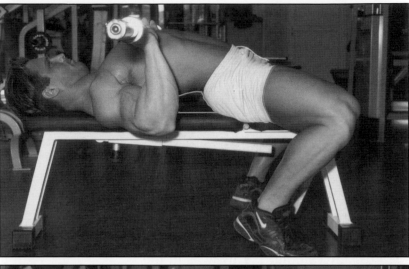

Comparison of the degree of arch in the lower back while bench pressing. Up on toes (top), feet flat on the floor (middle), and feet on a 4" platform (bottom). The greater the arch, the more dangerous the stress on the spine.

Barbell bench press, bar at the pec line: Hands too wide (above), producing forearms that are not vertical. The left photo shows the right spacing for the model.

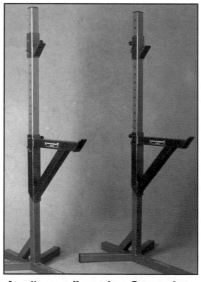

The last rep of a set of dumbbell bench pressing, and the return to the seated position.

An "open" rack—Scorpion Gym Equipment's "Safety Squat Racks."

A length of hose being slipped over a rack pin. The hose helps to prevent the bar from slipping.

3

Cable row

Main muscles worked
lats, upper back, biceps, brachialis, rear deltoid

Capsule description
sit and pull to your waist a bar fixed to a cable running from a low pulley

Introduction
Use a cable that runs parallel and close to the floor. Sit and hold a bar attached to the cable. Pull the bar to your waist and then return it to arm's length.

Setup and positioning
Use a supinated grip on a straight bar or a bar with a straight middle and ends that are slanted up, or use a parallel grip on a special purpose-made bar. One of the most common mistakes in this exercise is doing it with hands too close. A shoulder-width grip produces a much better effect than does a narrow grip. With a parallel grip be sure to grasp each handle in the center.

For the parallel grip, try to persuade the management where you train to get a shoulder-width bar if it does not already have one. If you are unsuccessful, buy your own bar, or get one custom made, and take it with you when you are going to do this exercise. Aim for a grip spacing that keeps your forearms parallel to each other throughout the exercise. Fix your leg flexion and sitting position so that you do not bang the handles or bar on your legs.

Performance
Sit on the floor, or on a built-in low seat, with your legs bent a little and feet against the foot restraint or support(s). If where

you train does not have a foot support near the floor pulley, improvise so that you have a solid foot brace that lets you space your feet as you need to. Pull the handle to the starting position that has you seated with your torso vertical, back flat, and arms pulled out straight by the resistance.

With a shoulder-width grip, smoothly pull the bar into your abdomen and crush your shoulder blades together. Do not let your elbows drift out to the sides. Your elbows should be equally spaced throughout each rep. Arch your back slightly as you pull your shoulders back and *down*. This means that your elbows must not rise when you are in the contracted position. They should actually go down a little as you crush your shoulder blades together. Hold the contraction for a second or two, and then let the resistance pull your arms straight in a controlled and deliberate way.

Involve *a little* forward movement of your torso during the negative phase, and then return to the vertical position during the completion of the positive (or pulling) part of each rep. This slight movement will help to reduce fatigue in your lower back. But do not round your back as you lean forward a bit. In the contracted position, do not bend back beyond where your torso is upright and perpendicular to the floor.

Top and left: Good form in the cable row using a parallel grip on a shoulder-width bar.

Incorrect contracted position, with the shoulders rounded and elbows raised.

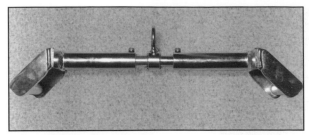

An adjustable parallel-grip bar from Scorpion Gym Equipment, which has the design rights. A single width grip will not suit all users.

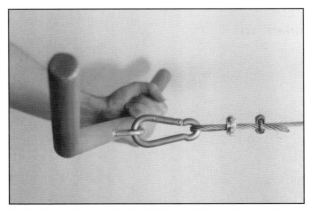

Relative to a straight bar, the slanted ends place the hands in a more natural position—for the cable row and pulldown. Shown here for the cable row, the ends are slanted upwards and a little away from you. Any skilled metal worker could cheaply make the slanted bar, and a non-adjustable parallel-grip bar.

Other tips for the cable row

If you lean back beyond the vertical, at least with a demanding weight, you will round your shoulders, be unable to crush your shoulder blades together, and rob yourself of working the target muscles.

The fullest-range movement involves your arms and shoulders relaxing between reps, to permit a full stretch. Doing this puts great stress upon the rotator cuff muscles at the back of your shoulders, and will set you up for an injury. *Do not do it!*

Keep your shoulders "tight" and your head up when in the stretched position. Never drop your head and let the weight stack yank on your arms and shoulders.

Put chalk on your hands for all your work sets. If the bar you use is smooth, the chalk will not help you as much as it will on a bar with knurling. To help your grip on a slick bar, place a palm-size piece of neoprene between each hand and the bar. (Neoprene is a synthetic rubber with many uses. Get some small pieces from a scuba gear shop, an engineering storeroom on campus, or a hardware store.)

Spotting

Spotting is not essential here because the resistance cannot come down on you. (But if the cable snaps you could have a serious accident.) But spotting is desirable for ensuring that the final rep or two of a set is/are done in good form. Form becomes ragged when your shoulders start to slump. Immediately, a spotter should pull on the weight stack cable just enough to let you get the rep out in good form.

Adding weight

Selectorized cable units, and selectorized machines in general, usually have weight increments of 10 lbs or 5 kgs. This is too much weight to progress by at a single jump. Where you train may have special weights of 2.5 lbs or 5 lbs designed to fit on the top of a weight stack. (If it does not, get your own from an exercise equipment store.) Use them to work from one pin setting to the next. Alternatively you could place a second pin through a small barbell weight plate and position it above the first pin. Though the second pin cannot go fully into the weight stack, it may go through enough to hold the small barbell plate securely. Or you could use magnetic small plates. But always check that the setup is secure before you perform a set.

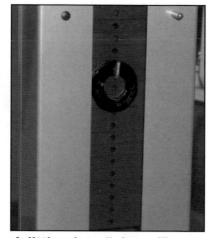

A weight designed to fit on top of a selectorized weight stack.

A little plate "pinned" to the stack, for a small increase in weight—a microload.

On the far left are the smallest plates that are usually found in gyms— 1.25 kgs (or 2.5 lbs). The other plates here are true small discs—the "little gems," i.e., 0.5 kg, 0.25 kg, and 0.1 kg. Use these to add microloads.

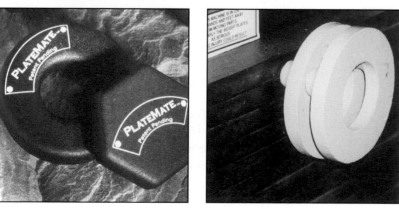

Magnetic PlateMate® weight plates come in 0.625-lb, 1.25-lb and 1.875-lb sizes. These are especially useful for applying microloads to selectorized weight stacks, and fixed-weight dumbbells and barbells. In pairs they produce 1¼-lb, 2½-lb and 3¾-lb increases.

4

Calf raise

Main muscles worked
gastrocnemius, soleus

Capsule description
stand or sit with the balls of your feet fixed, and lift and lower your heels

Introduction

Variations of this exercise are often called heel raises. Confusingly, they are also sometimes called toe raises even though the toes do not actually rise.

Calf raises come in four main varieties: standing involving both legs, standing with one leg exercised at a time, donkey style, and the seated version. Stay clear of the leg press machine for calf work. This offers nothing that other straight-legged calf exercises do not provide, but it reduces your control because your feet can easily slip out of position.

Keeping your legs straight in calf work heavily involves *both* the gastrocnemius and soleus. The soleus is underneath the gastrocnemius and is only visible around the edges of the calf. Though not very visible, the soleus contributes significantly to calf girth. Bent-legged calf work takes the gastrocnemius out of play according to the extent of leg flexion, and focuses the work on the soleus. But bent-legged calf work is less productive than straight-legged work for *overall* calf growth.

Setup and positioning

In all calf work, place the balls of your feet on a stable block. If the block is free standing, i.e., it is not attached to a calf machine, then fix it to a board that has a larger area. This will prevent the block from flipping over. For example, get a 4" x 4" x 20" length of wood and nail it to the center of a 1" x 10" x 22" board. Round one of the top two long edges of the block, for the side where you will place your feet. As an alternative to a wooden block, at least for one-legged calf raises using a dumbbell for resistance, you can use any suitable immovable object, e.g., a step.

How deep your heels should go is an individual matter. Like in many exercises, a range of motion one person can safely and productively use can injure another person. If you can use a full range of motion in the calf raise without experiencing any post-workout foot problems, then use it. But if the full range of motion produces foot problems, cut your range of motion by an inch or two. Find the maximum range of motion that is safe for you.

If the block or platform is moveable, then use one, or an improvisation, that is the ideal height for you. To reduce your range of motion, instead of the standard block of about 4" high, try one of no more than 2". The latter, when you wear shoes with a regular-thickness heel, will reduce your range of motion by an inch or two relative to the high block. Even if you can safely do the full heels-all-the-way-down range of motion, try at least one training cycle of three months or longer where you use a reduced range of motion, more poundage, and lower reps (no more than 10). Work hard, give it a fair try, and see if you get improved gains.

The use of partial reps in calf work, and a reduced rep count, means that you can immediately use much more resistance. This is great for providing more load to contract your calves against. But even if you could jump 100 lbs or more, and get straight into intensive work, *do not.* You must *gradually* increase the resistance so that you can adapt to the greatly increased load. Take at least two months. Make no big jumps in weight.

The need to work progressively into the bigger poundages over at least a couple of months is not just for the sake of your back. Your ankle joints and feet also need time to adapt to the increased load.

If you have back problems, the option of partial and lower reps for calf work may not be practical because you will not want to place very large weights over your shoulders. Holding a dumbbell at your side for one-legged calf raises should be a safe alternative. But once you work into very heavy weights you will need big dumbbells, which may not be practical, depending on the equipment available.

Depending on the soles of your shoes and the surface of the platform or block you stand on, your feet may slide out of position during the course of a set. If this happens, quickly reposition your feet, and next calf workout try using different shoes or a different platform or block so that your feet do not slip.

Perform your reps with a smooth and deliberate motion. Get as high as possible on each rep. The fully-contracted position is the most important part of the exercise. Briefly hold the contracted position of each rep. Descend under control, gently touch or reach your bottom position, and then drive

out of it. Never bounce at the bottom of a rep. If you use a reduced range of movement *and* actually touch your heels to something at the bottom of each rep, you could take a brief pause before driving into the next contraction. But in doing that there is a danger of spine compression. How to avoid spine compression will be described later in this section.

Keep your legs straight except in the seated calf raise. In all calf work, keep your big toe pointing directly forward or *slightly* outward. Avoid extreme foot positions.

If your Achilles tendons are tight, and you are using the full-range movement, then progressively increase the depth of descent over a few weeks. But do not get carried away. The purpose of the calf raise is to stimulate growth in your calves, not make your Achilles tendons into a pair of elastic bands.

Standing calf raise

A machine is needed for the conventional standing calf raise. An alternative is to use a barbell over your shoulders in a power rack, with the bar moving against the inside of one of the rack's two pairs of uprights. Position a stable foot block so that when you stand on it with the bar over your shoulders, you face out of the rack with a slight forward lean. This should ensure that the bar does not come away from the uprights during the movement, and that you do not lose control.

Take the bar off pins set at about shoulder height. When you are elevated on the foot block, that will take the bar clear of hitting the pins. But it is very important to set the pins at the appropriate height so that the bar touches the pins a fraction of an inch *before* your heels reach their bottom position, assuming that it is possible for your heels to reach the floor. If your heels touch the floor before the bar rests on the pins, the weight of the loaded bar will

Calf raise using a standing calf machine.

Calf raise in a power rack. *Be very careful not to compress your spine. See text for an explanation.*

Do not round your back while doing any standing calf raise using a machine or barbell.

compress your spine. This is very dangerous. The pins are also there for when you reach muscular failure, or lose control, and need to bend your legs and quickly put the bar down.

Possible compression of the spine also applies to the standing calf machine. If possible, set up the machine so that the resistance rests on a support before your heels touch the floor at the bottom of the movement. Alternatively, never touch your heels to the floor between reps. This is easy if you use a block sufficiently high so that it is impossible to touch your heels to the floor even at full stretch.

But if you use only a small elevation for some of your calf work, as recommended here, then it is easy to touch your heels to the floor before the resistance is set down. If you cannot ensure that you do not risk compressing your spine, change the type of calf raise you perform so that you *can* guarantee spine safety.

When working both legs at the same time, the standing calf raise has a big weight potential. If you get into the starting position incorrectly, or do your reps in a sloppy way, especially if you use more weight than you can handle correctly, you will hurt yourself.

Be very careful when you get positioned for the first rep of any standing calf raise. Do not round your upper back. And be sure to distribute the weight symmetrically over your back and legs. Put the pads or bar in position on your shoulders, pull your shoulder blades back, bend your knees, and place your feet in position on the foot board. None of the stress of the weight is taken on your shoulders yet. Now arch your back a little, "lock" your torso and straighten your legs. Then you will safely be in the starting position for the first rep, with the weight bearing down on you.

Never take the full load of the resistance on your shoulders and then shuffle into position on the block. You must be correctly in position on the block before you take on the stress of the resistance.

Your hands must hold the barbell if you are doing the power rack calf raise. With the standing calf machine, hold the gear firmly. This will help you to keep your balance *and* maintain a rigid torso. In either case, use a hip-width foot placement rather than a close stance. This will further help you to keep your balance.

During the course of each set, never allow your back to round, torso to relax, or legs to bend. If you have to bend and straighten your legs during a rep, you are using too much weight.

One-legged version

The one-legged calf raise is done while holding a dumbbell on the same side as your working calf, or by using a standing calf machine. Do not do one-legged calf raises with a barbell over your back, even inside a power rack. Balance is too tricky that way.

If you use a dumbbell, hold something that is fixed and rigid with your other hand, to keep your balance. If you hold a power rack upright, *do not* put a finger

One-legged dumbbell calf raise, holding a horizontal bar for balance.

The one-legged calf raise using a calf machine.

through one of the holes in the upright. If you do, and if you lose your balance, you could very seriously damage that finger.

During the dumbbell calf raise, rather than hold something that is vertical, hold something horizontal at about shoulder height; e.g., face a bar set at the right height in a power rack. Then balance is easy to maintain. Set yourself up for the calf raise so that you can hold the horizontal bar with your free hand—in front of the shoulder of the arm concerned, or a little to the outside. Keep your working leg straight during each set.

For low-rep calf work for a strong male trainee, a range of dumbbells over 100 lbs will be needed; or an adjustable dumbbell using a long rod could be loaded as needed. A standing calf machine, if available, may be more practical.

Donkey calf raise

This exercise can be used for variety, but it works the calves in the same way that the standing calf raise does.

The donkey calf raise is done while bent over at your waist. Hold something for balance and keep your legs vertical and straight. Resistance is traditionally applied by having a training partner sit on your hips. The partner can hold extra weight when needed.

Basic position for the donkey calf raise.

Resistance can also be applied by hanging weight from a belt or, in some gyms, by using a purpose-made machine.

For low-rep calf work for a very strong trainee, being able to load enough resistance may become a problem in the donkey calf raise. The calf raise using the standing calf machine is likely to be a much more practical exercise.

Seated calf raise

Bent-legged calf work should be reserved for the seated calf raise. This can be done on a purpose-built machine, or by placing a barbell over your lower thighs while you are sitting with your legs bent. Place some padding under the barbell. If you use a purpose-built machine, adjust the height of the padded surface to suit you. Place the padded surface, or the padded barbell, above your knees in the position that is most comfortable and effective for you.

In both versions, position your feet about hip-width apart. Your legs should be bent at about a right angle when at the

The setup for the seated calf raise with a barbell, and the machine version.

bottom position. Apply the exact same guidelines on range of movement, toe positioning, rep control, and stress on the contraction, as in other calf work.

Pivotal general points to remember

❏ *Please study the text of each exercise very carefully. Even just a handful of details can make the difference between an exercise being productive or destructive.*

❏ *With few exceptions, the exercises that are not included in this book are either dangerous, only of marginal value or no value, require machinery that is not commonly available, or are technically so demanding that expert hands-on coaching is needed. Grip training is an exception to this generalization.*

❏ *If you cannot achieve your physique, strength or fitness goals by using the exercises described in this book, then using any other weight-training exercises will not improve your situation. In such a case it would not be the exercises that would be limiting you, but what you are doing with the exercises, i.e., the program design, level of effort, and progression scheme you are using.*

❏ *Stick to the safe forms of exercises as described in this book, protect your joints, and then you will be able to train consistently over the long term. Being able to train consistently over the long term should be your priority, because without being able to do so you will never achieve your physique, strength or fitness goals.*

5

Close-grip bench press

Main muscles worked
triceps, deltoids, pectorals

Capsule description
lie on your back, shoulder-width grip, lower bar to your chest, then push it up

Introduction
This exercise is very similar to the standard bench press. The principal differences are in the grip spacing and the bar pathway. The section on the bench press should be studied together with this one on the close-grip bench press.

Setup and positioning
The traditional close-grip bench press has the hands either touching or very close together. This is a joint wrecker. The safe close-grip bench press is not actually very close. Just make it about 5" closer than your regular-grip bench press. Depending on torso girth and arm length, about 16" between index fingers will probably be fine for most men, and about 12" for women. Find what feels most comfortable for you. If in doubt, go a little wider rather than narrower. Apply the bench press rule of keeping your forearms vertical—vertical as seen from the front and from the sides.

Position yourself on the bench like in the standard bench press, with your feet elevated, and do not use a thumbless grip.

Performance
Take your grip on the bar and get a handoff to help you to get the bar out of the saddles. Keeping your arms straight, move the bar into the starting position above

your lower chest, and pause briefly. On each rep, turn your elbows in a little as you lower the bar. This will keep your elbows directly beneath your wrists—maintaining this relative positioning is very important. The bar should touch your chest at the line of your lower pecs, or a tad lower. The bar path is not the same as in the regular bench press. In the close-grip bench press, press and lower the bar in a vertical up and down manner.

Instead of taking the bar out of saddles, and having to return it to them, do the close-grip bench press from off rack pins. As in the regular bench press you have the choice between touch-and-go pressing and from-the-bottom rack pressing.

Other tips
The narrowed grip relative to the standard bench press can cause excessive extension of the shoulders, especially in long-limbed lanky trainees. If the close-grip bench press bothers your shoulders, and you are doing the exercise as described here, you need to modify the movement. Do the exercise in a power rack with pins set so that you reduce the range of motion by a few inches. That will reduce the extension of your shoulders and make the exercise safer.

Fatigue occurs very suddenly in the close-grip bench press. If you train alone,

A comparison of the hand spacing of the standard bench press (left) and the safe close-grip bench press (above right). In this case the difference is only about 5". The bar is at the pec line in both cases. The elbows should be directly beneath the wrists.

be very careful, and be sure to use a setup that will safely catch the bar if you have to dump it. Terminate a set as soon as your elbows start to drift out of position despite your best efforts to keep them in position.

Spotting

See *Bench Press*—similar guidelines for spotting apply here. But because fatigue occurs more suddenly in the close-grip bench press, your spotter must be very alert. He must be ready to help you when the bar stalls, or when your elbows start to drift out of position.

Having your hands this close is very dangerous. It will damage your elbows and wrists. The elbows are nowhere near to being directly below the wrists.

6

Crunch abdominal work

Main muscles worked
abdominal wall, especially the rectus abdominis

Capsule description
curl your shoulders towards your hips, or your hips towards your shoulders

Introduction

Abdominal work is needed not just for aesthetic reasons. Strong and well-developed abdominal muscles are very important for keeping your lower back strong and resistant to injuries. Take your abdominal work very seriously, and develop a strong set of abs.

Crunch abdominal work comes in two basic types. The first, the regular crunch situp, curls the shoulders towards the hips. The second, the reverse crunch, curls the hips towards the chest. Crunch-style abdominal work usually takes some getting used to because most trainees are used to banging out "abdominal" exercises that predominantly use hip flexion.

Most people get poor results from crunches for two main reasons. First, they use poor form. Second, they are locked into doing excessively high reps with light weights. With better form, lower reps, and a focus on progressive poundages, good results will come. Whether or not you will *see* your improved abdominal development will depend on how much fat you have covering your midsection.

Basic crunch situp

Lie on the floor with your knees bent at a right angle, and your calves resting on a bench. Do not cross your legs. Just before you do each rep, tilt your pelvis so that your lower back is pressed onto the floor. Keep your chin on your chest and curl your shoulders off the floor. You cannot get your shoulders very far off the floor without making it into a hip flexion movement. The crunch is a short-range exercise and the lower half of your spine retains contact with the floor. Never jerk into the movement. Keep the tension on the muscles by using a slow ascent, and then exhale and hold the contraction for a second. Slowly lower your upper back to the floor, inhale, press your lower back against the floor, and repeat.

The basic crunch situp, with a dumbbell held on the chest.

A common mistake is putting your hands behind your head. This leads to pulling on your head that can cause neck problems. Instead, cross your arms and rest your hands on your chest or shoulders, or in your armpits. When you need resistance, hold a dumbbell across your chest, with the handle parallel to your shoulders. You could hold small plates on your chest, but large plates held there will spoil the exercise because they will obstruct the proper groove. Once you have progressed beyond using small plates, move to a dumbbell. Be consistent in how you hold the dumbbell on your mid to upper chest, so that you apply resistance in the same way each time. If you vary the position of the dumbbell, e.g., sometimes high on your chest, and other times low, you will vary how you perceive the same weight.

Overhead pulley crunch

Kneel on some padding in front of the cable of an overhead pulley. A pulldown setup with a fixed seat and knee restraint may obstruct the performance illustrated overleaf. (Use an overhead cable from a crossover machine instead.) But a pulldown machine with a restraint bar may work well for the crunch if you are seated and pinned down by the restraint bar. (Not illustrated in this book.)

Attach a bar to the cable. To reduce stress upon your elbows when using a straight bar, use a supinated grip rather than an overhand grip. You could use an inverted v-shaped bar—one that has the handles running close to parallel, not merely sloping down slightly. Your palms should be near to parallel to each other when using this bar.

The most comfortable and versatile grip is a parallel one using a rope attachment designed for pushdowns. If one of these attachments is unavailable, attach your own sturdy but flexible strap or rope (or even a bathrobe's belt) to the cable's connection. Put a knot at the bottom of each end of the rope or whatever you use.

Hold the bar behind or just above your head, according to which position is the most comfortable and helpful. The rope attachment can be held at the sides of your neck. With the rope attachment you can easily do the exercise with your back to the cable, which may give you the best effect.

The more you bend your arms, the greater the stress you may feel in your elbows. If your elbows feel uncomfortable, reduce the degree of arm flexion.

Maintain an angle behind your knees of less than 90°. Keep your hips and lower back fixed. Starting with your spine vertical or leaning slightly forward of vertical, flex or curl it until your *upper* back gets close to being horizontal. Perform each rep quite slowly so that muscular tension is sustained. Never pile on weight so that you just yank on the cable without the correct "crunching" flexion. Exhale as you crunch, and then hold the contraction for a second before slowly returning to the top position. For variety and a different effect on the midsection musculature, perform each rep with a twist. Move your right shoulder to over your left knee, or vice versa.

To simplify form, and focus even more on your abdominal wall—assuming that you have no knee limitations—sit on your ankles as you do the overhead pulley crunch. Relative to the other interpretation, this style may necessitate a reduction in poundage. You may also need to position yourself a little closer to the pulley.

You may need to experiment in order to find the specific interpretation that most effectively focuses the work on your abdominal wall. Only when you have the groove embedded should you add weight and really start working intensively.

While learning the form, do the exercise alongside a mirror, to observe yourself.

Two interpretations of the overhead pulley crunch, both facing the pulley. The bottom one is the harder of the two because the hips are almost touching the heels. With a rope attachment, try the exercise with your back to the cable and hands holding the attachment at the sides of your neck.

The overhead pulley crunch can be a dangerous movement if, after the "crunch," you let the resistance jolt you up. Do the exercise smoothly and under control both up and down. The exercise can be harmful for your elbows if you do not use a comfortable grip.

Machine crunch

If you use a machine for crunch-style situps, be sure that you use it correctly. Flex the upper half of your spine. The aim is not to pile on as much weight as possible and just heave your whole torso forward. Exhale as you flex your spine, and briefly hold the contraction.

Reverse crunch

This works the abdominal muscles by bringing the hips towards the shoulders, rather than bringing the shoulders towards the hips as in the regular crunch.

Lie on your back on a horizontal bench. Tightly hold the bench behind your head. Bend your legs fully, and keep them that way during the exercise. Keep your thighs vertical and tilt your pelvis so that your lower back is flattened against the bench. Initiate every rep, not just the first one, by pressing your lower back onto the bench. Then curl your lower back off the bench. This is a short-range movement in which you focus on moving your pelvis.

Incline reverse crunch

Reverse crunch on a horizontal bench. Note how the knees move up.

Machine crunch

Your knees must move *above* their starting position while your thighs remain *vertical*—push your knees towards the ceiling as you move your hips. Do not bring your knees to your chest, do not try to lift your upper back off the bench, do not throw or straighten your legs, and do not use momentum. Lift and lower your hips in a controlled way, keeping continuous stress on your abdominal wall.

To increase resistance, use an incline bench. In the starting position your torso must be higher than your hips. Start with a very slight incline and increase the angle of inclination as you gain in strength.

Regularly review "Critical General Factors," which starts on page 17. Those sixteen factors are of crucial importance for all exercises.

7

Curl

Main muscles worked
biceps, brachialis, forearms

Capsule description
standing or seated, arms hanging, lift the weight by bending at your elbows

Introduction

As simple and popular as the curl is, it is usually performed incorrectly. As a result, not only does it yield poor results in terms of muscular development, it produces elbow problems.

The curl can be done with a barbell or dumbbells, and while standing or seated. If done seated, you need to use dumbbells in order to extend your arms fully.

The biceps flex the elbows *and* supinate the hands. To supinate your hands, rotate them from a palms-down to a palms-up position. You cannot do this with a barbell. But the biceps muscle is not the only major arm flexor. There is the brachialis too, which is also worked by the curl.

Barbell curl

Stand with your feet about hip-width apart. Keep your knees slightly unlocked, to reduce the potential for cheating. Use a supinated (palms-up) grip on the barbell, with hands spaced a little wider than hip width. Fine-tune to find the hand spacing that is most comfortable for your wrists and elbows. Many trainees use too wide or too narrow a grip.

Throughout the curl, keep your wrists and hands in a straight line, i.e., in the neutral position. This is important. If you do not maintain the neutral position you

The correct straight or neutral position of hands and wrists (top), and the incorrect position (bottom).

will set yourself up for wrist and elbow problems. If you cannot maintain the neutral position, then take a break from curls for a couple of months and focus on grip and forearm work instead.

The correct (left) and incorrect (right) top position of the curl.

Curl the bar up, do not swing it up. Start with your elbows at your sides so that your upper arms are vertical when viewed from the side *and* from the front. Never let your elbows move backwards or outwards as you curl. As you curl, your elbows may come forward only *very slightly*. At the top position, your hands should be several inches *short* of where they would be to make your forearms vertical. Your hands may come to shoulder height, but no higher. You should not be able to rest at the top of this exercise.

You can only get your hands higher than the position just described if your elbows come forward and you get your front deltoids heavily involved. Most trainees let their elbows come forward and well out in front of their torso. This does not increase work for the arm flexors but does increase stress on the elbows, shoulders and lower back.

Watch yourself side-on to a mirror and familiarize yourself with what is the correct top position in the curl. Curling in a strict and proper fashion will force you to reduce your usual curling poundage. But you will then apply more resistance to your biceps and brachialis than you were when using more weight, but with your deltoids doing so much of the work. Curl in good form and no longer will your deltoids be sore after a set of intensive curls.

Take a brief pause at the contracted top position. It is not possible to rest at the top of a *properly* performed curl. You can only rest if you move your elbows well forward, get the bar under your chin, and take tension off your arm flexors and place it on your elbows and shoulders. Do not use any of that improper form.

Lower the bar under perfect control. At the bottom of each rep, take a short pause before starting the next rep. Take a breath or two, hold your last breath, and then immediately perform the next ascent starting from a dead stop. Exhale during the ascent, or very briefly hold your breath if you prefer, and exhale on the descent.

If the straight bar irritates your elbows or wrists, try a slightly closer or wider grip. If that does not correct the problem, try an EZ-curl bar, or use dumbbells. But if you cannot keep your wrists in the neutral position on a straight bar, as noted earlier, you need to strengthen your forearms.

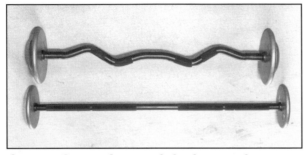

Comparison of a straight bar and an EZ-curl bar.

Use a 2"-diameter or thicker bar with great caution in the curl. A thick bar will increase the stress on your elbows. Start very light and progress slowly.

Curling with your hips, back and head against a vertical post will help eliminate cheating. But with a barbell, your thighs will get in the way at the bottom. Dumbbells would be a better choice. Another option is to do the barbell curl on a *vertical* preacher bench. Get the top ridge of the bench in your armpits and then have the bar handed to you. Be very careful not to lose control at the bottom. You must not hyperextend your elbows. Have a spotter watching in case you need assistance. While the preacher bench will tighten up your curling form, forget the myth that it will "lengthen" your biceps. That is just one of a host of deceptions that are widespread in the training world.

The barbell curl can be done while seated. This makes the movement into a partial curl because your thighs will

obstruct the barbell and prevent the full extension of your arms. For back support and to keep your form tight, brace your back against a vertical bench. Briefly pause at the bottom of each rep. Do not bounce the bar off your thighs.

Dumbbell curls

With dumbbells you can do the curl one arm at a time, alternately, or both together, and while either standing or seated. Different wrist positions produce differing effects on the arm flexors, and apply stress differently to the elbows.

One of the alternatives is to keep your thumbs up all the time, in the hammer curl. This uses a parallel grip, which is probably the most natural for the curling motion. If you have had wrist, elbow or shoulder problems, the hammer curl will probably be the most comfortable curl.

Hammer curl

In all dumbbell curls, use the same elbow positioning as in the barbell curl, and keep your wrists in a neutral position.

A supinated curl keeps your hands in the supinated or palms-up position during the entire exercise. The supinating curl moves you in and out of the supinated position during each rep.

Do the supinating curl while standing. Take two dumbbells and start with each hand pronated, i.e., with your palms facing to the rear. The inside half of each dumbbell should be touching its corresponding thigh. Rather than perfectly centering your hands on the dumbbells, position each hand slightly off center to the *outside*. You may find that this helps the exercise more than does a perfectly centered grip.

As you raise the pair of dumbbells, rotate your hands so that at the top of the curl your palms face up. Do not supinate and then curl. The supinating and curling happen together. Do not let your elbows drift out to the sides or to the rear. And always keep your hands in a straight line with your wrists.

The later you initiate the supination, the harder it will be to keep your elbows in the right position next to your torso. Curl into the same top position as in the barbell curl. If the weight is too heavy, the exercise will turn into more of a partial power clean than a curl. Resist the temptation to

Supinating curl

cheat in order to use more weight. Cheating will take the stress away from the muscles you are targeting.

Be sure to lower the dumbbells very deliberately, and gradually pronate your hands during the descent.

Spotting

Form deterioration in the curl is shown by leaning back and bringing the elbows too far forward. As soon as your torso goes back beyond the vertical, you should be urged to straighten up and get more serious. But on the next rep, a little assistance will be needed if you are to complete the rep in good form. Assistance should be applied with two hands and in a symmetrical way. Just enough help should be given to keep your torso and upper arms vertical.

As noted already, a spotter is essential if you use the preacher bench for curling.

Caution!

The curl works a very small area of muscle, which can get a lot of work from some of the major movements for the upper body, so do not get overly concerned with the curl. But when you do curl, do it in proper form. Get hung up on the big movements and then you will do a lot to improve your physique and strength.

8

Deadlift (bent-legged)

Main muscles worked
erectors, glutes, front and rear thighs, lats, upper back, forearms

Capsule description
with legs well bent, and a flat back, lift the resistance from the floor

Introduction

To perform the conventional deadlift, start with bent legs, medium-width stance, arms straight and positioned just outside your legs, flat back, and hips much lower than your shoulders. Lift a barbell from the floor until you are standing erect with your hands at your thighs.

Bottom position for the sumo deadlift. The conventional deadlift places the legs between the arms.

Properly done, the bent-legged deadlift is safe and super effective—it is one of the most productive of all weight-training exercises. But use poor form, abuse low reps, overtrain, or try to pull a too-heavy lift, and you will hurt yourself. Learn to deadlift properly before you concern yourself with poundage, and add weight slowly while maintaining perfect form.

Before you can deadlift with good form you need to be flexible enough to be able to adopt the necessary positioning. You especially need to have flexible Achilles tendons, hamstrings, thigh adductors, and glutes. Women who usually wear shoes with high heels are especially likely to have very tight Achilles tendons.

If currently you are inflexible, then invest 4–6 weeks progressively and carefully increasing your flexibility before you start learning how to deadlift. The deadlift itself will help you to become more flexible, but you will not be able to adopt good form for a while. Thus you will practice bad habits that will have to be "unlearned." This is why it is best to be flexible in the first place.

If you have had a serious back injury, do not deadlift without the clearance of a sports-orientated chiropractor. If you have had any minor back injuries, still get a chiropractor's clearance.

There is the straight bar deadlift, and the Trap Bar deadlift. The straight bar deadlift will be detailed first. Most of the technique also applies to the Trap Bar deadlift. Technique points specific to the Trap Bar deadlift will be discussed separately. Two other variations of the bent-legged deadlift—the sumo deadlift and the modified straddle lift—will also be covered in this section.

Setup and positioning

Deadlift using a bar with a 20-kg or 45-lb plate on each end. If you do not have the strength for this, and/or have to use smaller-diameter plates, then set the plates on blocks of wood so that the height of the bar from the floor is the same as it would be if it was loaded with 45-lb plates. Some suppliers of powerlifting and Olympic weightlifting equipment sell plates the same diameter as 45-lb ones, but with only a fraction of the weight. These can be used by people who have yet to develop the strength needed to handle 45-lb plates.

If you deadlift with raised heels you will encourage form defects. When you get very serious about deadlifting, you should wear non-slip footwear with the absolute minimum of a sole and heel. If you deadlift wearing shoes with a heel, choose solid and sturdy shoes. Soft and spongy ones will not give you the solid support you need because as you deadlift your feet will move slightly on the soft underneath structure. A sturdy pair of walking shoes or boots may give you better support than a pair of high-priced athletic shoes.

For best control of the bar, especially if you set the bar on the floor and stand between reps, do not train on a slick surface or bare concrete. Otherwise the bar will easily move around when set down, and there is also the chance that your feet will slip. Deadlift on rubber matting or construct a simple deadlifting "platform"

by affixing hard wearing carpet to the top surface of a 7' x 3' x 1" piece of wood.

Place your feet about hip-width apart with toes turned out. Fine-tune the heel spacing and degree of toe flare to find the precise stance that helps your lifting technique the most. Just a slightly different stance may help you to deliver smoother and more efficient deadlifting technique. Your hands should just touch the outside of your lower legs at the bottom of the lift.

With the stance fine-tuning what you are looking for is a foot placement that spreads the stress of the deadlift over your legs, glutes and back. Do not try to focus most of the stress on just one body structure. You must deadlift without your lower back rounding or your torso leaning forward excessively. You want your heels to remain firmly planted on the floor. You need to feel stable at all times, with no tendency to topple forward. You also need to be able to push through your heels, not the front of your feet. And you want your knees to stay tracking over your feet rather than tending to come in as you ascend.

Neither stand too far from the bar nor too close. If you pull the bar into your shins on the ascent, you probably started too close to it. If you are too far from the bar it will travel away from your legs and you will place excessive strain on your lower back, risk losing the rep and, perhaps, injure yourself. Position yourself so that the bar brushes against your legs throughout the ascent. Find the foot positioning which, when your legs are bent at the bottom position, has the bar touching your shins. But when you are standing erect before squatting down, your shins will be a little in front of the bar.

Closely related to how near you stand to the bar, is your arm positioning. Your arms should hang in a straight line with no bending at your elbows. Your arms just link your torso to the bar. In the deadlift with a

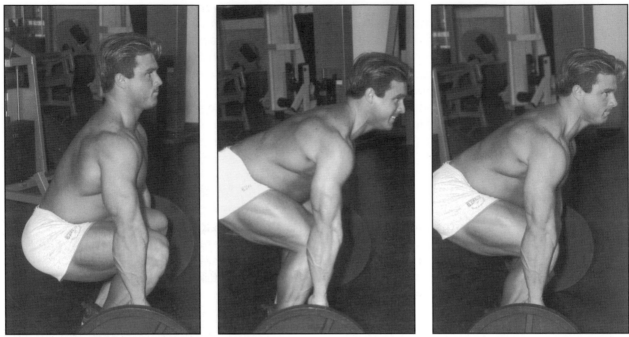

For an even distribution of stress over the legs, glutes and back, correct hip positioning is critical in the deadlift. Hips too low (left), hips a tad too high (middle), hips correct (right).

straight bar, your arms should be vertical or near vertical throughout the lift.

Use a pronated grip. If you are training for powerlifting competition, use a reverse grip only during your final weeks of preparation. The reverse grip produces an asymmetrical distribution of stress, and some torque. The pronated grip is safer. But no grip is safe if you lose it. A bar slipping out of one hand can result in a lot of torque. If you cannot hold onto a bar, do not try to lift it.

Perhaps, no matter how much you work on your grip, the pronated lifting style still lets you down when you use your heaviest deadlift weights. In such a case, and assuming you are using plenty of lifting chalk, use the reverse grip. But only use it for your heaviest sets, and alternate from set to set which way around you have

your hands. For one set have it left hand under and right hand over, and the next set have your right hand under and your left hand over. In this way you will avoid always applying the asymmetrical stress in the same way, and both sides of your body will get their turns.

The asymmetrical loading from this type of deadlifting is likely to be less than what it is during heavy side bends. Unless you have a history of back problems you should not encounter difficulties from doing the side bend, so long as your form is good. You should, therefore, not have problems from the reverse grip deadlifting so long as you do it as advised here.

Each foot must be exactly the same distance from the bar. Even if one foot is just slightly ahead or behind the other, relative to the bar, this will produce an asymmetrical drive and a slight twisting action. For symmetrical form you must have symmetrical foot positioning.

The bar must be exactly parallel to a line drawn across the toes of your shoes. If the bar torques slightly and is touching one leg but is an inch or two away from the other, then the stress upon one side of your body increases dramatically, as does the risk of injury.

All fine-tuning needed to determine your ideal deadlifting form must be done with a relatively light weight. Learn the technique *before* you start training hard.

Performance of the deadlift

With your feet and the bar in the right position, stand and get ready for the first rep. Straighten your arms and place them at your sides ready to "drop" straight down into position on the bar. Take your final breath, hold it, "lock" your back, and descend under control and until your hands touch the bar. Like in the squat, the first downward movement is to bend at your knees and then you will naturally move into bending at your hips. Keep your bodyweight pressing over your heels. But do not rock back and lose your balance.

If you have to fiddle to get your grip spacing right on the bar, you risk losing the rigid torso and flat back you need for a safe pull. Learn to get your grip right without any fiddling around. To help here, get two pieces of garden hose about an inch long each. Slice them open and tape one in the correct position on each side of the bar so that when your index fingers brush against them, your hands are in the right position. In this way you do not even need to look down as you deadlift. You descend, immediately place your hands into position, and then start the ascent.

At the bottom position, set yourself up with bent legs, hips *much* lower than your shoulders, bar close to your shins, head up, and your bodyweight felt mostly through your heels. The deadlift is done by the legs and back *together*. Do not try to deadlift with your legs or back alone.

If you try to start the deadlift primarily with your legs, your legs will straighten too

quickly and the movement will turn into a dangerous form of a stiff-legged deadlift. If you try to start a deadlift with very little leg involvement, you will not get very far unless it is only a light weight; but you will expose your lower back to a very dangerous degree of stress.

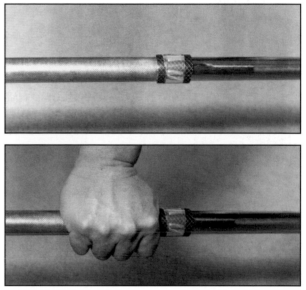

Two pieces of hose appropriately placed on a deadlift bar enable each hand to be positioned without having to look down to check. See text. Here is one of those pieces of hose. For clear viewing, the legs were kept out of the photos.

The degree to which you have to flex your legs largely depends on your arm and leg lengths, and their lengths relative to your torso. Consider an individual with relatively short limbs and a long torso. He will need to bend his legs more than will someone who has a more typical structure, in order to adopt the right position to lift the bar from the floor with a flat back and lots of leg involvement.

Hold the relative positions of your head, shoulders and hips during the lift, i.e., keep your back flat throughout. A flat

Common errors that cause injuries in the deadlift. Left: The legs have locked out too quickly and the bar has gone adrift from the legs. Right: The legs have locked out too quickly and the back has started to round.

back does not mean forcing an arch. Deadlifting with an exaggerated arch puts huge stress on your vertebral column. Leading with your head and shoulders will help you to deadlift with a flat back.

The first part of the ascent is to shrug your shoulders vertically (not forward) against the bar. While you will not lift the bar unless it is very light, this shrug "locks" your back into a solid position for the pull. Then "squeeze" the bar off the floor by simultaneously pushing with your legs, through your *heels*, and pulling with your back. When you pull, make it a smooth pull, even on the slow side for the first few inches. Do not snatch at the bar.

Snatching at the bar leads to bending your arms, moving you forward, raising your hips too quickly, losing the groove, and increasing stress on your back.

Once the bar is off the floor and moving, try to accelerate its speed. Push through both your heels with equal force. If you favor one leg you will produce a dangerous corkscrew-like motion. Think of pushing your feet "through" the floor.

Never look down as you initiate the pull from the floor. Keep your jaw parallel to the floor and look forward or slightly up. And never look down during the course of the ascent.

Slowly exhale during the ascent and always keep the bar moving next to your legs. If necessary, wear something over your shins to prevent abrasions. Absolutely *do not* let the bar move out and away from you—this is critical.

If the bar drifts even an inch forward of your ideal groove you will be in trouble, at least in low-rep work. In medium and high-rep training there is room for a *small* deviation from the ideal groove without causing any trouble, unless it is on the very final rep or two.

Over the final few inches of the ascent, pay very special attention to keeping your shoulders pulled back and your scapulae (shoulder blades) retracted. If your shoulders slump forward, your back will round severely, stress on your back will be hugely increased, and you will set yourself up for a serious injury. Incline shrugs will help you to develop the strength needed to keep your shoulders pulled back.

Never lean back at the top. Just stay vertical at the top of the lift. Having your hips in front of your shoulders causes hyperextension in your lower back, and very dangerous compression of your intervertebral discs.

As you stand, keep your scapulae retracted, lower back slightly arched, weight felt through your heels, and shoulders, hips and ankles lined up vertically.

Lower the bar in perfectly controlled and symmetrical form, with a synchronized flexion of your legs and forward lean of your torso. Always maintain a flat back. Lowering a straight bar can be awkward, depending on your structure. For tall people the descent may be dangerous because the torso has to be leaned forward so much to get the bar around the knees. Find the minimum of forward lean needed to get a straight bar around your knees.

For the descent with a straight bar, first slide the bar down your thighs to your knees, mostly by bending at your knees. Then bend forward the minimum needed to get the bar around your knees. Then bend further at your knees and lower the bar to the floor. As soon as the bar is below your knees, keep it as close to your shins as possible, to reduce the stress on your lower back. Descend quite slowly in order to keep perfect control over the bar—take 2–3 seconds for each descent.

A technically easier descent is just one of the many ways in which the Trap Bar deadlift is safer and more productive than the straight bar deadlift.

With the weight gently set on the floor or platform, keep your hands in position, your torso tensed and tight, and your eyes looking forward. Take a breath or two, and immediately do the next rep. As the cycle progresses, and the perceived weight becomes ever heavier, you may need to

take more breaths between reps. If so, stand between reps to take the breaths, with the bar on the floor. While you stand, ensure that your feet are in the right position relative to the bar. Do the reps one by one, making a perfect descent for each.

The bent-legged deadlift just described is the conventional style. There are two other styles of deadlifting—the Trap bar deadlift, and the sumo deadlift.

Trap Bar deadlift

The Trap Bar, developed by Al Gerard, is a terrific aid for the deadlift and is much superior to a straight bar. It reduces spine stress relative to the straight bar deadlift, and puts the arms and hands into a near-perfect position. It also makes the lowering of the bar a reverse of the ascent. With a straight bar, lowering the weight can be a problem. This is because the knees get in the way more on the descent than they do on the ascent. The extent of this depends on individual structure. This rhombus-like bar lets users get the best from the deadlift while keeping technique problems to a minimum. It is an outstanding bar. Urge the management of where you train to get a Trap Bar. All who use it will benefit.

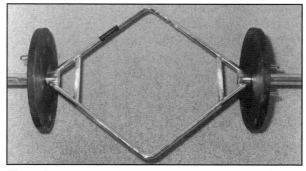

Trap Bar

If you are a competitive powerlifter and thus must use a straight bar at meets and in most of your training, a Trap Bar can still be a valuable "off" season training tool. It greatly reduces unnecessary stress but while developing strength that *may* have carry-over value to the straight bar deadlift (or even squat). Before a competition you would need to return to straight bar work for a cycle to "translate" any Trap Bar gains over to the straight bar deadlift (or squat).

With the Trap Bar deadlift you can involve more leg flexion if you want to make it more of a squat than a deadlift, hand spacing is determined by the gripping sites (about 22"–24" apart depending on the manufacturer), a parallel grip is used, and the bar does not drag against your thighs. The pathway of an imaginary straight line joining the ends of the bar can run "in" your body, rather than in front of it as with a straight bar. As a result of these differences, in the Trap Bar deadlift (done correctly) your arms will not be as near to vertical at the bottom of the exercise as they are in the deadlift with a straight bar. Your hands will be behind an imaginary vertical line dropped from your shoulders. The extent of this will be determined by your body structure and how deep you position your hips. Your arms, though, should still be straight.

Because a Trap Bar permits more leg flexion than does a straight bar,

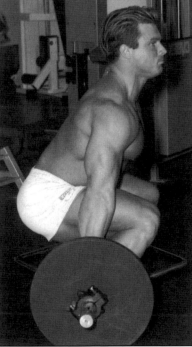

Trap Bar deadlift involving a lot of leg flexion.

the Trap Bar deadlift can give more work to your quads than can the straight bar deadlift. The Trap Bar deadlift can increase thigh involvement even further if it is done from off a raised surface of an inch or two. The two critical provisos are that your lower back can be kept flat in this extended range of motion, and you have no knee limitations.

Unless you use a wide stance in the squat, use your squat stance in the Trap Bar deadlift (see *Squat*). Fine-tune if you feel the need, but your squat stance should be your starting point. If you use a wide squat stance you will have to narrow it so that your legs just fit inside your arms when your hands are in position on the handles. If you cannot safely use this narrowed stance, then the Trap Bar deadlift is not suited to you.

With the spacing of your heels determined, you need to place your feet inside the rhombus in the best position for you. As a starting point, place your feet so that the center of the ends of the bar runs through the bony prominence in the center of the outside of each of your ankles, as you stand with your legs *straight*. While this foot positioning will suit some people, for many people it will be a little too far forward. Try it with a very light weight and see.

Two 15-kg plates, smooth sides up, can be placed side by side under a Trap Bar, to produce a raised, roomy and stable surface from which to deadlift for increased quadriceps involvement.

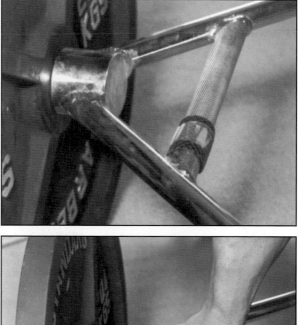

A piece of garden hose of the right size, and appropriately positioned, permits hand centering on a Trap Bar's handle without having to look down to check. See text. The legs were kept out of the photos so as not to obstruct viewing.

Then move your feet back an inch, and see how that works out. Then move another inch back, and try that. If that does not feel right, try a tad further back. Ideal foot positioning for most people will likely fall somewhere in that short range of variation.

Exactly where optimal foot positioning for you will be, heavily depends on your body structure and degree of leg flexion you use. You may need several workouts of practice before you can settle on the optimum foot positioning for you. What you should look for is being able to apply a vertical pathway to the bar with no horizontal movement. If you are positioned too far to the rear, you will probably be bent forward too much and the bar may swing a little to the rear as soon as you drive it off the floor, and there will be excessive stress on your back. On the other hand, if you are positioned too far to the front, the bar will probably swing to the front as soon as you drive it off the floor.

Once you have the foot positioning that works best for you, you need a reference point so that you can consistently adopt the right setup. Use the position of the front rim of your shoes relative to the front of the rhombus. Of course your eyes need

to be viewing from the same point each time. For example, as you stand upright, look down and perhaps the front rim of your shoes is directly below the inside edge of the front of the rhombus. Perhaps it is an inch inside. Get inside a Trap Bar and see for yourself.

If both of your hands are off center on the handles, the Trap Bar will tip. If just one hand is off center, dangerous rotational stress may result. You need to keep both hands perfectly centered, and the rhombus parallel to the floor.

Here is a tip for how to center your hands on the handles without having to look down and lose the tensed torso and correct "get-set" position. Slice open two pieces of garden hose that are each about 1.5" long. Tape one on each handle, flush against the front bar, so that when you feel your hand touching the edge of the hose you know that your hand is centered.

Sumo deadlift

The first-choice type of deadlift for anyone should be with a Trap Bar. But if you have no Trap Bar, experiment with the sumo deadlift and see if it works better for you than the conventional deadlift.

The sumo deadlift uses a straight bar and wide stance, with the hands holding the bar between the legs. Some people have body structures that are better suited to the sumo deadlift than the conventional straight bar style. People who prefer a wide stance in the squat, and who have good leverages for the squat but not so favorable ones for the deadlift, may prefer the sumo style. Tall people who have poor leverages for the squat and conventional deadlift may be able to sumo deadlift very efficiently. The key factor is being able to maintain a flat back. The sumo style may enable some people to keep a flat back at a lower position than they can in the conventional deadlift, and hold that flat back with less difficulty throughout the lift.

In the sumo style, the torso does not usually tip forward as much as it does in the conventional deadlift, when comparing the two styles on the *same* lifter. There may be a bit more leg flexion to balance the more upright torso. As in the conventional deadlift, the erector muscles are worked primarily through static contraction, and not through much of a range of motion. (Back extensions and stiff-legged deadlifts

work the erectors through a greater range of motion.) Though the back is heavily involved in the sumo deadlift, the glutes and thighs take relatively more stress.

Though the sumo deadlift looks radically different from the conventional deadlift, the two styles are very similar in actual performance, and pathway of the bar. It is the radically different stance that distinguishes the sumo deadlift. The grip is a little closer, but not greatly so.

Sumo-style powerlifters, at least in competition, may benefit from an extreme width of stance that has their feet almost touching the plates. This reduces the range of motion to the minimum. But for general training, that extreme stance is not desirable. Use a moderately wide stance.

For example, if you are a man of about 5' 10", use a stance with about 22" between your heels as the *starting* point, with your toes turned out at about 45°. Fine-tune from there. Try the same flare but a slightly wider stance. Then try a little less flare but the same wider stance. Keep fine-tuning until you find what helps your lifting technique the most. After a few weeks of experience you will probably want to fine-tune your stance further. By then you may find that just a slightly different foot positioning will help you to deliver improved sumo technique.

As in the conventional deadlift, find the foot positioning relative to the bar which, when your legs are bent at the bottom position, has the bar touching your shins. But when you are standing erect before bending down, your shins will be a little in front of the bar.

For the first descent, follow the same basic format as given for the conventional deadlift. Descend until your hands touch the bar, and then take your grip. Do not grip the bar so closely that your hands are on the smooth part of the bar. Use a hip-width grip as a starting point, with your

Sumo deadlift

hands on the knurling, and fine-tune from there. If your grip is too close you will find it hard to control the bar's balance.

For the drive from the floor, ascent, lockout, descent, and breathing, follow the same guidelines as in the conventional deadlift. You may find that descending with the bar in your hands is easier in the sumo style than the conventional straight bar style. Your knees may be less of an obstacle to get around, because of the wider stance. You may therefore find that you bend forward to a lesser degree in the sumo deadlift than the conventional style.

Do not immediately introduce heavy wide-stance deadlifting. That would be a road to injury. Continue with conventional deadlifting and progressively work into the sumo style, starting with a very light weight. If you do not have the flexibility to move straight into even a moderately wide stance, move there progressively over a few weeks. Some supplementary stretching for your thigh adductors, hamstrings and glutes may be needed, to give you the flexibility to adopt your optimum stance.

Once you have settled on the right setup for you, progressively add weight. Once you are close to working intensively, which may not be until 10–12 weeks after introducing the sumo deadlift into your program, drop the conventional deadlift and focus on the sumo style. After another month or two, if not already, you should know whether the sumo deadlift is for you.

Other tips for the deadlift

When experimenting to find your optimum stance in any deadlift style, you cannot precisely remember the stance variations you are working with unless you have something in black and white. During the learning period, while using light weights, stand on cardboard when you deadlift. When you have settled with whatever stance you are using on a given training day, for whichever style of deadlift you are working on, draw around your feet with a marker. Then next session, stand on your footprints and you will know where you were positioned last time. If you revise your positioning, draw a new pair of footprints. Eventually you will settle on a stance that works best for you. Mark that position on cardboard and then you will be able to refer to it when needed.

For work sets, use chalk on your hands to improve your grip on the bar. Do not use straps. With a few months of specialized grip work if needed, chalk, and working up in poundages slowly, you will be able to hold any weight you can deadlift.

Always deadlift with collars on the bar. This is critical for keeping the plates in position and ensuring a balanced bar.

During both the descent and ascent, keep the stress of the lift *off* your toes. Otherwise the bar will tend to move away from you during each rep. This will greatly increase the stress of the exercise and the chance of your form breaking down.

Critical reminder
Photographs alone cannot explain good exercise technique. Please do not skip any of the text. Study it all very carefully.

Do not bounce the weights on the floor. If you rush the reps, and do them in a continuous style, you will risk banging the floor with the plates on one or both sides. This will disrupt your balance, produce asymmetrical pulling, and stress your body unevenly. This is dangerous.

Never turn your head while you are lifting or lowering the bar. If you do, the bar will tip slightly, your groove will be ruined, and you could hurt yourself.

Pull and lower the bar symmetrically. Do not take more stress on one side of your body than the other.

If you cannot complete a rep without your shoulders slumping, lower the weight immediately. *Do not try to get that rep. End the set of your own volition before you get hurt.*

Never drop the weight, even if you have to dump it due to feeling your back starting to round. Protecting the equipment and floor is only part of the reason for always lowering the bar in a controlled manner. A bar slamming onto the floor or platform, or onto rack pins, can injure your back, shoulders, elbows or wrists. You may not feel it immediately, but just wait a few days. Lowering the weight too quickly also leads to rounding the back and losing the important flat-back position.

If you deadlift inside a power rack while facing a mirror and using a straight bar, the position of the bar relative to the rack's uprights will help you to be aware of the path of the bar during the lift.

Once you are training hard, never work the deadlift to absolute failure. Always keep the "do or die" rep in you. And do not do forced reps or negative-only reps. If you go so near the limit that it takes you 10 seconds or more just to get the final few inches of a rep, especially when doing very low reps, the stress upon your lower back will be colossal. This type of lifting can cause *very* serious injuries. Do not do it!

Do not deadlift while your lower back is still sore from an earlier workout or some heavy manual labor. Rest a day or few longer, until the soreness has left.

Using a lifting belt is optional for low-rep deadlifts, but inhibiting in high-rep work because of the heavy breathing. A strong midsection is the best type of belt.

A flat back is *vital* for safe deadlifting. As seen from the side view, get feedback from a training partner or assistant, or record yourself with a video camera.

Discover your relative hip, shoulder and head positions. This is critical because the form you think you use is almost certainly not what you actually use.

Once you have mastered deadlifting technique you must still give 100% attention to ensure that you deliver perfect form for every rep you do. Never become overconfident and think that you can deliver good form even if your focus is not 100%. Even a slight slip of concentration can lead to lowering the bar slightly out of position. This will ruin your groove, make the weight feel heavier, make your reps harder, cause frustration, and risk injury.

To make plate changing easy, there are several tips. With a straight bar, do the deadlift from off rack pins set at the height so that at the bottom position the barbell plates are a fraction of an inch off the floor. Alternatively, and for both a straight bar and a Trap Bar, you could load only a single full-size plate (45 lbs or 20 kgs) on each end, and use smaller-diameter plates outside the large one. Another option for plate changing is to use multiple full-size plates at each end but first roll the bar so that only the inside plate rests on a small disc. Other full-size plates can then be added or removed easily. Then roll the bar back into position for lifting. For a straight barbell, a lever bar (a sort of "jack") is available that can lift one or both ends off the floor when you need to change plates.

Deadlifts and any other heavy grip work cause callus buildup on your hands. If this is excessive, your skin will become vulnerable to cracks and tears. Both may temporarily restrict your training.

Avoid excessive build up of calluses. Once or twice a week, after you have showered or bathed, use a pumice stone or callus file and gently rub the calluses on your hands. Do not erase the calluses, and do not try to cut them away with a blade or scissors. Just keep the calluses under control so that they do not cause loss of elasticity on the skin under and around them. To maintain the elasticity of the skin of your palms and fingers, use hand cream when necessary—but never immediately before training.

Deadlifting from the top

In both straight bar and Trap Bar deadlifts, the exercise can be done from the top. The bar is first taken off a support while you are standing, and the brief pause between reps is taken at the top.

Take the loaded bar from off boxes or, just in the case of the straight bar, from off saddles set at mid-thigh height in a power rack. If you use boxes, the plates loaded on the bar will roll easily if they are placed on a surface that is horizontal and slick. A slightly hollowed surface, or some hard wearing carpet or rubber fixed to the top of the boxes, will increase your control over the bar when the plates are on the boxes.

You want to have the bar set at a little below the height of the middle of your thighs, depending on the length of your arms. Put your feet under the bar, take your grip, arch your back a little, and then straighten your legs. Then shuffle back a quarter pace, akin to how you would back out of a rack if you were going to squat. Then you are ready to start a set.

By starting from the top, and with a perfect descent as described in the form of the regular "from the bottom" deadlift, you will be properly set up for the pull from the floor. There are three alternatives for the "turnaround" at the bottom. First, and probably the best, is to very briefly and gently set the weight on the floor, stay tight and immediately drive up. You must not relax your body, not even for a split second. Second, lower the bar to an inch or so above the floor and then start the ascent. Third, just touch the plates to the floor and immediately drive the bar up. There is no

In position to start deadlifting from the top. The bar was taken from off saddles set at mid-thigh height in the rack. This was followed by shuffling back just enough so that the rack's uprights could not be struck during the deadlift.

pause. This third option is risky because you are more likely to lose the groove, especially if you touch only one side of the plates to the floor. Regardless of how the turnaround is done, the pause between reps for a breath or few is taken at the top while you have the bar in your hands.

There is likely to be a grip limitation if you move straight into your top weights for this style. If, though, you build up your weights gradually, from a moderate start, if you hold the bar between your palms and fingers rather than just in your fingers, if you use chalk, if you have been doing some serious thick-bar grip work for a few months, and if you avoid high reps, then your grip should not be a major limitation.

To hold the bar between your palms and fingers, place it in the middle of your palm before wrapping your fingers around it. If the bar is at the base of your fingers when you wrap your fingers around it, your grip will not be as secure.

This "from the top" deadlifting is especially suited to a Trap Bar because that bar makes the deadlift a more efficient exercise. Regardless of which bar you use, pay special attention to ensure that you do not get out of the groove in the descent. Never lower the bar casually. But if you do get the bar out of the groove, set the bar on the floor and reposition yourself so that you are in the right position for the next ascent. Even though you are not supposed to stop at the bottom in this style, it is best that you break this rule if you have lost the groove and are in danger of hurting yourself on the next ascent.

One of the big advantages of starting each deadlift from the bottom is that you get the opportunity to check foot and bar positioning. By standing between reps, with the bar on the deck, you can correct any errors in foot or bar positioning so that you are perfectly set up for the next deadlift. In addition, there will be less compression of your spine because there is no exaggerated pause at the top position while you hold the weight. A further advantage of the from-the-bottom style is that a greater poundage can be used.

Deadlift in action

There are several ways to see the deadlift in action and discover the positive and negative impact of changes in technique. First, watch the impact of alterations in someone else's form. Second, see the impact on your own form by video taping yourself. Third, have someone else describe the effect of form changes on your own

technique, and work with you for a few sessions to get to grips with technique. This can apply to all forms of the deadlift: conventional, Trap Bar and sumo.

Start by discovering the influence of different positions of your hips before starting the descent. If your hips are pushed too far back at the start of the descent, the position that results for the start of the ascent will be poorer than if you had started the descent with your hips on an imaginary vertical line drawn between your shoulders and ankles (but with your lower back still arched a little). Your knees should bend *before* you bend at your hips. Get it the other way around and your form will be the worse for it.

When performing a set's first deadlift from the floor, if you did not previously make a good descent—with an imaginary weight in your hands, tensed torso, hips in the right place, stress over your heels, and back locked—that first rep will probably not be in the right groove. But the second rep of a multiple-rep set, provided that you made a proper descent and kept hold of the bar continuously, will be better than the first rep. Many people will find that this is true because a descent with a barbell is taken much more seriously than when a descent is made to a waiting barbell on the floor. Another factor has to do with muscle recruitment/activation being different in a descent with no weight relative to one with weight. Descending with a weight needs better lifting mechanics than descending without any weight. These are arguments in favor of starting the deadlift set with the bar in your hands at the top. But with practice you should be able to descend correctly *without* having the barbell in your hands, if you know what you are doing.

The descent of a rep, *if out of the groove*, will impair the ascent of the next rep, and contribute to acute and chronic injuries. This is especially so for the biggest lifts.

Pay very careful attention to a proper and controlled descent of every rep you do.

Look out for rounding of your lower back at the bottom of the deadlift. If you are very tall, have unusual leverages, or your body is (temporarily) very inflexible, you may not be able to deadlift from the floor without rounding your lower back. If this applies to you, you need to raise the bar in order to preserve a flat lower back. This can be done by setting the weights on a small but sturdy platform at each end, or by doing the exercise in a power rack with the pins set at the appropriate height.

With your lower back arched, but not excessively so, and your shoulders, hips and ankles in a straight line, compare the results from having the stress of the exercise felt through the front of your feet, and the rear. Do a few reps with a light weight felt through the front of your feet, and then a few reps with the weight over your heels and the pushing done through your heels. With the latter, your body will be nearer to perfectly vertical while you are standing, the forward lean during the exercise will not be as pronounced, and you will have more power potential.

To be sure that you have the weight over your heels at the bottom of each rep ready for the ascent, you must have it over your heels during the descent. If you descended with the stress over the front of your feet you will not be able to shift it to the rear once you are at the bottom, at least not when you use demanding weights.

If you have a Trap Bar handy, compare the Trap Bar deadlift with the straight bar deadlift. Notice how the former keeps the weight moving through a more vertical line than the latter, how the knees do not get in the way, and how a Trap Bar keeps the stress of the weight going "through" your body rather than in front of it.

Also notice the advantage of a Trap Bar for enabling you to get your hips in a better position for the descent. With a straight bar, the bar pressing against your thighs at the top position stops your hips moving the extra inch or two forward that they really need to before the next descent.

If you can do it without a negative reaction in your lower back or knees, notice how Trap Bar deadlifting while standing on a raised surface an inch high (only you are raised, not the barbell) causes the *top* of your thighbones to descend slightly *more* than the extra inch. Trap Bar deadlifting off a raised surface produces considerably increased thigh work.

With a very light weight, do a few reps that have your hips rising faster than your shoulders during the first part of the lift. Notice your form and the disproportionate stress on your lower back relative to the light poundage used. Compare this to form where, at the get-set position at the bottom, you shrug hard (with straight arms) against the stationary bar and *then* drive your heels into the floor while *simultaneously* driving your shoulders back. With the latter technique your hips will not ascend quicker than your shoulders.

Also compare the difference made by snatching at the weight (usually with slightly bent arms) as against the correct "squeezing" of the bar off the deck with straight arms.

Modified straddle lift

The straddle lift with a barbell is an awkward lift that is not recommended. But a modified version of it may be a fine alternative to the deadlift or the squat, according to how precisely it is done, and depending on the individual. The modified straddle lift can simulate the degree of flexion of the full squat, or the reduced leg flexion of the deadlift.

A loading pin is all that you may need before you can get going with the modified straddle lift. Get a loading pin made locally, or buy one ready made. Choose the thickness of pin according to the size of hole in the plates you use. (The loading pin is also needed for some of the grip work promoted elsewhere in this book.) The loading pin costs a small fraction of a Trap Bar, and yet the modified straddle lift provides some of the key advantages of a Trap Bar. You can deadlift using a natural parallel grip, without a bar getting in the way of your knees, and while keeping the pathway of the resistance close to your body. But in the modified straddle lift you can use a wider stance than you can with a Trap Bar, if you need to.

The top position of the modified straddle lift, prior to descending as if performing a deadlift. The legs straddle the weight.

Use a pair of very close parallel-grip handles. The greater the space between the handles, and the larger the gripping unit is, the more of an obstruction the handles will provide. This will tend to throw the pathway of the resistance forward, which should be avoided.

Attach the handles to some links of strong chain, or two or more carabiners linked together. This will provide "give" between your hands and the resistance if the weight hits the floor. (A carabiner is a D-shaped ring with a spring catch on one side, used in mountaineering for fastening ropes. Carabiners can be bought from suppliers of mountaineering gear.)

The boxes or benches you stand on should be of the same height, and must be stable and strong. Set their spacing so that there is plenty of room in which the resistance can move. By not using the largest-diameter plates you will reduce the potential for the resistance striking whatever you stand on. You must have plenty of room for the resistance to move in so that even if it swings a little it will not hit anything and ruin a rep.

Use your squat stance, or a little wider, and determine the degree of leg flexion you want to use. Make the movement into a deadlift or a squat, according to your purpose. But as in the squat, never put a board or plate under your heels. Adjust the length of chain, or number of carabiners joining the handles to the loading pin, so that when the resistance just touches the floor, you have reached the depth you want. But this length adjustment may not be practical. You may need to place a low platform or some plates on the floor, to raise the height from where you lift the resistance. Place some protection on the surface that the weights will strike.

You may need to widen your stance a little if you find that your upper legs get in the way of the handles at the top of the lift.

A loading pin and several carabiners linked together.

Keep your arms straight and the resistance moving in a vertical line. Exercise under control so that the resistance does not swing as you perform a set. And apply the other technique tips given for the deadlift, e.g., keep your head up, shoulder blades retracted, back flat, and push hard through your heels.

Keep the handles as close as possible to you throughout the exercise. With the Trap Bar deadlift, the path of the center of resistance can be kept a little farther back than it can in the straddle lift. This is because with a Trap Bar you hold the resistance at the side of your legs, but with the modified straddle lift you hold the resistance in front of you. Because of this, if you perform a deep descent, to mimic a squat more than a deadlift, you will probably deliver more stress on your knees than you would with a Trap Bar using the same depth of movement and resistance. In short, the straddle lift is likely to be more stressful on your knees and should be used with caution, and not by everybody.

Another potential problem arises from the close grip used in the straddle lift. The narrow grip may tend to pull your shoulders forward. If your back is weak relative to your thighs and hips, you will end up rounding your back. If this is a problem, focus for a few months on building back strength from stiff-legged deadlifts, and incline shrugs. This will bring up your back strength to match that of your thighs and glutes. Then you will be able to forge ahead with the straddle lift, in good form and with a flat back.

The Trap Bar and Shrug Bar—comments and qualifiers

The trap and shrug bars are not just terrific for many people who *do not* squat well with a bar over their shoulders. They are also terrific for people who *do* squat well, but perhaps do not straight-bar deadlift well because of their favorable leverages for the squat. For home gym trainees on a tight budget and no squat stands or safety setup to "catch" the bar, should they get stuck at the bottom of a squat, the trap/shrug bar deadlift is a perfect substitute for the squat. (The parallel bar dip could substitute for the bench press.)

However, depending on your leverages, the trap/shrug bar deadlift may not work your lower back adequately enough by itself. Stiff-legged or partial deadlifts may be needed too. For some people, the trap/shrug bar deadlift is a great substitute for the squat, but *not* for a straight-bar deadlift. And strength built by the trap/shrug bar may not necessarily carry over to the straight-bar deadlift, *depending on the individual.* Also, because the gripping sites on the trap/shrug bar limit the width of foot placement, some people—especially large men, and any trainees who must use a relatively wide stance for the sake of their knees—*may* find the *standard* trap/shrug bar too restricting for safe bent-legged deadlifting/squatting, and thus require a custom-made bar with gripping sites placed wider apart.

Different grips

Pronated grip (top) and supinated grip.

The two reverse grips, one hand under and one hand over in each case.

A medium-width parallel grip without a bar (top), and a wider parallel grip on a Trap Bar.

Grip confusion

A "palms facing away from you" description of a pronated grip only applies when you have your hands overhead such as in a pullup, or arms flexed like in the top position of a reverse curl—the reverse curl has the knuckles on top of the bar.

For exercises where the arms are not raised or flexed, such as the deadlift and shrug, a pronated grip has your palm facing towards you; and a supinated grip has your wrist turned so that your palm faces away from you.

In the bottom position of the reverse curl, a pronated grip (like in the deadlift) has your palms facing you. But in the *top* position of the reverse curl, when your arms are fully flexed, the pronated grip has your palms facing away from you.

9

Decline bench press

Main muscles worked
pectorals, deltoids, triceps

Capsule description
lie on your back on a decline bench, lower bar to your chest, then push it up

Use this exercise with special caution. It can be very severe on the shoulders. It also encourages exaggerated arching of the back. Arching should be minimized as much as possible in decline, horizontal and incline pressing, if not almost eliminated. Exaggerated arching increases the stress on the lower back to a dangerous level.

The decline bench press, relative to the torso, uses a different bar pathway than does the standard bench press, and a reduced range of motion. But the decline bench press is a riskier exercise. Partial bench presses in the rack, or dips, perhaps done as partial reps, are safer alternatives.

To do the decline bench press, use a decline of no more than 30°. Place yourself on the bench so that you do not struggle to unrack the bar from its supports, or struggle to rack the bar at the end of a set. Use the same grip and breathing pattern as in the regular bench press.

With a handoff, take the barbell out of the stands. Lock out, pause briefly, and then lower the bar under control to your lower chest well below your nipples (on the side of your abs). Pause very briefly at your chest, keep yourself tight, and then push the bar straight up. Your forearms should be vertical throughout the lift.

The decline bench press does not give the latitude for the bar pathway used in the regular bench press. Get more than just slightly out of the vertical-up-and-down groove and you will risk missing the rep and injuring yourself.

Never lower the bar to your mid chest or, even worse, to near your clavicles. And do not exaggerate the arch in your lower back—keep your butt fixed to the bench.

At the end of a set, have your spotter give you a guided return of the bar to the weight stands, so you do not lose control.

Spotting
A spotter is essential for this exercise. See *Bench Press*—similar guidelines for spotting apply to the decline bench press.

Spotting is so vital here because the groove of the decline bench press can be lost very easily. Further, fatigue can strike suddenly in the decline bench press, which makes the likelihood of losing the groove even greater. Losing the groove can be very dangerous. This applies even if you do the decline bench press in a power rack, with pins properly positioned for safety. The pins will catch the bar at the bottom of the exercise, but if you lose the groove before the bar is set down on the pins, you may hurt yourself. If you cannot do the decline bench press in 100% safety, with an alert and strong spotter in attendance, find an alternative exercise.

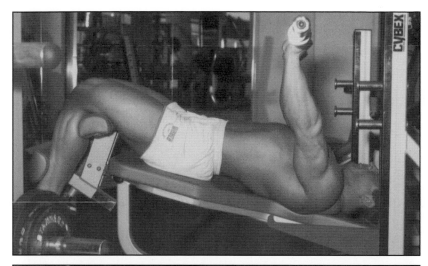

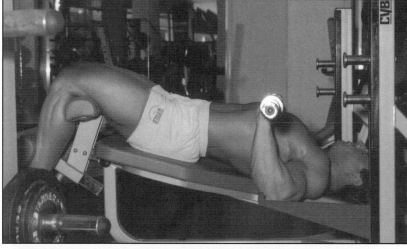

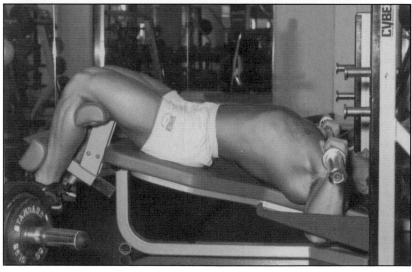

Top and left: The correct bar path of the decline bench press.

Never use this position.

10

Dumbbell row

Main muscles worked
lats, upper back, biceps, brachialis, rear deltoid, forearms

Capsule description
with one hand braced on a bench, take a dumbbell and pull it to your hip

There are two basic setup options. First, place your right knee and entire lower right leg on a horizontal bench. Brace your right hand on the same bench. Bend that arm slightly as you bend at your hips until your upper body is almost parallel to the floor. With a dumbbell on the floor below your left shoulder, keep your left leg almost straight, and positioned to the rear and out of the way.

An alternative setup is to brace your right hand on a bench, but keep your right foot on the floor. Your right leg must be well bent and your right foot well ahead of your left. Your left leg should be almost straight and your torso near to parallel with the floor.

The performance of the exercise is the same in both formats. Grab the dumbbell from the floor with your left hand. Keeping your elbow *in*, pull the dumbbell until it touches your left hip. Pull in an arc, not straight up, and with control. Do not yank it up by rotating about your spine and twisting your torso. Reduce the weight and do the exercise properly. As you pull the dumbbell, move your wrist so that the groove is as natural as possible. Hold the top position for a second, and try to crush your shoulder blades together. Your forearm should be vertical throughout the exercise. This method works your left side.

To train your right side, reverse the procedure. For breathing, inhale during the descent or while your arm is straight, and exhale on the ascent.

Unless there are small-diameter plates on the dumbbells you use, the plates will get in the way and obstruct a full range of motion. For home-gym trainees, consider having a local metal worker construct a Montini collar-free dumbbell rod. This is named after its designer, Art Montini. Due to the shape of the handle your hand is kept above the center of the weight plates. This allows you to use large plates but without the plates getting in the way like they would on a straight dumbbell rod. Another alternative is to use a kettlebell handle attached to a dumbbell rod. For home-gym trainees in particular, a local welder could cheaply make you a kettlebell handle to fit your dumbbells.

To reduce the size of the weight jumps between fixed-weight dumbbells, you can use the same approach described for dumbbell bench presses (see page 41). But in the dumbbell row, using wrist weights (obtainable from a sporting goods store) may be a good option for progressively working from one fixed-weight 'bell to the next. The wrist weights should not spoil your balance in the dumbbell row, unlike in pressing movements.

Two setups for the dumbbell row.

The correct (top photo) and incorrect contracted position.

Dumbbells with kettlebell handles.

Collar-free Montini dumbbell rod.

11

Finger extension

Main muscles worked
finger extensors

Capsule description
against resistance, open all the digits of a given hand

The finger extension is an essential exercise. It strengthens the muscles that extend the fingers whereas gripping exercises work the muscles that flex the fingers. A strength imbalance between these opposing muscles can cause elbow problems. Perform the finger extension at least once a week.

Get some elastic bands that are about 3" long when not stretched. Take just one of them to learn the exercise. Put all five digits of your right hand inside the elastic band so that the band rests approximately on the joints nearest your finger nails. Stretch out your fingers as far as you can without the elastic band slipping down. Find the degree of curvature in your fingers that is needed to keep the elastic band in place throughout the exercise.

When you can open your fingers fully against the resistance for 20 or more consecutive reps, add another band next workout and build up over a few weeks to another 20 or more reps in good form. Do two or three sets with each hand.

You will need to find elastic bands of various strengths so that you can add *gradual* resistance. You will also regularly need to replace the bands because, with use, they lose their strength and elasticity.

To help keep the bands in position, twist them around your middle finger before putting your other digits inside the

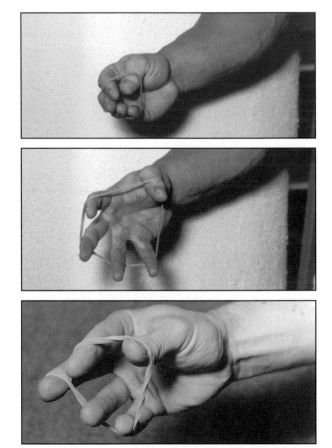

The bottom photo shows the bands wrapped around the middle finger.

bands. This will increase the tension on the bands and reduce the number of them you can use unless you switch to longer bands.

More pivotal general points to remember

❏ *Excellent exercise technique is needed not just to avoid training injuries. The use of first-class exercise form is one of the pivotal requirements for delivering the fastest rate of muscular development and strength gains.*

❏ *It is impossible to learn improved form at a stroke and immediately apply it to your usual working poundages. You must first practice the improved form using light weights for several workouts, and then progressively build your poundages back to where they used to be. How much time you will need to do this largely depends on how many bad habits you have to "unlearn."*

❏ *Training injuries come from at least three main sources—bad exercises, overtraining, and good exercises done in poor form. Descriptions of bad exercises are not included in this book, and overtraining comes as a result of poor program design.*

❏ *As critical as good exercise form is, for it to yield good results it must be combined with first-class training program design. If you overtrain, even using good exercise technique, you can still hurt yourself. But program design is not within the scope of this book. This book's concern is with teaching you how to perform the good exercises using first-class technique.*

12

Grip machine training

Main muscles worked
forearms, finger muscles

Capsule description
close a moveable bar to a fixed upper bar by using only your fingers

Introduction
A good grip machine is more comfortable, adjustable (for accommodating individual hand sizes, and changing resistance), and effective at developing crushing strength than are fixed-strength grippers. Grippers that are adjustable are much closer to the versatility of a grip machine. Fixed-resistance grippers can be fun to use, but depending on your hand size and strength they can be uncomfortable and awkward, and perhaps favor one hand more than the other, depending on the design.

Setup and positioning
While using a proper grip machine is the ideal, it is not a necessity. A grip machine can be simulated using a power rack. Set the two pairs of pins in the rack so that, with a bar set upon each pair, the space between the two levels of pins is right for squeezing the lower bar from extended fingers until it touches the top pins. If the distance is too great—and the next pin setting makes it too little—then, in the "too great" setting, fix something on the lower pins so that the lower bar starts from the correct position. Moving the lower bar up and down against the rack's uprights will help you to keep the bar in the right groove. The bar resting on the upper pins should not be so long that it gets in the way of the plates loaded on the lower bar. Get in a power rack and see how you can make this method work.

A better mock-up needs a special bar with hooks, as illustrated. Any skilled metal worker could easily make such a bar.

Performance
Regardless of whether you use a grip machine or a mock-up of it, use it *only* for your gripping muscles. When the weight is very demanding, the exercise can become more of a shrug from the trapezius than a squeeze from the grip. Keep your hands fixed to the top of the unit during the exercise. If your hands rise off the top bar, you have started to assist your grip by shrugging the weight up. Avoid this. Doing the exercise while seated helps ensure strict form and keeps the target muscles involved to the full. And be consistent with how you position your feet—braced *or* unbraced.

The grip machine is typically used with the thumbs around the top, and the other digits doing the movement. The exercise can also be done with the thumbs on the bottom, while seated or kneeling. This is a weaker squeezing position because the thumbs alone have to do the work. Finish off each grip machine session with a set of thumbs-below work, to ensure that all five digits of each hand get plenty of work.

A heavy-duty grip machine from Scorpion Gym Equipment.

Thumbs-down work.

Two mock-ups for a grip machine. The bottom one needs a bar with hooks.

13

Incline bench press

Main muscles worked
pectorals, deltoids, triceps

Capsule description
lie on your back on an incline bench, lower bar to your chest, then push it up

Setup and positioning

Use a heavy-duty adjustable bench, and preferably one that has an adjustment for tilting the seat—to prevent the user slipping out of position. Use a low-incline bench that has an angle of about 30° with the horizontal. Many if not most incline benches are set too upright for this exercise.

Ideally, do the exercise in a power rack, with pins properly positioned for safety. You can then do the exercise from the bottom position, off the pins, and not have to be concerned with getting the bar in and out of saddles. Alternatively you can do the exercise in a purpose-built incline bench press unit. If you do the exercise outside of the safety of a power rack, be sure to have a spotter attentively watching you in case you get stuck on a rep. The spotter is also needed to help you to get the bar out of the saddles safely, and return it to the saddles after the set is over.

Use the same grip as in the standard bench press. Do not use a thumbless grip—wrap your thumbs around the bar securely. Do not lower the bar to as low on your chest as in the regular bench press. Due to the inclination of the bench, a low position of the bar on your chest would lead to excessive and unsafe extension of your shoulders, and reduced control and power coming off the bottom. Nor should you lower the bar to your neck or near your clavicles—that positioning is very dangerous for your shoulders. But the lower the incline, the lower the bar can safely go on your chest.

> **To demonstrate exercise form clearly, the model did not wear a shirt, and weight stands and safety bars were often not used. This was only for illustration purposes. When you train, wear a shirt and always take the proper safety measures.**

Rather than wonder where to place the bar on your chest at the bottom of the incline press, look at it in terms of your forearms and upper arms. Your forearms should be vertical at the bottom—vertical when viewed *both* from the side and from the front. At that position your upper arms should be at about a 45°–60° angle to your rib cage. The precise angle will vary from individual to individual, largely due to arm length and torso girth variations. Get your forearms in the right position and you should automatically find the ideal placement of the bar on your chest.

An incline bench press unit with adjustable safety bars built in.

Once you have practiced the technique with a bare bar, to discover where the bar should touch your chest, you can proceed with the exercise.

Performance

Position yourself on the incline bench and plant your feet solidly on the floor, or on a foot brace if provided. Keep your feet fixed in position. Do not lift them. With a handoff, take the barbell out of the stands. Lock out, pause briefly, and then lower the bar under control. Touch your chest at the position explained earlier, and pause briefly. Keep yourself tight during the pause, with your abs contracted. Then press up and slightly to the rear, using one of the pathways described for the bench press, but with reduced horizontal movement. After locking out over your face, pause briefly, move the bar forward a little, and then lower it for the next rep. Use the same breathing pattern as in the bench press on a horizontal bench and, like in that exercise, never exaggerate the arch in your lower back.

You need to have vertical forearms when the bar is at your chest. Too wide (top), too narrow (middle), perfect (bottom).

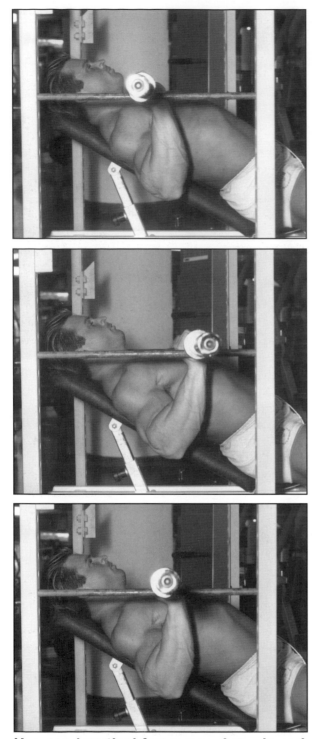

You need vertical forearms when viewed from the side. Bar too high on the chest (top), too low (middle), fine (bottom).

Dumbbell incline bench press

The incline bench press can also be done with dumbbells. Once the 'bells are in pressing position, the technique is basically the same as in the barbell version, but harder to implement.

A big advantage of dumbbells is that you can use whatever wrist positioning is most comfortable, rather than have your wrists fixed by a barbell. But there are handling difficulties getting the 'bells into position. See page 40 for some of the pros and cons of dumbbell bench pressing.

To perform the dumbbell incline bench press you need a method for getting the dumbbells into position ready for pressing. See pages 41 and 111–113 for how to do this. Use the method which is the most appropriate for the slope of the bench you use for incline pressing.

During the pressing, pay special attention to keeping the dumbbells from drifting out to the sides, go no deeper than in the barbell version, and keep the 'bells moving in tandem. Go easy for the first few workouts to get the feel for the exercise, and to find the wrist positioning that best suits you. This may be a parallel or near-to-parallel grip at the bottom of the movement, and a pronated or near-to-pronated grip at the top.

See page 41 for tips on how to progress gradually from one pair of fixed-weight dumbbells to the next.

Spotting

See *Bench Press*. The same guidelines apply to spotting the incline barbell press. The spotter needs to be elevated, to apply assistance with least difficulty.

Spotting someone who is incline pressing dumbbells can be tricky. One hand should be used to apply force under each elbow. But this is strictly for assisting a lifter to get a tough rep up in good form. A single person cannot simultaneously take

Dumbbell incline bench press

a pair of 'bells from someone who fails on a rep. Two spotters are needed then. With any type of dumbbell pressing, key markers of form deterioration are the 'bells drifting out to the sides, and one hand getting above, in front of, or to the rear of the other. Like in the dumbbell bench press, do not push this exercise to total failure. Stop a little short of failure so that you do not risk losing control of the 'bells.

Caution!

To help prevent back injuries when you incline press, you need to minimize if not almost eliminate the arch in your lower back. Here are three strategies for minimizing arching, each of which must be enhanced by keeping your abdominal muscles tightly contracted during each rep.

First, with your feet flat on the floor, keep your heels *in front* of an imaginary vertical line dropped from your knees. Wear shoes with non-slip soles, to avoid

your feet slipping. Trainees usually have their heels behind an imaginary line dropped from their knees, and thus they exaggerate the arching of their backs. But if the seat of the bench is too high, or if you have short legs, this first strategy will not work well enough.

For the second strategy there must be a foot rest attached to an extension from the end of the bench. If so, keep your feet on that rest when you perform the incline press. That will reduce the arch in your lower back so long as the design of the bench does not place your hips too high.

For the third strategy, place a non-slip block or platform under each foot, with your heels slightly in front of an imaginary line dropped from your knees. The blocks or platforms need to be high enough so that the arch in your lower back is reduced. Start with blocks or platforms about 4" high. If they do not reduce your arch, try something a little taller. A wide single platform would also do the job. The wider your feet are, the greater your stability.

Leg press

Main muscles worked
quadriceps, glutes, thigh adductors, hamstrings

Capsule description
with your feet against the foot plate, bend and straighten your legs

Introduction
The leg press can be done while seated or lying, depending on the model of machine. The major problem is the need for a safe machine. Some leg press machines (especially the vertical models), at least for some if not many trainees, are destructive. Great care must be given to ensure that you use a machine that does you no harm.

There are several types of leg press machines. Each can stress the musculature of the thighs and glutes slightly differently because of the differing angles of body positioning. *What is most important is finding a safe way of leg pressing over the long term.*

If used with perfect *controlled* form by a person with *no injury limitations whatsoever,* some vertical and 45° models *may* yield good results. But for most people, the leg press machine of choice will be of the leverage-style, e.g., the models produced by Hammer Strength®.

A few leg press machines, e.g., one of the models produced by Hammer Strength, have independent foot plates, one for each foot. These machines can be used one leg at a time, or alternately, i.e., "iso-laterally," as against the usual "bilateral" machines that have a single foot plate for both feet. (A bilateral machine can be used one leg at a time, but the non-working leg will not be properly braced as it can be on a true unilateral machine. But a bilateral machine cannot be used in alternate-leg fashion.) The unilateral leg press machine gives you the option of working both legs bilaterally, though each leg will have its own resistance to deal with. If you have the chance to use a unilateral leg press machine, do so. It may be especially valuable if you have one leg shorter than the other.

Here are key form rules to apply in the leg press, regardless of which model of machine you try.

Setup and positioning
Be sure the leg press machine is positioned on a perfectly horizontal surface. Check the floor's surface and, if necessary, have the machine repositioned.

Wear shoes with non-slip soles. The exercise may, however, be less stressful for your knees and back if you do it without shoes on (and thus zero heel elevation). But if you leg press without shoes, your stocking feet are likely to slide out of position. Doing the exercise in bare feet is an option. Quality non-slip shoes with no heel elevation relative to the balls of the feet is, however, the ideal.

Center yourself, from side to side, on the seat or bench. Place your feet on the middle or, better yet, on the higher part of the foot plate(s). The lower your feet are, the greater the knee stress. Some leg press

Never use a very low foot placement (left). While this positioning will minimize rounding of the lower back, it will maximize stress on the knees. Right: A much safer foot placement.

machines have foot plates that can be adjusted, to find the best angle of "fit" for the user. But most have set-position foot plates. If you use an adjustable machine, set the angle of the foot plate so that you can push through your heels during each rep.

If you do not push through your heels, then knee problems will be the likely result, sooner or later. Even if over the short term you do not suffer knee soreness from the leg press, though you are pushing heavily through the balls of your feet, knee problems will come later on. Correct your form now so that you do not have knee problems over the medium or long term. Take good care of your knees.

As with the deadlift and squat, even a small change of foot spacing or flare can have quite an impact on knee comfort. To begin with, using a very light weight, try a hip-width heel placement, with the inside "edges" of your feet perfectly parallel to

each other. Then try flaring your toes out just a few degrees. Then try a bit more flare. Then try a slightly different heel positioning in the different positions of toe flare. Find the heel spacing and angle of flare (if any) that feel the most comfortable and natural for you. The foot positioning you use must help to keep your knees tracking in a plane directly over your feet. Never let your knees buckle in, not even once. Start out right, and keep it right.

Without weight on the machine, find the depth of leg pressing that causes your lower back to round just slightly off the back support. If the seat is adjustable, fix your setup position so that you cannot go lower than an inch or two short of the point where your lower back would start to round. This assumes that your knees can handle that degree of leg flexion. If the machine is not adjustable, find or place a marker to let you know when the carriage is at your safe maximum depth. Perhaps place a restraint block in the correct place.

How much your legs can safely flex will be influenced by the type of machine you use, and the condition of your knees. The greater the flexion, the less weight you will

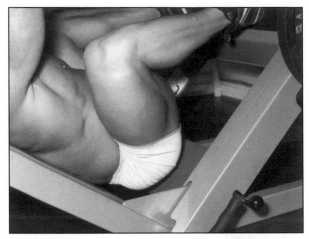

Do not use a range of motion that makes your lower back round, like in this photograph. Your lower back must maintain contact with the back support.

need to use to exhaust your thighs, but the greater the stress will be on your knees. But reduce the leg flexion too much and you will need such a large poundage to exhaust your thighs that you may put your back at risk. Find the degree of flexion that is safest for your back *and* knees.

As in the squat, avoid excessive forward travel of the knees. The knees should never travel beyond the line of the toes. Best to keep the knees *behind* the line of the toes, as in the right photo on the previous page.

Performance of the leg press

If you use an excessive range of motion your lower back will come off the back support. (This is an example of when the fullest range of motion is bad for you.) Rounding your lower back off the back support exposes you to the risk of a serious back injury. Never mind that it may give your thighs more work.

Keep your head stationary, and fixed against the head support if one is built into the machine and it is comfortable to rest against. Never turn your head to either side during a set. Maintain your body's stability

by holding the machine's hand grips. If there are no hand grips, hold onto some rigid parts of the machine clear of the moving carriage. Hold somewhere that does not encourage your back to arch. If you have options of where to hold, find the one that helps most to maintain a flat back.

With your feet flat on the foot plate, push through your heels, not the front of your feet. Never slam into the locked out position. Brake just before your knees lock out, and never force an exaggerated locked out extension. Better yet, stop the movement just short of the point where your legs are completely straight.

Never lose control of the descent. Lower under complete control, taking *at least* two seconds to make the descent..

As you reach the maximum safe depth for you, stay tight and press straight out of it. But *never* bounce out of it. If practical, set the weight down at your safe bottom position and do each rep from a dead stop.

Other tips

If your knees are easily irritated you should never fully lock out your legs in the leg press. You will not be able to use as much weight as you could if you locked out fully on each rep, and took a short rest pause between reps, but knee care should be your priority. You can still stimulate lots of growth with this conservative approach, if you work hard and progressively.

Never deadlift or stiff-legged deadlift intensively before you leg press. Do not fatigue your lower back and reduce its potential as a stabilizer in the leg press.

On a bilateral model, provide an even application of force. On a machine that has unilateral potential (i.e., can exercise one leg at time), use it bilaterally if the unilateral style is hard on your knees or back, but keep your legs moving in perfect unison. But when used unilaterally, a unilateral machine may not be a problem even if you have a back that is easily injured. But you must start out light, use excellent form, and take a few months to build up the weight and effort level before training full bore.

For unilateral use keep your non-working leg extended while your other leg completes a set. This may not be practical if you have knees that are easily irritated. On a unilateral machine you can also press your left leg while you lower your right, and vice versa, i.e., alternating fashion.

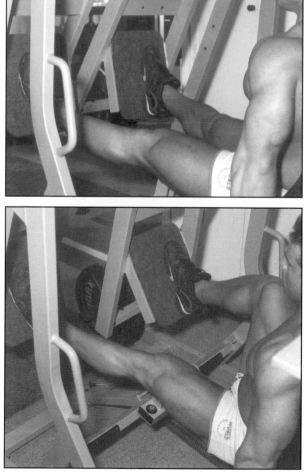

Hammer Iso-Lateral Leg Press

Due to the shearing forces on the knees, and the compression and possible torsion on the spine during the leg press, avoid a very high per-rep stress. Keep reps above 8. This will help reduce the potential downside of the exercise.

The problems associated with holding your breath—headaches, dizziness and even blackouts—can be especially felt in the leg press. Inhale on *each* descent, and exhale during *each* ascent. While your legs are extended between reps, take several quick deep breaths if you feel the need.

Leg press application

Never go full bore early on in a cycle when using the leg press for the first time, or after a month or longer away from it, or when using a model you have not used before. Focus on finding the foot position, form, range of motion, and groove that are optimal for you. Optimal for you includes no knee or lower-back aching and soreness on the day or days after the workout. Never persist if something does not feel right. Be very alert to warning signs that your knees and lower back are starting to protest. If this happens, modify your form and/or change the machine you use.

If you cannot get the available machine to work safely—by adjusting your setup position, range of motion, and form—then *do not* persist with the leg press.

If you can get a leg press machine to work for you, start light and add weight gradually. Take at least 6–8 weeks from first starting to experiment with it, before you push poundages that are hard work. Then you will set yourself up for a long and productive period of leg pressing. But if you move to demanding weights before you prove that the exercise is safe for you, you will set yourself up for injury and frustration. While adapting to the leg press, continue with your usual thigh work, to maintain your leg strength.

15

Lever bar work

Main muscles worked
forearms

Capsule description
with arm straight, lift a bar by moving at your wrist (and perhaps shoulder)

First are the two basic movements shown on the next page. Take a dumbbell rod and load only one end with a few pounds. With your arm hanging straight by your side, hold the unweighted end. With the weighted end to the front, move the rod up and down only by moving at your wrist. Do not bend your elbow or move at your shoulder. Do maximum reps to the front, and then do the same with the other hand. Then repeat but with the weighted end to the rear. The second action is stronger than the first, so you will be able to do more reps to the rear when using the same weight. Alternatively you can use a heavier weight for the stronger action, and target the same rep count for both movements.

You do not have to use a dumbbell rod or a purpose-made lever bar. You could use a cricket or baseball bat, a sledge hammer, or a broomstick with a broom attached. If you cannot handle the whole length of the fixed-weight item with one hand, grip it down the length a little and, over time, progress to the end. As an alternative you could use both hands and hold the item at its full length. Progress to exercising each hand separately once you have developed sufficient strength from training with both hands working together.

There are many variations of the two basic lever bar movements. You do not have to do the exercise while standing. You could, for example, kneel and pick up the lever tool from the floor in front of you. Raise it until your arm is parallel to the floor, keeping your arm straight and the lever bar parallel to the floor. From the front, use one hand at a time or both together. With the lever bar behind you, you could squat down, take the bar, and stand while keeping the bar parallel to the floor and your lifting arm straight and vertical. Or you could take the bar from a bench rather than the floor. Use your imagination and you will find a number of ways to work your forearms and wrists to their limit with a lever bar.

Lever bar work where you raise your arm in front until it is parallel to the floor is very demanding on the elbow and wrist. Take several weeks of gradually increasing resistance and intensity before you start to train with maximum effort. If you rush into intensive lever bar work of this sort, you are likely to injure yourself. Lever bar work with a vertical arm is much safer.

Small discs, i.e., plates lighter than 2.5 lbs or 1.25 kgs, have great practical value for all exercises. But for exercises that do not have a big poundage potential, like lever bar movements, the little discs are essential. Without them you will be unable to apply a gradual increase in resistance.

An example of lever bar work to the front, using a dumbbell rod loaded at one end.

An example of lever bar work to the rear.

16

L-fly

Main muscles worked
shoulder external rotators, rear deltoid

Capsule description
keeping an elbow bent and fixed, move its hand outwards against resistance

Introduction

This is an *essential* exercise because it strengthens the shoulder external rotator muscles, which include the supraspinatus, infraspinatus, subscapularis, and teres minor (see pages 24–25). The tendons of these muscles fuse with tissues of the shoulder joint, at the rotator cuff.

The L-fly is needed to reduce the strength imbalance between the external (weaker) and internal (stronger) rotator muscles of the shoulders. An excessive strength imbalance between these opposing muscles is a major contributing factor to shoulder problems.

To distinguish between the external and the internal rotators of your shoulders, imagine that you are shaking someone's hand with your right hand. Keep your right arm bent at a right angle, and your elbow fixed at your side. Moving your right hand to the right is external rotation. Moving your right hand to the left is internal rotation.

The book THE SEVEN-MINUTE ROTATOR CUFF SOLUTION by Dr. Joseph M. Horrigan and Jerry Robinson alerted me to the importance of specific exercise for the shoulder external rotator muscles.

Small discs are especially critical in the L-fly, to ensure that progressive resistance is applied gradually.

Lying L-fly

To do the lying L-fly, lie on your right side on a bench while placing your right hand on the floor for balance. With a small plate or very light dumbbell in your left hand, form a 90° angle at your left elbow. Then put your left elbow on your left oblique muscles (or hip, depending on your body structure). Lower the weight until your left forearm rests against your abs, then raise your left lower arm as far as possible. Always keep your left elbow against your side. Inhale on the descent, and exhale on the ascent. Finish the set, turn around, and then work your right side.

Do the exercise slowly—at least two seconds for the lifting phase and another two seconds for the lowering phase. And use a weight which permits you to perform at least 8 reps.

Start with no more than 5 lbs for a man, or half of that for a woman. Add weight *very slowly*. Depending on training experience, a man may need a year or more to build up to using just 10 lbs. This is quite a lot of weight for this movement; and 15 lbs may be enough for even a very strong man.

Never train shoulder external rotation to failure. Keep the very last rep in you. Never get to the point where you need to raise your elbow or roll backwards a little.

The lying L-fly can help your shoulders. But push it too much or too quickly, and you will irritate your shoulders. After a few months of consistent work on the lying L-fly you can progress to the standing L-fly, or even use both movements in a program—one work set of each per arm.

Lying L-fly, start and midpoint positions. Lift the forearm as near to vertical as possible.

Standing L-fly

Stand alongside an incline bench. The top of the bench should be positioned at the height of your nipples. Bend at your knees or raise the height of the bench to achieve this positioning.

With a small plate or very light dumbbell in your left hand, rest your left lower triceps on the top edge of the bench. Then place your right hand on the bench directly under the lower triceps of your left arm. Keep your left elbow bent at a right angle throughout the exercise. The angle between the bench and your shoulders should be about 60°, and certainly less than 90°.

Starting with your left hand pointing to the ceiling, slowly lower the plate or dumbbell to a little below the point where your forearm is parallel to the floor. At this point your left forearm will be down on the opposite side of the bench to where you are standing. Then *slowly* raise the weight to the upright position. Inhale on the descent, and exhale on the ascent. During each set you must maintain the initial setup that has the top edge of the bench level with your nipples. Do not lift or lower your torso. When you have finished training your left side, change over and work your right side.

The safety rules of the lying L-fly apply to the standing version: Use slow and controlled form, avoid low reps, do not change your elbow positioning or angle during a set, and do not work to total failure.

Standing L-fly

17

Neck work

Main muscles worked
neck musculature

Capsule description
seated, lying or standing, move your head against resistance

Perform some neck work once or twice a week. As well as improving your physique it will increase your resistance to neck injuries from training and accidents.

At the minimum, provide the resistance yourself, perhaps with the help of a towel held between your hands, or get someone sensitive to your resistance needs to do it. But do not do bridging-type exercises because they carry a high risk of injury to the cervical vertebrae. Bridging exercises are done by supporting your weight only on your head and feet, either facing the floor or the other way around. One type of these movements is often seen in wrestling, and is called the wrestler's bridge.

If you have a four-way neck machine available, use it. A neck-strap device is an option, though clumsy to use.

An easy way to work your neck is to follow Dick Conner's suggestions in HARDGAINER issue #40. Buy a large-size and *soft* playground ball for resistance. This can work well if the ball is of the right composition. Hold it between your head and a narrow upright. If you use a wall as the upright you will not be able to stabilize yourself by holding with your hands. Use something that lets you hold it at its sides, e.g., a door jamb. But hold just enough to stabilize yourself, not to make it easy for your neck. Press your forehead into the

ball. Do a set of *slow* reps. Go easy on the first few reps of each set, and then start pushing hard against the resistance of the ball. Turn around, and do the movement to the rear. Turn to the sides to do lateral flexion. Progressive resistance comes from applying more force to the movement.

One example of a bridging exercise. Avoid this type of movement.

A simple neck exercise is done by lying on your back with your head and neck off the end of a bench. Place a plate on a folded towel and rest it on your forehead. Lower and raise your head, using your hands to hold the weight in place, not to help raise it. Then turn around, face down, and place a plate on the rear of your head, to exercise the back of your neck. Perhaps a safer alternative to plates is to apply manual resistance with your hands. Here, after the first few warmup reps, apply enough resistance to make each rep hard work.

Work into neck exercise carefully and progressively. If you eventually work hard against resistance in four directions (front, back and both sides) once or twice a week, that can get your neck to grow substantially, so long as you work against increasing resistance as the months go by. You need to take neck exercise seriously if you want some visible gains in neck girth.

Use resistance which permits moderate to high reps—consider 10 reps as your minimum. Do not use an exaggerated range of motion. Use *slow* form, and take it very easy on the first few reps of each set. Never use jerky movements. Do each rep smoothly.

The neck, while being very responsive to training, is easily injured, especially in lateral flexion. If your neck is particularly prone to injury, just stick with front and rear flexion.

Because neck work does not have a big poundage potential, small discs are critical when weight is used for resistance. Then you can apply progressive resistance gradually and carefully.

Examples of neck work that require minimal equipment.

18

Overhead lockout

Main muscles worked
deltoids, triceps, traps

Capsule description
seated, with arms overhead, move the bar up and down a few inches

Introduction

To focus a lot of work on the lateral head of the deltoids while using a big lift, use the partial overhead press, i.e., the top 3"–4". This overhead lockout works more than just the lateral head of the deltoids. The whole of the shoulder-cap muscle is involved. Use this exercise as an alternative to the full-range overhead press.

Setup and positioning

Set up an adjustable incline bench inside a power rack or Smith machine. Be sure that the bench is sturdy, heavy and stable. Set it up so that the angle between the horizontal and the back of the upright part of the bench is about 75°–80°. If the seat is adjustable, set it at the position next to horizontal so that you are less likely to slide out of position during a set.

Place the bench so that your eyes, when your shoulders and head are against the bench, are a little in front of the barbell as it rests on pins and *against* the front or rear uprights of a power rack. This assumes that you use the type of power rack that enables you to set a bench inside it in the position you need. The rack's uprights should be *behind* the bar as you look at it while you are in position against the back support. Alternatively your eyes could be a little in front of the bar of a Smith machine. Exactly where your eyes will be, relative to the bar, will be determined by factors including the angle of the back support of the bench, arm length, and how much your head is tilted. Find the best positioning for you.

The bar must be set at a height only 3"–4" below the position where it would be if your arms were fully extended and locked-out overhead. Position the pins of a power rack appropriately for you, and then load your bar while it is across the pins, not while it is on the weight saddles. This will be your starting position. Never take the bar out of the saddles of a power rack and do the exercise without pins set in place. That would leave you with nothing to catch the bar if you failed on a rep.

Chalk your hands before each work set, to prevent your hands slipping on the bar. Use a shoulder-width grip, *never* a wide grip. But if your grip is too close you will easily lose balance of the barbell.

In a power rack the bar should, preferably, travel up and down *against* the uprights. This keeps you in the right groove. If you are doing the exercise in a Smith machine, the bar will already be locked into position.

With a Smith machine it is critical that you can safely "rack" the bar. At the end of a set your shoulders and arms will be very fatigued and you will not have full control

Overhead lockout in a power rack. Whether using a rack or Smith machine, your arms should be vertical or near vertical throughout the exercise—NOT at the same 75°–80° of the bench. Arrange your setup position accordingly.

over the bar. Set up the machine so that your bottom position is where the latches are at rest. Keep the latches inside the guided pathway during each set. Then you will be able to move the bar up and down the guided pathway without ever twisting your wrists to take the latches out. Then, even if you lose control, the bar will come to rest safely. This is possible only because the lockout is a partial movement.

The overhead lockout can be done without the vertical guide of the rack uprights, or a Smith machine. But still use a power rack, with pins set in the same position as for the guided style. If done with insufficient control in the unguided style, there is a greatly increased risk of injury because the bar can easily move out of the right groove due to one hand getting in front of the other. This causes dangerous asymmetrical stress. If you cannot keep control over the bar in the unguided style, then only use the guided pathway method.

Performance of the lockout

Do not do the reps in a non-stop touch-and-go style because that is an easy way to lose the horizontal balance of the bar, and stress one shoulder more than the other. This can cause injuries. Very briefly set the bar on the pins between reps so that you can keep the groove more easily.

Do the reps with control. Avoid just blasting the bar off the pins, because that will cause you to lose the groove. It will also make you slam into the locked out position. That is harmful for your elbows. And the excessive momentum will take some of the stress away from the primary target muscles—the deltoids.

As you do the lockouts, you may want to let your head come forward slightly so that the bar is moving up and down behind your head.

After your final rep, with your arms fully locked out, shrug your shoulders up (and hence raise your arms). Though the bar will only move an inch or so, the shrug will add further stress to your deltoids. Do as many overhead shrugs as possible.

A harder method is to shrug at the top of *each* rep. To optimize this style, set up two pairs of pins 4" apart. Arrange the height of the pins in the rack so that the first 3" of the movement *completes* the lockout. The final inch is only for the shrug. You must not be able to lock out for the entire 4". For each rep you must lock out *and* shrug in order to be able to touch the bar to the upper pair of pins, with the barbell sliding up and down against the rack's uprights.

Warm up well, practice the groove with a light weight, and then carefully build up the weight from workout to workout. Poundage potential is influenced by factors including the range of motion you use, and whether you shrug on each rep or just at the end of each set.

During the overhead lockout you need to minimize the arch in your lower back. See page 93 for tips on how to minimize the arching.

Spotting

The groove can easily be lost, especially if the exercise is not done using a guided pathway. The spotter should look out for the bar tipping, one hand getting forward of the other, or the bar being pressed off center, and provide help to prevent serious form deterioration.

Using a Smith machine, a spotter is essential unless you never take the latches out of the guided pathway. At the end of a hard set, if you have moved the latches forward, you may have trouble putting them back in the locked position. When fatigued at the end of a hard set, it is easy to lose control of the movement. A spotter would then be critical, to ensure that you do not lose control over the bar.

The Smith machine has few uses for safe training. The overhead lockout, because it uses a short range of motion, is one of the safe applications if done as described here. But do not do any type of full-range press in the Smith machine. The rigid vertical pathway of this machine is unnatural to the body for full-range pressing. It will set you up for chronic injuries.

19

Overhead press

Main muscles worked
deltoids, triceps, traps

Capsule description
seated or standing, push resistance from your shoulders to overhead

Introduction

The overhead press can be done standing, and is then called the military press. All the body is involved in holding the weight overhead. The overhead press can also be done seated, to reduce the tendency to lean back. And it can be done seated against a high-incline bench to remove much of the stress from the lower back. This is the most conservative form of the overhead press. Do not, however, use a perfectly vertical bench. Use one set at about 75°–80°.

Setup and positioning

For the military press, take the bar out of squat stands, or do it inside a power rack. The bar should be set just a little below the height from which you press. Both options spare the bar having to be cleaned from the floor to your shoulders before pressing.

For the standing press, place your feet about shoulder-width apart. For the seated press, place your feet a little wider, and flare them for greater stability.

For both the standing and seated press, chalk your hands and take a pronated grip on the bar that has your forearms vertical at the bottom position, when viewed from the front or rear. Start with a hand spacing a couple of inches wider on each side than your shoulder-width grip, and fine-tune from there. Do not use a thumbless grip.

To get into the starting position for the military press, grip the bar while it is on supports, get your feet under the bar, arch your back a little, dip your knees, get your hips under the bar, place the bar on your upper chest, and then lock out your legs. Step back if you took the bar from squat stands, and then you will be set to press.

For the seated barbell press, many gyms have purpose-built units, with fixed back support and built-in uprights to hold the bar. Some can be very good, but others have problems. The back support may be too upright, making the press in front of the face impractical. Because the uprights that support the bar are usually behind the trainee, a good spotter is essential for unracking and racking the bar. Taking the bar unassisted from behind your head is a very bad position for your shoulders, as is the press from behind neck.

Do not use a machine that forces you to use a perfectly vertical bar pathway, e.g., a Smith machine. That will lock you into an unnatural groove that, sooner or later, will cause shoulder problems.

With or without back support, do the seated press in a power rack for ease of getting the bar into position. Position the bench inside the rack so that you cannot hit the uprights with the bar. Load the bar on pins set at the height from which you press.

You can also do the seated press close to squat stands. Just position yourself and the stands so that you have minimum handling problems getting the bar out of the stands to start a set, and getting it back in the stands at the end of a set. Spotters should be used here so that you do not have to wrestle with the bar.

You can also do the seated press without stands or a power rack. Get two assistants to lift the bar up for you, while you are seated. Get them to take the bar from you when you are finished. If you are a purist you may even want to clean the

Note the two flaws in this starting position for seated pressing from off the pins of a power rack. The elbows need to be moved forward to produce forearms nearer to vertical. The lower back shows too much arching, largely because the heels are behind the knees.

bar into position yourself, shuffle back to the bench, and then sit down while holding the bar at your shoulders. But that will cost you energy and strength that would be better invested in actual pressing.

Using a power rack is the perfect way to do each rep in the from-the-bottom style, off the pins. Like in the bench press, you can do overhead pressing in touch-and-go style, or from off the pins. When done in a power rack from off the pins, set the pins at about the height of your clavicles (when you are in your pressing position), or a little higher. For shoulder comfort, long-limbed people will need a slightly higher starting position than will a short-limbed person. Starting too low will put excessive stress on the shoulder joints.

Pressing the bar from off the pins on every rep simplifies the press. You do not have to take the bar from saddles, or return it to them. Just set yourself up in the right starting position for you, and use that position on every rep.

Performance

Once in the correct starting position, drive the bar up, keeping the rest of your body braced. For the standing press, keep your legs straight. Do not use a "kick" from your legs to get the bar moving. In all overhead pressing, do not let the bar move forward. Drive it up near your face. But be careful not to slam the bar into your face. Apply force evenly with both arms and shoulders, to keep the bar moving without one hand getting ahead of or in front of the other.

Particularly in the standing press, keep all your body's musculature tensed as you press and lower the bar, especially your abdominals, thighs, glutes and back.

Lower the bar under control, do not lower it beyond your safe point, and do not bounce at the bottom. Very briefly pause at the bottom before driving the bar up, but do not relax at the bottom position. Keep yourself tight like a coiled spring. If you are doing each rep from off pins, then you can take a longer pause between reps, and even relax your body for a few seconds before tightening up ready for the next rep. The breathing pattern to use is the same as in the bench press.

Do not press from behind your neck. The press from the front is more natural, and much safer for your shoulder joints.

Other tips

The press while standing encourages leaning back. But with good form you can avoid leaning back excessively. The seated version reduces the potential for leaning back. This is one of the reasons why the press is commonly done while seated. For maximum control, do the exercise seated and with your back supported by a high-incline bench.

If you use a bench for support, tilt the seat a little (if it is adjustable) to help prevent slipping off the bench while pressing. With or without the seat tilt, keep your legs well spaced and solidly planted. And be sure any adjustable bench you use is sturdy, heavy and stable.

Dumbbell press

Dumbbells can be used for any of the three basic variations of the overhead press, i.e., standing, seated, and seated with back support. With dumbbells your hands can be parallel to each other, pronated, or somewhere in between. Move in and out of the pronated position during the course of each rep, according to what feels most natural. Try the hand position variations and find the groove that feels the strongest and most comfortable for you. You may find that your ideal groove starts with your hands parallel to each other at shoulder height and, during the top half of the movement, your hands move to or towards a pronated position.

A key point of control, when doing the dumbbell overhead press, is to keep the 'bells directly over your shoulders. Do not let them drift out to the sides, and do not overstretch at the bottom.

Dumbbell pressing can be done simultaneously, or by alternating hands. For the alternating dumbbell press, press with one hand as you lower with the other, or press and lower one dumbbell while the other "sits" at its shoulder. This produces asymmetrical stress and encourages some leaning from side to side. The simultaneous pressing is a safer option if you have a history of back problems. If you do not want to handle two dumbbells at the same time, do the one-arm dumbbell press.

Do the one-hand press standing or seated. Using both hands, get a dumbbell to your right shoulder. Hold the 'bell in your right hand, and hold onto something sturdy and stable with your left hand. While bracing yourself with your left hand, perform a set of presses with your right hand, using the groove that feels the strongest and most comfortable for you. Then reverse the procedure and exercise your left side. The braced position helps to maintain good form, and reduces the tendency to lean back.

Dumbbell pressing demands a lot of control and is a fine way to work your shoulders, upper back and triceps. It also heavily involves the trunk musculature if it is done standing. Probably its greatest benefit is that it allows you to find the wrist positioning and pressing groove that are most comfortable for you. With a barbell you have no flexibility with your wrist positioning because you are restricted to a pronated grip.

The downside with dumbbells is getting them into position and keeping control during the exercise. With a barbell inside a power rack, with pins positioned properly, the press is simpler and safer.

One-hand dumbbell press

Getting dumbbells into position

To get a pair of dumbbells into position ready for overhead pressing, obtain the help of an assistant or two, or use the "bench method." But if you intend to do seated pressing with your back supported, first set up a bench with an incline of 75°–80°, and tilt its seat if it is adjustable.

To perform the "bench method," stand immediately in front of a bench, feet about hip-width apart. Each dumbbell should be touching the outside of its corresponding foot, with the two handles parallel to each other. Bend your legs and take the 'bells from the floor with a parallel grip and good deadlifting technique. While standing, center the rear end of each dumbbell on its corresponding thigh just above the knee.

If you use dumbbells with protruding ends or collars, probably adjustable 'bells, place just the inside part of the bottom plate of a given dumbbell on the outside of its corresponding lower thigh. This will work if the radius of the dumbbell plate concerned is sufficient so that you can have the 'bell positioned vertically on your thigh while you are seated. But be sure that the collars are securely in place. A 'bell that falls apart during use could be disastrous.

Sit on the bench, with your butt against the bottom of the back support if you are using an incline bench. The 'bells will move into a vertical position as you sit down. The dumbbells must remain against your thighs just above your knees.

Once you are sat on the bench, thrust your right knee up and simultaneously pull vertically and vigorously with your right arm. This will get the dumbbell to your right shoulder. Then do the same for your left side.

Once you have a pair of dumbbells at your shoulders, you have three options. You can stand up and press while standing, do the exercise seated, or seated against back support. If it is the latter, then *without* arching, lean onto the back support. Then you will be in position for pressing while your back is supported.

After finishing a set of dumbbell presses, lower the 'bells directly to the floor, under control. Keep your knees together and the dumbbells well away from your legs.

Before actually doing any dumbbell overhead pressing, make the handling of the 'bells an exercise in itself. For a couple of workouts, do sets and reps with a relatively comfortable weight so that you can master the form needed to handle the dumbbells safely.

Another possibility for any type of dumbbell pressing—upright, incline or supine—is to suspend 'bells on adjustable chain fixed to an overhead bar. The 'bells should hang at the bottom position of the exercise. But make sure the setup is safe.

From the left is the "bench method" for getting dumbbells into pressing position. See text. Then, on the facing page, is pressing from a parallel to a pronated grip.

Spotting

At the end of a set of the overhead press, the groove can easily be lost. The first sign of form deterioration in the military press is excessive arching of the back. In addition to that, and for any type of barbell press, the spotter should look out for the barbell tipping, one hand getting forward of the other, or the bar being pressed off center. The moment that one of those markers occurs, the spotter should provide assistance to prevent serious form deterioration.

The spotter should stand on a box behind a *standing* presser, to be able to apply assistance easily. If the presser is seated, spotting is easier. The spotter must use both hands, and apply help in a balanced way.

Spotting someone who is pressing dumbbells can be awkward. One hand should apply force under each elbow. This is strictly for assisting the lifter to get a tough rep up in good form. A single person cannot simultaneously take a pair of dumbbells from a presser who fails on a rep. Two spotters are needed then. With dumbbell pressing, the key additional markers of form regression to look out for are the 'bells drifting out to the sides, and one hand getting above, in front of, or to the rear of the other.

Caution!

To help prevent back injuries while doing any type of overhead pressing (standing or seated), you need to minimize *but not eliminate* the arch in your lower back. In decline, horizontal and incline pressing, the arch can be almost eliminated, because the spine is not vertical or near-vertical, and thus not actually bearing the weight.

Instead, the shoulders and shoulder blades are bearing the weight. But when bearing weight with a vertical or near vertical spine, as in overhead pressing, it is important to preserve a *non-exaggerated* arch in the lower back. This is the natural weight-bearing formation.

To avoid exaggerating the arch in your lower back while performing the seated press, keep your feet flat on the floor, with your heels in front of an imaginary vertical line dropped from your knees. And wear shoes with non-slip soles, to prevent your feet from slipping.

Regularly review "Critical General Factors," which starts on page 17. Those sixteen factors are of vital importance for all exercises.

20

Parallel bar dip

Main muscles worked
pectorals, triceps, deltoids, lats

Capsule description
while on parallel bars, lower and raise yourself by bending at your elbows

Introduction

This can be a great major exercise. But it has been corrupted by those who promote extremes in order to focus the stress upon a particular area of musculature. An excessively wide grip, turning the hands in rather than using a knuckles-out grip, keeping the elbows out as wide as possible, a concave chest, and going for maximum depth are dangerous practices.

The dip is very demanding on the shoulders, even if done under good control and without bottoming out. But most people can do it safely if they use good form. If you have had shoulder problems in the past, and the dip still bothers you no matter how careful you are, then forget the dip. But while you may not be able to do the orthodox parallel bar dip safely, you may be able to do the machine version.

People who have the most difficulty with dips are frequently heavy. Other factors are rounded shoulders and adaptive shortening of the pectoral muscles. If you are tight in those areas, then before you start dipping you should work for a few weeks on gradually increasing your shoulder and pec flexibility.

Setup and positioning

If possible, try using parallel bars of slightly different width positions. About 22" between the centers of the bars is a good starting point for most men. Women and slender or small men will be more comfortable with bars a little closer. Very big men may prefer slightly wider bars. You can try v-shaped bars to find the optimum hand spacing for you. Face the part of the unit where the v-shaped bars come together, not where they fan out. Another option is to use a power rack. If its uprights are suitably spaced you can position a bar on saddles on the front uprights, and another bar on the rear uprights. Set the height of the bars at what is ideal for you.

Regardless of the type of setup you use, be sure the bars are securely fixed so they cannot wobble as you dip.

Find the strongest, most comfortable and natural dipping position for you. For joint safety and maximum overall gains, distribute the stress from the dip over *all* the involved muscles. Do not try to focus the stress onto one particular area.

Stand on a box or bench of the right height so that you can easily get into the arms-locked-out position. When you bend your legs and descend into the dip, your knees should graze the box or bench when you are at your maximum safe depth. If you are like most people, the maximum safe depth will be an inch or two above the very lowest point you could go down to. This is likely to coincide with the position where your rear upper arm is parallel to the floor. Some people can safely dip to a little below this parallel position, while some people need to stop a tad above parallel.

To find a depth marker to suit you, try different benches or boxes. To fine-tune, place something of the correct thickness on top of the best-fit bench or box.

Dipping so that your knees must graze something at the maximum safe depth for you is not just to prevent overstretching. It ensures accurate record keeping. Without a marker to ensure consistent rep depth, there is a tendency to shorten the reps at the end of a set.

Performance

Absolutely never bounce (or "pre-stretch" as it may euphemistically be called) at the bottom of the dip; and avoid doing reps in a rapid style. Go down slowly and immediately push up in a controlled way. Never relax or pause at the bottom.

Keep your elbows in the same plane as your wrists, or *slightly* to the outside of that plane. Take a brief pause between reps at the *top* position. Keep your legs fixed—no swinging them around. But your legs will not swing if you dip with control. And neither thrust your head forward nor throw it back as you perform each rep.

Do not descend on a deflated chest. Inhale before you descend, hold it, and then exhale during the ascent. Going into the bottom position of the dip on a deflated chest may increase your risk of injury, so keep your chest full during the descent and early part of the ascent. Keeping your chest stuck out will help to keep your shoulders pulled back and safe.

At the top of the dip—during the brief pause between reps, especially at the end of a set—do not let your shoulders slump as you

hold yourself on locked arms. Keep your head and shoulders up high. Stay tight.

Avoid extremes: *do not* use a wide grip, *do not* use a "reverse" grip where your thumbs are on the outside of the bars, and *do not* force your elbows out to the sides.

Other tips

Warm up for the dip very carefully. Start with some floor pushups. Then from the upright position of the dip, perform *partial* reps as you gradually work into *your* bottom position. Then, if you are able to dip with a heavy weight around your waist, warm up further with some reps using *your* full range of motion but only 50% or so of your work sets' extra resistance.

Find a method of attaching weights comfortably and securely. A belt designed for hanging weight from is ideal. An alternative is to wear a strong belt and put a dumbbell inside it by having the 'bell vertical and the belt across the handle. Another option is to use a strong piece of rope to attach a dumbbell or plates to your belt. Let the dumbbell or plates hang at the front of your thighs. But the resistance must not hang so low that it touches your depth marker before your knees do.

As the weeks go by, add weight slowly and in small increments. Attach one or more small discs in order to work from one fixed-weight dumbbell to the next, or use an adjustable dumbbell. Alternatively you can just use individual weight plates.

If a machine unit for dips is available where you train, try it. It may enable you to find your optimum dipping pathway. A slight change in torso or wrist position can produce a significant improvement in comfort. And the range of movement can be easily controlled. In addition, because resistance starts at nothing or nearly nothing, the machine unit for dips can be used by people who do not yet have the strength to do regular parallel bar dips.

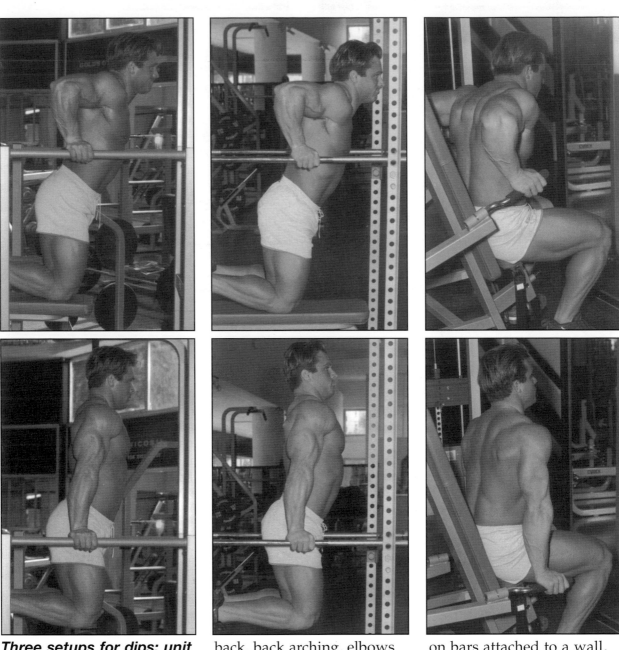

Three setups for dips: unit with v-shaped bars (left), in a power rack (middle), machine version (right).

Spotting

The main markers of form deterioration are legs moving, throwing the head back, back arching, elbows wobbling, and stalling. A big urge to get more serious should get the "warning" rep out in good form, but if another rep is attempted, assistance should be at hand. The spotter should stand behind you. If you dip on bars attached to a wall, dip facing the wall so that your spotter has plenty of room. The spotter should place his hands under your shins and apply the minimum of assistance that is necessary.

Six basics of excellent exercise form

❑ *Before you can apply good exercise technique you first need to know what good exercise technique is. Please study this book very carefully.*

❑ *Before a set, review the correct exercise technique that you need to use.*

❑ *Never charge into a set, grab the bar and then realize after the first rep that you took an imbalanced grip, the wrong stance, or are lopsided while on a bench. Get perfectly positioned for every set you do.*

❑ *Be 100% focused and attentive while you train—always. Never be overconfident or casual.*

❑ *Lift the weight, do not throw it; and lower the bar, do not drop it. Use control at all times. Regularly perform the "pause test" (see page 17).*

❑ *For each work set you do, only use a poundage that lets you just squeeze out your target reps in good form. Most trainees use more weight than they can handle correctly. This leads to "cheating" and a loss of control.*

21

Partial deadlift

Main muscles worked
erectors, lats, upper back, forearms

Capsule description
with a flat back, straight arms and slightly bent legs, lift a bar from knee height

This is an exercise rarely used outside of powerlifting circles, but one that has a big potential for muscular gains.

In a power rack, find the pin setting that puts the bar at just *above* your knee caps when your legs are bent as they would be at that stage of the *stiff*-legged deadlift. That is your bottom position. Alternatively you can set a loaded bar on boxes (see tips on page 76). Set it at the height so that the bar's starting position is the same as in the power rack setup.

Stand with your feet under the bar, heels about hip-width apart, and toes flared a little. Take a shoulder-width or a little wider overhand grip. Bend your legs *a little* and adopt the starting position. With a flat back and straight arms, shrug against the bar and pull your shoulders back. The bar will not move unless the weight is very light, but the shrug will "lock" your back into the pivotal flat position. Now while looking forward or upward, use a back pull to move the bar. Your legs should straighten as you complete the lift. *The bar should brush your thighs at all times.* Do not lean back at the top. Stand straight, pause, keep your scapulae retracted, then lower the bar to the pins by bending your legs *slightly* and simultaneously leaning forward. Due to the *minimal* leg flexion advised for this exercise, it is really a partial *stiff-legged* deadlift.

Briefly pause on the pins or boxes, and reset your starting position if you got out of the groove on the descent. Take a breath or few as the bar rests on the pins, and relax your grip for a few seconds. Then hold the last breath, shrug and "lock" your back, and do the next rep. Do not bounce the bar or rush the reps. Alternatively, do not rest the bar on the pins at the bottom position. Instead, briefly pause *just above* the pins, akin to a Romanian deadlift.

Exhale during the ascent, or at the top. Then either inhale and make the descent, or inhale as you actually descend.

Lift and lower symmetrically, and do not turn your head. And never let your shoulders round. If your shoulders start to slump, and you cannot pull them back, dump the bar instantly (but with control).

The exercise can be done with a straight bar or a Trap Bar. With a Trap Bar it has to be done from boxes because the bar is not long enough for use inside a power rack.

Even with plenty of chalk you may eventually be forced to use a reverse grip. If so, then from set to set alternate which way around you have your hands.

The partial deadlift can be done from just *below* the knee caps. But with a straight bar the knees get in the way, especially for tall and lanky trainees. Using a Trap Bar will fix this problem.

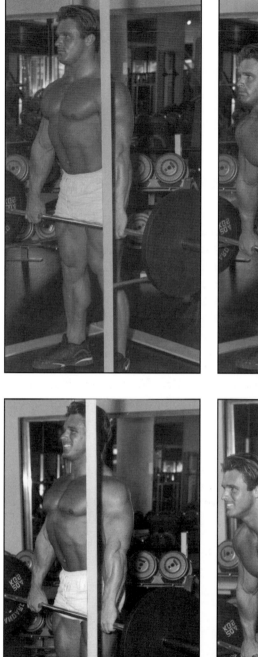

Partial deadlift in a power rack, from pins set just above the knees.

Partial deadlift from pins set 4" lower than in the example above.

Pinch-grip lifting

Main muscles worked
forearms, finger muscles

Capsule description
lift resistance while holding it with only your pinch-grip strength

Introduction
Lifting using your pinch-grip strength is one of the best grip, forearm and finger exercises. Never mind that you may never have seen anyone do it. There are many terrific exercises that are unheard of in most gyms.

Setup and positioning
If you do not have a purpose-built pinch-grip device, rig up something that does the job. Get a 2" x 4" block of wood about 24" long, for pinching across the 2" width, and bore a hole through its center. (Use a 2" x 5" block if you have huge hands.) Pass a strong cord through the hole, and suspend a loading pin with plates on it, or an adjustable dumbbell. With a longer board you could have a large hook securely fixed near to each end, on the underside. The board could then be hooked around a regular barbell. By lifting the pinch board, the barbell will be lifted off the floor. The longer board is needed to reduce the problems with balance that can arise when the device is hooked up to a barbell.

You could get a welder to produce a pinch block for you out of metal. Have matt paint put on the metal to help reduce the likelihood of slipping.

A 2" thickness is a good standard, but you could use a slightly thicker or thinner thickness if you prefer. If the gripping surface is too smooth, you can fix it for easier gripping by securely affixing some rough material such as canvas.

Another equipment alternative is to fix a couple of plates, smooth sides out, to a metal or wooden rod. Fix them together with collars. This becomes your gripping site. Outside the inside collars, load plates as you need them, with further collars used to hold the plates in place. Here is an example that uses a thick wooden wrist roller handle as the loading rod.

An easily-made and adjustable pinch-grip device using a 2" wooden rod.

To protect your feet, stand the weight on a low platform. This will keep the resistance above your feet. Put some rubber matting or thick cardboard under the weights, in case you drop the pinch-grip device. Keep your feet well to the sides of the area that the weights move above. To help in this respect, avoid using full-size weight plates—stick to small and medium-diameter plates. Be safety conscious.

Pinch-grip sliver bar

To train your finger-tip pinching strength, rather than that of your entire fingers, get a thin but strong flat piece of wood and find a way to suspend weight from it. As an alternative, get a metal worker to weld a piece of 10" x 1" flat bar to a hook. You can then attach the hook to a loading pin. Pinch grip the sliver with both hands, or with one at a time. Put the thumb(s) on one side and the other digits on the other side. Find a specific grip and site on the bar you are comfortable with, make a written note of it if necessary, and use the same grip each time you use the sliver bar.

A 2" x 4" x 22" metal pinch-grip block, loading pin, and sliver bar.

Using the sliver bar, in addition to the grip that involves all your digits, you can exercise any pair of a thumb and one finger from the same hand. You can use this piece of equipment to mimic pinching a coin attached to resistance. There is potential here for a lot of challenging fun.

Performance

Regardless of what pinch-grip device you use, do either reps, singles, or timed holds. You can train one hand at a time, or both together. But when you lift, bend at your knees and keep your back flat.

With the pinch block, and for each hand, put the full length of your four adjacent fingers down one side of the block, and the length of your thumb down the other side. Grip with the entire length of all your digits, not just the tips. Find the most comfortable and secure gripping site for you, and stick with it. Use the identical way of gripping your device each time you use it. (This matter of form consistency applies, of course, to each exercise you do, whether grip work or otherwise.)

When pinch-grip lifting an item from the floor, do not snatch at it. To reduce the chance of the object slipping out of your fingers—even a weight you know you have the strength to handle—squeeze hard and then *ease* it off the floor.

Pinch lifting, for timed holds, is considerably easier if your hands are held against your thighs rather than out away from your thighs. Be consistent in the form you use, or use both styles. Use more weight in the against-the-thighs style, or hold the same weight for more time.

When your grip is close to failing in any pinch-grip work, make a deliberate effort to try to bend whatever you are holding. While you cannot possibly bend it, that attempt to can extend the life of your grip. And do not just try to hold the pinch-grip device, try to *crush* it.

Three pinch-grip devices in use: two plates locked together, smooth sides out (left); 2" x 4" block (middle), and sliver bar.

Keep accurate records of the weights you lift and the style(s) you use. If you use the against-the-thighs style, be sure you keep your legs locked and your torso either vertical or tilted forward slightly. If you bend your thighs and/or lean back as you do the pinch-grip lifting, you will cheat because the weight will be partly supported on your thighs, thus defeating the object of the exercise. If you always keep your hands off your thighs, then you will eliminate this problem.

The value of chalk

❑ *Do not underestimate the value of chalk. Though chalk is not used much outside of powerlifting and Olympic weightlifting circles, that does not mean it is not useful for other types of weight trainees.*

❑ *Once you have used chalk for a few weeks you will wonder how you ever managed without it.*

❑ *Use chalk everywhere you need the help, especially in back exercises, upper-body pressing movements, and specialized grip work.*

❑ *See page 27 for how to obtain and use chalk.*

Prone row

Main muscles worked
lats, upper back, biceps, brachialis, rear deltoid, forearms

Capsule description
while lying face down, pull resistance to your abdominal region

Introduction
The prone row is a much safer version of the conventional but potentially dangerous barbell bent-over row, and T-bar row.

Setup and positioning
Elevate a bench, or securely place a plank (or an old-fashioned padded bench for situps) across pins in a power rack. You want the height so that when you are lying face down on the bench you can just manage to take the resistance from the floor. Fine-tune the gap between the bench and resistance by placing a weight plate of the correct thickness under each end of a barbell, or under each dumbbell.

With a barbell, choose a pronated or supinated grip according to which is the most comfortable for you. Start with a shoulder-width grip and fine-tune from there. You may find that both the pronated and supinated grips are uncomfortable and impractical.

As well as grip difficulties, there are other drawbacks with the barbell prone row. First, your chest gets compressed and breathing can be constricted. This is common to any prone row, but can be tolerable, especially if you can briefly set the resistance on the floor between reps.

Another drawback, especially for trainees with short arms and barrel chests, is the reduced range of motion due to the barbell striking the bench before the shoulder blades are fully retracted. The deeper the underside of the bench, the greater the disadvantage. This can be corrected if you fix a pair of kettlebell handles in position on the barbell.

A solution that gives you a greater range of motion than a barbell, and a much more comfortable grip, is to use dumbbells. Dumbbells let you use a natural parallel or near-parallel grip. But with dumbbells, the plates, depending on their diameter, can get in the way and force your hands outwards in order not to strike the bench. Small-diameter plates will reduce this problem, as will using a parallel grip rather than a pronated one.

Perhaps a better solution, like in the one-arm dumbbell row (see *Dumbbell Row*, page 84), is to use a kettlebell handle on each dumbbell, or use a pair of Montini no-collar dumbbell handles. Then you can get a full range of motion at the top without having to use small-diameter plates, and without the plates getting in the way.

Performance
Pull the barbell or, preferably, dumbbells to alongside your abdominal region, and crush your shoulder blades together and back. If you cannot hold the top

The starting position for the dumbbell prone row. Keeping your forearms perpendicular to the floor, pull the dumbbells as high as possible.

position for a second, and simultaneously pull your shoulders back, then you are using more weight than you currently have the strength to handle correctly. Find the groove and grip spacing that suit you best and which preserve the important vertical position of your forearms. Always lower the resistance under control, and do not let it yank on your shoulders at the bottom of each rep. Keep your shoulders tight.

A seated row machine mimics the prone row but without gravity pulling on your torso. If you have such a machine available, try it. Your lower back will be as well protected as it is in the prone row, and there will be little compression of your chest. But because you will be locked into the machine's groove, you may not have the necessary freedom to make the adjustments needed to find the pathway that feels most natural for you.

Depending on the seated row machine you use, you may have the choice between a pronated and a parallel grip. The parallel grip, however, may be too close. Your forearms should be parallel to each other

Seated row machine using a pronated grip. Note how the shoulder blades have been crushed together.

throughout the movement. Choose the grip that best approximates that. Then adjust the seat's height to find the position that lets you keep your forearms parallel to the floor, and a slightly arched back when in the contracted position.

Pulldown

Main muscles worked
lats, upper back, pectorals, biceps, brachialis, forearms

Capsule description
sit in front of the cable of an overhead pulley; pull resistance to your chest

Setup and positioning

Before you use a pulldown apparatus, check that the cable and connections are in good condition. If the cable snaps or a connection breaks as you are pulling, you could smash the handle into yourself.

Sit just in front of the cable of the pulldown apparatus. The cable should run vertically during the exercise, or slightly out of the vertical on the side of your torso. Brace your thighs under the T-shaped restraint that has been set at the correct height for you.

If there is no restraint bar, find another way to avoid being pulled off the floor. While seated, a barbell of sufficient weight could be placed on your lap. Your hips would need to be lower than your knees, so that the bar cannot roll off. A heavy dumbbell could be jammed vertically between your thighs, or sufficient weight could be hung from a belt. Someone could press down on your shoulders, but that method tends to disrupt the exercise. Another alternative is to kneel on some padding on the floor and roll a sufficiently heavy barbell to over the back of your calves. If you use plates of the appropriate diameter, this will "lock" you to the floor.

There are several bar and grip options for the pulldown. Use the one which lets you use the most resistance over the fullest but safe range of motion. With a straight bar, start with a supinated and shoulder-width grip, and fine-tune your hand spacing for wrist and elbow comfort. Or use a supinated grip on a bar that has a straight middle and ends that slant up *and* a little *towards* you, or use a parallel grip on the appropriate bar. (See page 46 for photos of these bars.) For the parallel grip, a shoulder-width spacing produces a better effect than does a close grip. Be sure to grip each handle in the center. The parallel grip, however, results in a smaller weight potential than does a supinated grip.

If a supinated grip is uncomfortable, and the bar for a shoulder-width parallel grip is unavailable, try a pronated grip using a *straight* bar. Take it 2" or 3" wider on each side than your shoulder-width grip, so that your forearms are vertical at the contracted position of the exercise. For the parallel and supinated grips, use a width that keeps your forearms vertical during the exercise. Regardless of the bar you choose, never use a very wide grip, and do not pull to the rear of your head.

Use chalk on your hands. If the bar you use is smooth, the chalk will not help you as much as it will on a bar with knurling. To help your grip on a slick bar, put a palm-size piece of neoprene between each hand and the bar—see page 46.

Starting position for the pulldown.

Performance

Look forward or upward, and smoothly pull the bar until your hands are at your upper chest or a little lower, according to wrist and shoulder comfort.

During the descent, lean back a little but never round or hump your back. If you have to round your back and/or crunch your abs to help, the weight is too heavy. If you round your shoulders you will be unable to pull your shoulder blades down, and will thus rob yourself of thoroughly working the target musculature.

Arch your back somewhat during the descent. If you cannot pull your hands to below your clavicles, the weight is too heavy and you will be unable to pull your shoulder blades down fully. Make a special effort to pull your shoulder blades down. But do not pull beyond what is comfortable for your shoulders and elbows. To provide the same range of motion you will need to use about 15% less weight with a parallel grip than with a supinated grip.

Briefly pause in the contracted position and then let your arms straighten under full control. Never let the weight drop rapidly. The weight stack must never yank on your arms or shoulders.

Inhale while your arms are straight. Hold the breath as you pull the bar down, and exhale as your arms straighten out. Alternatively you can exhale as you pull the bar down. Towards the end of a tough set, take a few quick breaths between reps.

Keep your shoulders tight when your arms are extended. Never relax in order to get extra stretch. While in the top position do not let your head protrude forward.

Spotting

Spotting is not essential here because the weight cannot come down on you. But spotting is desirable for ensuring that the final rep of a set is done in good form. Form starts to become ragged when your shoulders start to slump or round a little. A spotter can push down on the bar or pull on the weight stack.

Adding weight

Selectorized cable units, and selectorized machines in general, often have minimum weight increments of 10 lbs or 5 kgs. This is too much weight to progress by at a single increment. See the note on page 46 for how to get around this problem.

Pullover

Main muscles worked
lats, pectorals, triceps, abdominal wall

Capsule description
move resistance from behind your head, with bent or straight arms

Introduction
There are two types of pullover—the muscle-building one, and the rib cage enlarging one. Both involve moving resistance from behind your head. The former has your elbows bent while the other keeps your arms straight.

Muscle-building pullover
Use a machine, not a barbell, dumbbell, or pair of dumbbells. Assuming that you have a pullover machine available, find the best setup for you according to your torso and arm lengths. Experiment with adjusting the machine and yourself to find the body and arm positioning that enables you to work your musculature hard without producing any joint soreness. You may or may not be able to get a given machine to work well for you. Some pullover machines are much better than others. If you can find a machine that suits you, exploit it to the full. It will enable you to train your lats without your arms being a limiting factor.

The danger in this exercise primarily comes from an excessive range of motion for your shoulders. Strap yourself in properly, and with a very light weight on the machine, discover how far back you can take your arms before your back starts to arch. Your starting position should be an inch or two short of the point where your

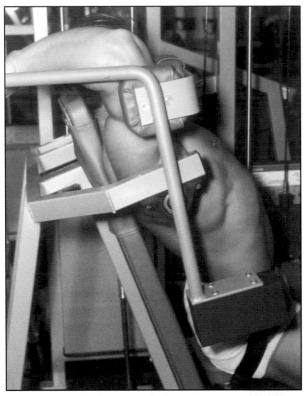

An exaggerated and dangerous starting position for the machine pullover. Note the arch in the lower back.

back starts to arch. Then always keep your back flat against the machine's back support. And if even this less-than-full-range of motion irritates your shoulders, reduce it until there is no irritation.

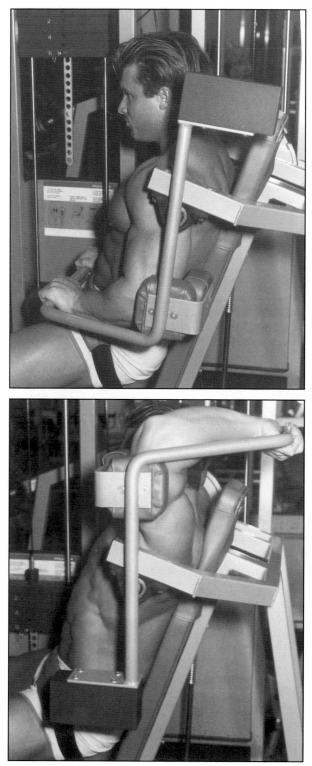

A reduced and safer range of motion.

Apply force through your rear upper arms, not your hands and forearms; and do not grip tightly. Face forward and keep your head still. Inhale as your arms move back, and exhale either during or at the end of the positive (or contraction) phase.

Though not essential, use a spotter if possible. As soon as a rep grinds to a halt, the spotter should apply a tad of help. This will keep the rep moving and prevent you from loosening your form.

The "breathing" pullover

The "breathing" pullover is an alternative to the Rader chest pull that is described later in this book. Both of these exercises aim to increase the size of the rib cage.

Rib cage enlargement is a controversial issue. Some people are adamant that it is not possible. Others are equally adamant that it is possible for *all* ages, and especially for very young trainees. I am sure that I benefited from the many "breathing" pullovers I did as a teenager. At the minimum, all teenagers and trainees in their early twenties should use this pullover (or the Rader chest pull) for possible rib cage enlargement. Rib cage enlargement will produce a deeper and broader chest and, as a bonus, perhaps help improve posture.

This is strictly a stretching and forced breathing exercise. Use only 10–15 lbs to begin with—a short and unloaded bar, a pair of very light dumbbells, a single dumbbell, or just a barbell plate. (The pullover machine is not to be used for the "breathing" pullover.) After a couple of months, you can increase to 15–20 lbs, but stop there unless you can bench press over 250 lbs, in which case you could progress to 25 lbs. When you can bench press over 300 lbs, use a maximum of 30 lbs for resistance. Do not exceed these poundage ceilings—do not use progressive resistance in the "breathing" pullover. The use of

"Breathing" pullover

heavy weights will defeat the purpose of the exercise, as well as be harmful to your shoulders. If in doubt over which weight to use here, use the lighter one.

Holding the resistance, lie lengthwise on a bench, *not* across it. Keep your feet on the bench. This will prevent excessive arching of your back, and excessive stretching of your abdominal wall. Hold the resistance at arm's length above your upper chest. Take a shoulder-width grip, or closer if you are using a single dumbbell or a weight plate. Keeping your arms stiff and straight throughout, *slowly* lower the bar and simultaneously inhale as deeply as possible. Do not inhale in one gulp, but in a steady stream. Spread your ribs as much as possible. Lower your arms until they are parallel or only *slightly* below parallel with the floor. Do not go down as deep as possible. At the safe bottom position, take an extra gulp of air. Briefly pause and then return your arms to their starting position, simultaneously exhaling. Repeat for at least 15 slow reps. There is no need to count reps. Just keep going for a while, focusing on stretching your rib cage.

Experiment with a different positioning. Do the same movement but with your head just off the end of the bench, as illustrated. This may produce a better effect on your rib cage than with your head fully on the bench. The exercise can also be done on the floor. Though this style will reduce the range of motion a little, it can still produce excellent results. This was how it was done in the old days, long before benches for bench pressing became standard in the weight-training world.

Keeping your arms completely straight and locked out may irritate your elbows. If so, then very slightly bend your elbows. But keep this to the absolute minimum or else you will reduce the expansion effect on your rib cage. Elbow irritation may, however, come from using more weight than has been recommended, or from not introducing the exercise into your program carefully enough. So before you bend your elbows, first cut back your poundage, and take a few weeks to work into the exercise before doing lots of reps. Elbow irritation

may also come from using a straight bar, whereas a parallel grip on a weight plate, or dumbbell(s), may remove the irritation.

For heavy muscle-building pullovers it is essential that your elbows be bent, but not so with the "breathing" pullover. Do the "breathing" pullover as described and you should not get a bad elbow reaction.

The "breathing" pullover, and the Rader chest pull, are traditionally done immediately after an exercise that gets you heavily winded, e.g., high-rep squats, deadlifts or leg presses. But you can do the rib cage work whenever you want to, and without having done any exercise before it. You may even find that if you are heavily winded you will not be able to do the "breathing" pullover properly.

Do a set of rib cage work every day if you are serious about enlarging your rib cage. It is not high-intensity systemically-demanding work.

Go easy at the beginning, especially if you are not doing the pullovers when winded from a heavy leg exercise. The forced and exaggerated breathing may make you feel dizzy unless you work into it over a period of a few weeks. Your chest may get very sore, too, if you do not work into the exercise gradually.

Pullup/chin

Main muscles worked

lats, biceps, brachialis, pectorals, upper back, abdominal wall, forearms

Capsule description

holding a fixed overhead bar, pull yourself up to touch your chest to the bar

Introduction

Once you can do pulldowns in good form to your upper chest with about 5% over your bodyweight, or a bit less if the pulldown machine you use has a lot of friction, move onto pullups/chins. Achieving this level of strength in the supinated-grip pulldown is within the capabilities of most men, given enough time and effort, and a good training program. An important factor influencing your chinning ability is your body fat percentage, and your bodyweight in general. The more body fat you have, and the heavier you are, the harder chinning and the target pulldown poundage will be.

Setup and positioning

If your overhead bar is adjustable, e.g., if you use an Olympic bar placed on saddles in a power rack, then set the height so that you can grab the bar when standing on your toes. The knurling on the Olympic bar will help your grip, especially if you have chalk on your hands. The perfect positioning will let you pause for a few seconds, by taking your weight on your toes, to give your grip some respite before each of the final few reps of a set. Then you can give your all to each rep.

If you have a fixed and high overhead bar, then arrange a box or platform of the appropriate height so that you just have to stand on your toes to grab the bar. During the exercise, keep your legs straight and your toes pointed. When your toes touch the box or platform, you will have come to the bottom. This will ensure that you never overstretch.

If you set a bar over pins set high in a power rack, you will have to use flawless form to prevent the bar rolling as you chin.

First try holding the overhead bar with a supinated grip. Start with a shoulder-width grip and fine-tune to find the slightly narrower or wider grip that feels best for you. If you cannot find a workable supinated grip, try a pronated one. Take a pronated grip that is 2" or 3" wider on each side than your shoulder-width grip, so that your forearms are vertical at the contracted position. Regardless of the grip you choose, never use a very wide spacing, and do not pull to the rear of your head. Pulling to the front is safer for your shoulders and neck.

Some chinning units provide the option of using a parallel grip. This may be more comfortable than a supinated or a pronated grip on a single bar. But the parallel handles may be too close to produce a good training effect. You can do the pullup while hanging from bars designed for parallel bar dips, preferably bars set a bit wider than shoulder-width apart. This setup will enable you to use a parallel grip. This setup will only work if the bars are set far enough above the floor so that you can perform a full or nearly full-range pullup. You will need to keep your legs bent. Ideally your knees should just touch the floor, or something placed on it, at the arms-extended position.

Perhaps a better choice for chinning with a parallel grip is to use a power rack. If its uprights are appropriately spaced you can position a bar on saddles on the front uprights, and another across the rear uprights. Set the height of the bars so that when your arms are straight, your knees touch a bench placed beneath you.

Another option is to use a slanted bar like that suggested for the cable row and pulldown—see photo on page 46. Such a bar, if fixed overhead, could work well for chins, which use a supinated grip; but do not use it for pullups (pronated grip).

A Smith machine has a bar that is adjustable for height, and which may be well knurled. It may be perfect for pullups.

Performance

Pull until you touch the bar to your collar bones, or lower on your chest. Comparing the same resistance and degree of effort, you will be able to pull your hands to a lower point with a supinated or pronated grip than with a parallel one. Fully contract your lats by pulling your shoulder blades down, like in the pulldown. How low you can go will depend in part on your grip spacing and arm length, in addition to your strength and bodyweight. Do not pull beyond what is comfortable for your shoulders and elbows. Your back should be arched at the top of the exercise. If you have to hump your back in order to finish a rep, you are using too much resistance.

Inhale as you lower yourself, and either briefly hold the breath on the ascent and exhale at the top, or exhale during the ascent. Trying to catch your breath during a pause at the bottom position is usually counterproductive unless you can briefly stand or kneel while you breathe.

Never drop into the bottom position, or relax and stretch while you are hanging. Keep your eyes looking up slightly and do not turn your head. Keep your shoulders tight and your head tilted back, but do not throw your head back.

Pullups on a Smith machine. Note the pronated grip. Chins typically use a supinated grip. See page 81 for grip info.

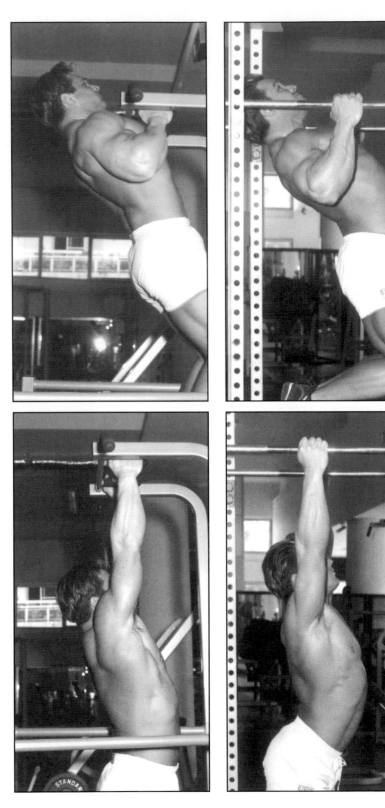

Right: Chinning using a parallel grip that is too close for best effect. Far right: Chinning in a power rack, with a grip a little wider than shoulder width.

Find a way to attach weights securely and comfortably. Either a shoulder harness or a belt designed for hanging weight from is ideal. An alternative is to wear a belt and put a dumbbell inside it by having the dumbbell vertical and the belt across the handle. Another option is to use a strong piece of rope to attach a dumbbell or weight plates securely to your belt. Let the dumbbell or plates hang either in front of your thighs or to the rear.

Add weight slowly and in small increments. To work from one fixed-weight dumbbell to the next, gradually add weight to the lighter dumbbell using small discs; or use an adjustable dumbbell. Or alternatively you can just use individual weight plates.

Spotting

Though not essential for the pullup, use a spotter if possible. When you grind to a halt a few inches short of touching the overhead bar to your upper chest, get a spotter to assist. Enough pressure should be evenly applied with both his hands to your back. The assistance should push you up in your regular groove, not push you forward and ruin the pathway.

Critical reminder
Photographs alone cannot explain good exercise technique. Please do not skip any of the accompanying text. Study it all very carefully.

27

Pushdown

Main muscles worked
triceps

Capsule description
using resistance from an overhead pulley, press down with elbows fixed

If you cannot do parallel bar dips or close-grip bench presses, and need a triceps exercise additional to your regular pressing, the pushdown is the one. You want your hands to be as close to parallel as possible. This removes stress from your wrists and applies stress throughout the triceps akin to how the parallel bar dip does it. This style also protects your elbows because it helps to prevent wrist extension.

To get your hands into a parallel position, use a rope attachment. As an alternative, use an inverted v- shaped bar—but not a bar that has sides which merely slope slightly. But it is better that you get the best type of attachment. You could securely attach your own sturdy but flexible strap or rope to the cable's connection so that you can keep your hands parallel to each other. A bathrobe's belt works well. Put a knot at the bottom of each end to prevent your hands slipping.

Push down under control, hold the contraction briefly, let the bar back up under control, stay tight at the top, and repeat. Keep your wrists and hands in a straight line, and your elbows fixed at the sides of your ribs. Keep your torso and legs rigid, and focus on arm extension and flexion. Exhale as you push down, and inhale as you let the bar return to its starting position.

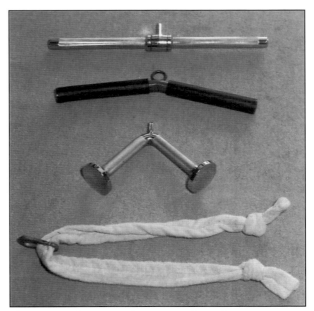

Four cable attachments for the pushdown, from a straight bar (poor) to the belt of a bathrobe (good).

As with all isolation exercises for the triceps—but most are useless even if performed safely—do not use a range of motion that causes your forearms and biceps to crush together. Stop the ascent of your hands just before your forearms and biceps meet. And never relax at the top of the pushdown. Keep tight control.

See the note on page 46 for how to add weight gradually to the pushdown.

Pushdown using a pulldown machine. Only use this exercise if you cannot do parallel bar dips or close-grip bench presses—the pushdown is an inferior exercise. Even the regular bench press is a far superior exercise to the pushdown, for the triceps.

28

Rader chest pull

Main structure worked
rib cage

This exercise was developed by Peary Rader. Teenagers and trainees in their early twenties should use it—or the "breathing" pullover, see page 129—for rib cage enlargement. Older trainees may benefit too, though probably to a lesser degree.

Stand at about arm's length from a vertical bar, with your feet hip-width apart. Alternatively you could use a sturdy and stable object that can be grasped at a little above head height. An upright on a power rack, or a door jamb, will do the job. Grab it at about head height, with straight arms. If you use an upright of a power rack, or a vertical bar, keep your hands together. If you use another object, keep your hands close together.

Keeping your arms straight, take a deep breath and, at the same time, pull down and *in* with your arms. Do not contract your abdominal muscles. Keep them relaxed. If you tense your abdominal muscles this will flatten your chest and defeat the purpose of the exercise. Done correctly, the exercise will raise your chest and produce a "pull" and slight discomfort in your sternum. If you do not feel this, you are not doing the exercise properly.

You may get a better effect if you bend your arms slightly, because this will let you pull harder. The harder you pull, the better the effect on your rib cage, so long as you are pulling in the right way.

Rader recommended that you tense the muscles at the front of your neck and then

Starting position of the Rader chest pull.

pull your head back. This should be done at the same time as you pull down and *in* with your arms. This neck involvement will provide further stretching and lifting of your rib cage. But do not apply this tip until after you have learned how to apply all the other instruction.

Once you get to grips with it you will feel a considerable stretching effect in your rib cage. It may, however, take a while to get the exercise right. You may have to fine-tune the precise height you place your hands, the spacing between your hands, the distance between your feet and the base of the object you hold, and the angle of pull that you use. Persist until you get the exercise right.

Hold your breath for as long as comfortable, and throughout the entire time you should be able to feel the "pull" and slight discomfort in your sternum. Do not, however, hold your breath until you are almost ready to burst, because you need to be able to perform up to 20 reps for a single set. How long you can comfortably hold your breath will depend on the state of your breathing prior to performing the chest pull (primarily whether or not you squatted prior to the chest pulls), and your general conditioning. With practice, over time, you will be able to hold each pull for a longer time, for a comparable level of discomfort. Somewhere in the range of 4-6 seconds per pull will be fine.

You can perform the Rader chest pull after an exercise that gets you heavily winded, or when you are not winded. As noted in the section on the "breathing" pullover, rib cage work can be done much more frequently than other weight-training exercises. It is not high-intensity systemically-demanding work.

Go easy to begin with, especially if you are not doing the Rader chest pull when winded from a heavy leg exercise. The forced and exaggerated breathing may make you feel dizzy unless you work into it over a period of a few weeks. Your chest may get very sore, too, if you do not work into the exercise gradually. Exercise caution and good sense.

Shrug

Main muscles worked
traps and entire upper back, deltoids, forearms
(in the bench shrug, the pectorals, deltoids and traps are heavily worked)

Capsule description
while holding resistance with arms straight, shrug your shoulders

Introduction

Shrugging movements are an underrated group of exercises. There are many types of shrugs, a number of which were developed by Paul Kelso. One type of overhead shrug is described on page 106. Here are three major shrugs: incline shrug, standing shrug, and bench shrug.

Incline shrug

Set a bench at about 45°. Lie on it face down. Let your arms hang vertically. The lowest point you can reach without forcing a stretch is where you want to be taking the resistance. Place a barbell over pins set in a power rack at this position; or place a loaded barbell or dumbbells on boxes of the appropriate height. A simpler setup is to position an adjustable bench at the lowest setting which, when you are face down, allows you to keep your arms straight and take dumbbells from off the floor without forcing a stretch. All three alternatives will prevent an excessive range of motion. This is an important precaution because heavy weights are possible in this exercise, eventually. You must avoid the possibility of the weight yanking you beyond the point that is safe.

While dumbbells or a straight bar can be used, a Trap Bar will bang against the underside of the bench you lie on and ruin the exercise. With a pair of dumbbells, use a pronated or a parallel grip, or one somewhere in between.

Do not jam your chin onto the bench. Keep your head lifted off the bench, or off the end of the bench, so that you keep stress from off your chin and neck.

While solidly on the incline bench, shrug your shoulders *and* pull them back. Do not shrug up and forward because that focuses the work on the upper traps rather than on the whole upper-back area. Try to crush your shoulder blades together. Then lower the resistance under control to the pins, boxes or floor as the case may be. Gently touch and then do the next rep.

It is important that you keep your arms straight. Nearly everyone bends their arms as they shrug. To help prevent this, use your bench press grip or slightly wider. A close grip, or moving too fast, will prompt your arms to bend. With a pronated grip, rotate your elbows in, and keep them in, to "lock" your elbows. Then shrug without any bending of your arms. If you use a straight bar you can use a reverse grip for added grip strength. From set to set, alternate which hand is supinated.

Start light in the incline shrug, get the form right, do not bend your arms, and

Dumbbell incline shrug

then you will build up resistance in good form and benefit from the exercise. But rush into it, add weight too quickly, and your form will become a mess.

In the standing incline shrug, keep your legs slightly unlocked. This will remove the excessive knee strain that accompanies having your legs ramrod straight while shrugging intensively.

Barbell incline shrug from off pins in a power rack.

Do not bend your arms as you shrug.

A variation of the incline shrug can be done on a seated row machine that has your chest braced. Position the seat so that your arms are parallel to the floor. While keeping your arms straight, shrug your shoulders back and down.

Starting position of the shrug on a seated row machine.

Standing shrug

This is the shrug that most trainees are familiar with. Stand, with your arms straight, and hold a bar as if you were at the top position of a deadlift. Without bending your arms, shrug up as high as possible. Lower under control, and repeat. Dumbbells and a Trap Bar are ideal for the shrug because they are not obstructed by your legs or groin, unlike a straight bar.

To avoid an excessive range of motion at the bottom of the standing shrug, use a rack or boxes akin to how they were used in the incline shrug.

Keep your body tight, a moderate arch in your lower back (*never* round your back), do not shuffle your feet around, and do not take more of the stress on one side of your body than the other. Keep the stress distributed symmetrically.

Keep your arms straight. Most trainees bend their arms as they shrug. To help prevent this, use your bench press grip or slightly wider. A close grip, or moving too fast, will prompt your arms to bend. With a pronated grip, rotate your elbows in, and keep them in, to "lock" your elbows. Then shrug without any bending of your arms.

If you use a straight bar, use a reverse grip for added grip strength. From set to set, alternate which hand is supinated.

Caution!

Regardless of which shrug you use for your upper-back musculature, do not use a circular action. The circular motion places unnecessary wear on your shoulder joints.

Keep your shoulders tight at the bottom of each rep—never let the weight yank your shoulders down. And keep a tight hold on the bar or dumbbells, using plenty of chalk for grip support.

Standing dumbbell shrug

Calf machine shrug

Over the years I have often had negative after-effects from shrugs performed using a calf machine—a "not quite right" discomfort in the traps during the following few days. I confused this with muscular soreness *until* someone gave me another explanation. On hindsight, the problem is obvious.

Previous printings of this book recommended the calf machine shrug. This was a mistake. For the calf machine shrug (not illustrated here), the resistance rests against the actual musculature that is primarily worked in the movement. So when the musculature contracts, the contraction is distorted due to the compression from the weight bearing down on it. Such an obstruction produces a skewed effect on the musculature, leading to possible damage in the tissue. *The musculature being worked should be free of compressive impediment to its contraction and relaxation.*

Because the calf machine shrug takes the grip out of the exercise, it enables greater resistance to be used than in the regular shrug. This further exaggerates the compressive effect on the traps, and the potential for harm. The traps are able to move a great deal of weight.

The negative impact of this exercise on the traps depends on the design of the calf machine, and the body structure of the individual trainee. How the machine's shoulder pads are positioned on the shoulders is critical. If someone has narrow shoulders, and the pads primarily rest on the bony prominences, that would put far less stress on the actual trap structures than if the pads were directly on the muscle, as they would be on a man with a large neck and shoulders. Machine design will play a role too, depending on the spacing between the pads. A machine with wider-spaced pads will place them less on the traps than would a setup with the pads closer together.

Though I have never suffered serious problems from this exercise, I have recently heard reports of cases of partial tears of the trapezius from the base of the skull.

There will probably be a severe pull at the base of the skull regardless of the size of the user or the design of the machine. *I recommend that you be conservative, avoid the calf machine shrug, and play safe. Use another type of shrug.*

Bench shrug: The arms must be kept locked out throughout the movement.

Bench shrug

Do this exercise while lying on your back on a horizontal bench positioned inside a power rack. Plant your feet on the floor or, better, on a platform as recommended for the regular bench press. Position the pins about 4" below your bench press lockout position. Take a shoulder-width grip. Do not use the grip you normally take for bench pressing because that will put your shoulders at greater risk.

Take the bar from the saddles or, much better, directly from off the rack's pins. Immediately lock out your arms. This is your starting position. Keeping your arms locked, pull your shoulder blades together. This will pull your shoulders fully onto the bench and cause the bar to be lowered a little. Now spread your shoulder blades and roll your shoulders off the bench, simultaneously exhaling. Your arms must remain locked throughout, and your upper back and head must stay in contact with the bench. As you roll your shoulders up, crunch your pectoral muscles together. The top position of the bench shrug will have your hands about 3" higher than where they would be at the lockout of a regular supine bench press.

Especially to begin with you may have trouble keeping the bar in the right groove. But if you do lose it, the pins are there to catch the bar. To make it easy to keep the bar in the groove, do the shrugging while sliding the bar up and down against the uprights of a power rack, like in the tip described on page 104 for the overhead lockout. This assumes that you use the type of power rack that enables you to set a bench inside it in the position you need.

To stay in the right groove you must keep both hands moving in unison. If one hand gets above or in front of the other, you will lose the groove and risk injuring yourself. Use slow and controlled form. Start with no more than 50% of your 10-rep bench press poundage, and progress carefully. Chalk your hands before each work set you do.

Using a Smith machine can give you excellent control in the bench shrug. This machine locks the bar in a fixed pathway. But the same cautions apply as noted in *Overhead Lockout*—see pages 104–107. You must be able to "rack" the bar safely. Ideally, set up the machine so that your bottom position is where the latches are at rest. Then you can move the bar up and down the guided pathway without needing to twist your wrists to take the latches out. Then, even if you lose control, the bar will come to rest safely. But if you move the latches out of the guided pathway, a spotter is absolutely essential, to ensure that you do not lose control over the bar.

The Smith machine has few uses for safe long-term training. The bench shrug, because it is a short-range movement, is one of the safe applications if performed as prescribed. But *do not* do the full-range bench press in the Smith machine because its technique would be corrupted by the pathway that the machine forces upon you. This will set you up for chronic injuries.

Side bend

Main muscles worked

erectors, quadratus lumborum, abdominal wall

Capsule description

holding resistance against a thigh, bend to that side, and return upright

Introduction

The side bend is a very valuable exercise for strengthening the girdle of musculature around your lower torso. This will help to keep you free of lower back injuries. It will not add inches to your waist measurement. It will add less than an inch of solid muscle to your waist girth if you build up to using well over 100 lbs for at least 10 good reps. But that extra muscle will do nothing but good for your overall strength, appearance and resistance to injury.

Setup and positioning

Space your feet about hip-width apart, but fine-tune this to best suit you. If you have a tendency towards groin strains, a close stance with your feet touching may be better. But balance is harder to maintain with a close stance than with a wider one. Another thing to try, if you tend to suffer from groin strains, is keeping your buttocks contracted during the exercise.

The side bend can be done with a dumbbell or with a barbell. The plates on a conventional dumbbell obstruct a smooth exercise groove, at least in the standing side bend. The dumbbell's gripping site needs to be held a little out from your thigh because the plates get in the way. With a barbell, your fingers can slide up and down the outside of your thigh. Even an Olympic barbell can be used, though balance is easier with a shorter barbell. So long as you hold the barbell in the right position, and use good controlled form, balance will be fine even with an Olympic barbell. In order to maintain balance, the bar must be kept horizontal and your form must be tight.

If the bar is long enough, do the barbell side bend inside a power rack. Set the pins an inch above the absolute lowest point you can go down to. The pins serve three important purposes. First, they ensure that you cannot overstretch. Second, they enable you to set the bar down briefly between reps when necessary. This lets you release your grip for a few seconds while keeping your hand in place. This provides your gripping muscles with brief respite before the next rep. Third, the pins will "catch" the bar if you lose control.

Before the first rep of a set using a barbell, check that you have gripped onto the bar so that the bar is horizontal when lifted off the pins. If it is not perfectly horizontal, set the bar down, reposition your hand, and start again. If it is not perfectly positioned to begin with, it is set up for becoming seriously imbalanced. This will cause you to terminate the set before its true finish.

A dumbbell can be used for the standing side bend, good form maintained,

Side bend in the rack.   **Dumbbell side bend**   **Seated side bend**

and the plates not be an obstruction, so long as the dumbbell is adjustable. But the plates need to be loaded so that there is space between the gripping site and the plates at each end. The space needs to be sufficient so that your fingers can slide against your outer thigh without the plates getting in the way. To achieve this you could jam something of the correct width in between both sides of the gripping site and the plates. The plates would then need to be situated nearer the ends of the bar. But if the dumbbell rod is short there may not be enough space at the ends to secure the collars in position.

Collars should be used on an Olympic bar, and are a necessity on a dumbbell. The plates only need to work their way slightly out of their starting position for the balance of the barbell to be ruined. Collars will prevent this.

A simpler way of doing the dumbbell side bend is while seated. Do it while seated at the end of a bench, across the middle of a bench with one leg on each side, or on a box. With a wide enough foot placement to maintain balance, the seated side bend can work very well. There will be no problem with the plates striking your legs and obstructing a smooth pathway. But be careful not to overstretch.

Performance

Take the weight in your right hand. Rest your disengaged hand (your left) on your left obliques and "tune in" with the muscles as they are worked. Bend to your right side as far as is comfortable. Then return to the vertical position. Do all your reps to the right side without interruption. To exercise the other side of your body, reverse the procedure. Face forward throughout each set.

There should only be lateral movement. Do not lean forward any, do not lean back, and do not overstretch.

Avoid taking too much of the load on your leg which is on the side that the weight is held, or else you will lose your balance and topple towards that side.

Do the reps carefully—about two seconds up and two seconds down, or use a slower tempo of about four seconds up and four down, and fewer reps per set. Avoid "snapping" into the movement. It is important to keep the form smooth, and the negative phase under control even after the final rep when you feel like putting the bar down in a hurry. Inhale on the descent, and exhale on the ascent.

After an intensive set of side bends, take a few minutes rest before working your other side. This will ensure that your performance there does not suffer greatly. From workout to workout, alternate the side you work first.

Other tips and A CAUTION

Carefully adapt to this exercise if you have not done it before, or if you have not done it for a long time. For two weeks, do it twice a week without added resistance. Do a couple of sets of high reps each time. Keep your hands by your sides, and then progress to placing them behind your ears. Focus on strict form free of snappy movements. Go down to a comfortable depth. If your flexibility increases you may be able to increase the depth a little over the first few weeks. Avoid twisting your torso in order to go down deeper.

To learn the groove, do the exercise side-on to a mirror. Keep your head turned to the side and scrutinize your form; and make it impeccable. But do not do any serious work with your head turned. You must have your head facing forward when you train intensively.

In your third week of doing the side bend, use a light weight and thereafter add poundage slowly and gradually, using small increments.

So long as the exercise is easy, it does not matter when you do it in your routine. But as soon as it becomes intensive, avoid doing it before your major exercises. Either do it afterwards, or on a different day.

Before doing an intensive set, warm up with a set without resistance, followed by a set with a light weight.

When you are training hard, use chalk and take each set almost to failure. Like with the deadlift and the stiff-legged deadlift, it is best to keep the very final rep of a set in you. Going for the "do or die" rep in the side bend could injure you.

As well as being a valuable movement for torso stability, the side bend provides a satisfying change of pace from the major lifts. And for a "little" exercise it is very demanding if you really work at it.

The side bend needs to be treated with caution if you have a history of lower-back injury or problems. If the side bend irritates your back, DO NOT persist with it. Try the side bend alternative instead. The latter can also be used in an occasional training cycle by trainees who *can* safely perform the side bend but who want some variety. But even the side bend alternative is demanding on the lower back. *Proceed with caution!*

Side bend alternative

This exercise does not train the quadratus lumborum like the side bend does, and thus cannot add lateral stability to the body like the side bend can. But it works the other midsection structures well.

Lie on the floor with your hips and lower back on a folded towel. Put your arms flat on the floor and perpendicular to your torso. Raise your legs so that they are straight and vertical. Keep them together and straight, and lower them to your left side until your left foot touches the floor. Then return to the vertical position and lower slowly to your right side. Then go to the left again, and so on. Do the same

Side bend alternative

number of reps for each side. When lowering your legs, keep them in the same plane as they were in the vertical starting position—do not move them to the front or rear. When you can do 20 perfect reps to each side, attach weight to your feet or ankles. Then use lower reps and get serious about building up resistance. An alternative to extra resistance, at least for the short term, is always to do this exercise immediately after an intensive set of crunch abdominal work. Then build your reps up to 20 before adding resistance.

31

Squat

Main muscles worked
quadriceps, thigh adductors, glutes, erectors

Capsule description
hold a bar over your shoulders, sit down, and then immediately stand erect

Introduction

This exercise is sometimes called the back squat, to distinguish it from the front squat. The front squat has the bar held at the front of the shoulders. As well as being a more productive exercise because it works more muscle mass, the back squat is much easier to perform than the front squat, especially with heavy weights. The back squat is a much better exercise and is the only squat promoted in this book.

In the conventional style of squatting you descend to the appropriate depth and then come up immediately. Safety bars or rack pins should be set a couple of inches or so below your bottom position. Then if you cannot complete a rep you can descend a little more than normal and safely set the bar down. But you do not touch the safety bars unless you have to. There is, however, another form of squatting. Here, while at the bottom position, you intentionally set the barbell down on safety bars before each ascent. In this style, i.e., rack squatting from the bottom, each ascent is started from a dead stop following a brief pause at the precise depth you squat down to.

Properly done, the squat is safe and super productive. But use poor form, abuse low reps, overtrain, or try to lift a too-heavy weight, and you will hurt yourself. Learn to squat properly before you concern

yourself with poundage, and add weight slowly while maintaining perfect form.

Before you can squat with good form you need to be flexible enough to be able to adopt the necessary positioning. You especially need to have flexible Achilles tendons, hamstrings, thigh adductors, and glutes. Women who usually wear shoes with high heels are likely to have tight Achilles tendons. You also need flexible shoulders and pectorals in order to hold the bar in the right position with ease.

> **To demonstrate exercise form clearly, the model did not wear a shirt, and weight stands and safety bars were often not used. This was only for illustration purposes. When you train, wear a shirt and always take the proper safety measures.**

If you are inflexible, invest 4–6 weeks progressively and carefully increasing your flexibility before you start learning how to squat. The squat itself will help you to become more flexible, but you will not be able to use good technique for a while. Consequently you will practice bad habits

A squat rack unit.

that will later have to be "unlearned." This is why it is best to be flexible in the first place. No matter how good or bad your leverages may be for the squat, a flexible body will improve your squatting form.

If you have had a major back injury, you must get the clearance of a sports-orientated chiropractor before you squat. If you have had any minor back injuries, still get a chiropractor's clearance.

Setup/positioning

Always squat inside a four-post power rack (see page 35) with pins and saddles correctly and securely in place. Alternatively you could use a half rack, sturdy and stable squat stands together with spotter racks or bars, or a squat rack unit that combines stands and safety bars.

In a power rack, the pins must be held securely in place. Once a pin is in position, put a piece of garden hose sliced down its length over the pin, especially if you are going to be doing rack squats from the bottom position. This will reduce bar rolling and sliding, and vibrations.

Always squat in solid and sturdy shoes. Soft and spongy ones will not give you solid support because, as you squat, your feet will move slightly on the soft soles and heels. A pair of walking shoes or boots may give you better support than high-priced athletic shoes. But do not use a shoe with a heel height above the norm, or with unevenly or excessively worn heels or soles. And keep the laces of your shoes tied.

A straight bar is fine for squatting, but a cambered squat bar is much better. (See the photos on page 21.) A cambered bar is one bent like that of a yoke used in some societies to drape over the shoulders, for carrying heavy objects with relative ease. Use a cambered squat bar if possible. Urge the management of where you train to get a cambered squat bar. Relative to a straight bar, the bent bar is easier to hold in position, "sits" better on your upper back, and is less likely to roll out of position. But whatever bar you use, one with center knurling will greatly help you to keep it in place during each set.

If you cannot squat intensively with a straight bar, a bent bar will probably not make enough difference to warrant the investment. But if you can train hard with a straight bar, you should be able to train even harder with a cambered bar.

Set the height of the bar on its saddles so that you only have to dip a few inches when getting the bar out. If the bar is too low you will waste energy getting it out. If it is too high you will need to rise on your toes to get the bar out. The too-high setting is especially dangerous when you come to return the bar after finishing a hard set of squats. You will have a serious problem putting the bar back in its saddles.

If you are used to squatting with a straight bar, and then move to a cambered bar, you will need to lower the position of the saddles, and that of the pins or safety bars set at the bottom position of the squat. This is because the ends of a cambered bar are lower than the center part that sits on your upper back. If you position the pins and saddles for a cambered bar as they were for a straight bar, you will have trouble unracking and racking the bent bar. In addition you will hit the pins before you reach your usual depth of descent.

Use little or preferably no padding on the bar. If you are a training novice you will probably have little visible muscle over and above your shoulder blades. After a few months of progressive training that includes deadlifts and incline shrugs you will start developing the muscular padding you need on your upper back. Then the bar can be held in position more comfortably.

The more padding that is around a bar, the more likely that the bar will be incorrectly positioned, or that it will move during a set. Tolerate the bar directly on the shirt over your traps. Wearing a thick sweatshirt rather than a thin T-shirt will give you some acceptable padding to cushion the bar. If more padding is needed, wear a T-shirt *and* a sweatshirt, or even two sweatshirts. But for body temperature control you may need to cut off the sleeves and bottom half of the outer shirt.

Before you center the bar on your upper back you must be holding the bar properly, with your shoulder blades crushed together. This creates a layer of flexed muscle on your upper back over and above your shoulder blades.

For low-rep work, especially if you have a relatively long back, you can position the bar as low as directly over the flexed muscle on top of your retracted shoulder blades. For medium and high-rep work, such a low bar position cannot be held for the duration of the set, especially if you have a relatively short back. Therefore, position the bar a little higher. Put it on the muscle just above the center of the top ridge of your shoulder blades, but *below* your seventh cervical vertebra. To find C7, tilt your head back and feel for the bony prominence at the base of your neck.

Use as low a bar position as you can maintain for the duration of the set. Practice correct bar positioning until you can do it automatically. What will initially feel very awkward will become relatively comfortable after a few weeks of practice.

Hold the bar securely in your hands, not loosely in the ends of your fingers. Do not drape your arms over the bar or your hands over the plates. You want a solid hold on the bar, to help it stay in position. The width of grip you use to hold the bar depends on your torso size, arm length, and shoulder and pectoral flexibility. For the best control over the bar, use the closest *comfortable* grip. But if your grip is too close it will be hard on your shoulders and elbows, especially for medium and high reps. The closer your grip, the more that flexibility is an issue and the greater the tendency for the upper back to round. Most people use a medium or wider grip.

If your grip is too wide, you will risk trapping your fingers between the bar and the safety supports or rack pins that are in position at the bottom of the squat. Be sure your hands are placed so that there is no chance of your fingers getting trapped.

Quite low bar placement for the squat (left). Bar too high and hands not holding it properly (right). A cambered bar may not drape over your shoulders properly unless there is weight pulling on it.

Regardless of the width of grip you use, be sure that both hands are the same distance from the center of the bar.

Following some experimentation using a very light weight, find *your* optimum width of heel placement, and degree of toe flare. As a starting point, place your heels a little more than hip-width apart, and turn out each foot to about a 35° angle from an imaginary straight line extending from your face. Perform some squats. Then try a bit more flare and the same heel spacing. Then try a slightly wider stance and the initial toe flare. Then try the wider stance with more flare.

The flare of your feet, i.e., how much your toes are turned out, is critical. If you do not have enough flare it is almost certain that when you squat intensively your knees will come in on the ascent. You will also lean forward excessively if your feet are not flared enough.

The combination of a moderately-wide stance and well-flared toes usually gives plenty of room to squat into, helps to prevent excessive forward lean, and lets you squat deeper without your lower back rounding. But too wide a stance will restrict how easily you descend. Keep experimenting until you find the stance that best suits you. Individual variation in leg length, torso length, hip girth, and relative lengths of your lower and upper leg, contribute to determining the squat stance that is ideal for you. This individual variation is why you must experiment until you find the stance that is best for you. Tall people usually need a wider stance than do people of average height.

What you are looking for is a foot placement that spreads the stress of the squat over your legs, glutes and back. Do not try to focus the stress on only your legs. You want to be able to squat without your lower back rounding or your torso leaning forward excessively. You want your heels to remain firmly planted on the floor. You need to be stable at all times, with no tendency to topple forward. You also need to keep forward movement of your knees

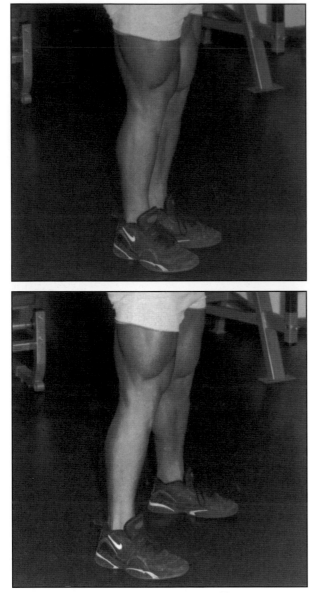

Two common stance errors: Feet too close (top), and feet well spaced but with insufficient flare (bottom).

to a minimum. And you want your knees to stay tracking over your feet. If your stance is good, you should be able to keep your knees where they belong. If you have a stance that is too close and/or have insufficient toe flare, then buckling is inevitable when you squat intensively.

It may take a few workouts before you find the best stance for you. With 50% or so of your 10-rep squat poundage, stand on some cardboard, adopt your new squat stance, and check it out. After a few reps, when you are sure your stance is correct, and while keeping your feet in position, get someone to draw the outline of your feet on the card. Then you will have a record of your stance for when you need to refer to it. Practice repeatedly until you can adopt your squat stance automatically. But at each squat session you may need to make tiny adjustments in foot placement to feel smooth for that day.

With poor squatting form your lower back will round earlier in the descent than it would had you used good form. With good form as advised here, and using a very light weight, find the depth of descent at which your lower back just starts to round. An assistant must watch you from the side, with his eyes level with your hips at your bottom position. Set your squatting depth at 2" above the point of rounding.

Performance of the squat

Face the bar so that you will have to walk backwards from the saddles before taking your squatting stance. Take your precise grip on the bar, and then get under it as it rests on the weight saddles or stands. Do not lean over in order to get under the bar. Bend your legs and get your hips right underneath the bar. Your feet can either be hip-width apart directly under the bar, or "split." If split, one foot will be a little in front of the bar, and the other will be a little behind the bar. Pull your scapulae together, flex the musculature of your back, and then correctly position the bar.

With the bar correctly held and in position, lower back arched a little, and hips directly under the bar, look forward, tense your entire torso, and then straighten your legs. The bar should move vertically up and out of the saddles or stands. Do not take it out in an inclined pathway. Stand still for a few seconds, without having moved your feet. Just check that the bar feels perfectly centered. If it feels heavier on one side than the other, put it back on the saddles. If it felt just a little unbalanced, stay under the bar as it rests on the saddles, reposition the bar and try again. But if it felt considerably lopsided, get out from under the bar, check that you have loaded the bar correctly, and make any necessary corrections. Then get under the bar again, position it properly, and unrack it. Never walk out of squat stands with a bar that does not feel properly centered on your upper back.

Step *back* the minimum distance so that you do not hit the uprights of the rack or squat stands during the ascent. Do not step forward after you have taken the bar out of its supports. If you do you will have to walk backwards, and look to the rear, to return the bar to its supports. This is more hazardous than returning the bar forward into the rack saddles or squat stands.

Slide your feet over the floor as you walk with the bar in position over your upper back. This keeps both of your feet in contact with the floor. Do not lift your feet. Put your feet in the stance you have drilled yourself to adopt. Do not look down.

Keep your jaw parallel to the floor at all times—both between and during reps. Your eyes should look straight ahead or slightly up, but never down. Fix your eyes on a spot and keep them riveted on it throughout the set.

The weight should be felt through your heels, *not* the front of your feet. But do not rock back on your heels and lose your balance. Always maintain a tight torso, and make a deliberate effort to tighten your torso further as you start the descent.

With the bar and the center of your hips and heels in a vertical line, weight felt

This stance for the squat, or something close to it, will work well for many if not most trainees.

through your heels, and your back flat and as tight as possible, start the descent by bending at your knees for a few inches while keeping your torso upright. Then you will automatically bend at your hips as you continue the descent. Do not bend at your hips first.

Descend symmetrically, under control, and with the weight felt through your heels. Take about 3 seconds to descend to your squatting depth. A perfect descent is needed before you can produce a perfect ascent. Take the descent very seriously.

Some forward movement of your knees and shins is a necessity, of course, but keep it to the minimum. Keeping the weight felt through your heels goes a long way to ensuring correct leg positioning. Assuming the use of good form, how much forward movement there is of your lower legs largely depends on your body structure and how deep you squat.

Descend until your upper thighs are parallel or just below parallel to the floor. If *your* lower back rounds before you reach the parallel position, you must not squat to parallel. The maximum safe depth for squatting, remember, is 2" above the point where your lower back starts to round. Squatting with a rounded lower back is very dangerous. But most people who are flexible enough can squat to parallel or a bit below without their lower backs rounding. Do not cut the depth of your squats unless you have to.

Even if you are able to squat below parallel *without* your lower back rounding, this is generally not recommended because it may increase the stress on your knees. Not only that, but the greater depth of squatting puts an increased stress on your lower back. Play safe: Squat to parallel or to the point just above where your lower back starts to round, *whichever comes first.*

I will make an exception here because the "squat to parallel" advice is a general recommendation. If you can squat to deeper than parallel *without* rounding your lower back, *and* without knee problems, then do so. But those are two very important preconditions.

While some people can squat safely to *below* parallel, they probably belong to a minority when the whole mass of trainees is considered, not just a limited group. But you may belong to that minority. Proceed with caution and absolutely never bounce at the bottom position. And never relax at the bottom so that your rear thighs collapse onto your calves. Keep tight at the bottom position. Squatting below parallel is called the "full squat." But the full squat does not mean going down to the point where your buttocks meet your ankles and your chest is at your knees.

For those people who do not round their backs when going below parallel, and who also have healthy knees, they may even experience less knee stress from going below parallel than they do when stopping at parallel. This is an individual matter, and you need to find out what is best for you. Keep in mind that the deeper you squat, the less weight you will need to exhaust the involved muscles.

Do not pause at the bottom unless you are doing rack squats where you actually set the bar down on the pins.

For the ascent, drive up while pushing through your heels. Drive with equal force through both feet. If you favor one leg you may produce a dangerous corkscrew-like motion in your ascent.

During the ascent, the bar, as seen from the side, should move as vertically as possible. It must not move forward before it moves upward. If you tip forward at the bottom of the squat, the bar will go forward before it starts to go up. The bar's pathway will then look rather like an inverted question mark, assuming that you complete the rep. This is one of the most common mistakes in the squat, and leads to lots of sprained and even seriously injured lower backs.

Your hips must not rise faster than your shoulders. Competitive powerlifters sometimes intentionally let their hips rise quicker than their shoulders when making the initial drive from the bottom. That is a specialized technique for specialized conditions, and *has proven to be ruinous for many people.* Do not use it yourself!

Focusing on pushing through your heels will help to maintain the proper ascent. Pushing through the front part of your feet will almost inevitably tip you forward and ruin your ascent. Making a special effort to keep your shoulder blades pulled back, and your chest stuck out, will also help you to keep your ascent in the right groove.

The ascent, just like the descent, should be symmetrical. The bar should not be

While standing between reps, preserve the natural curves of your spine (left). Do not round your back (right).

positioned off center on your back, the bar should not tip to one side, and you should not take more weight on one side of your body than the other. Keep the stress distributed symmetrically.

While standing between reps, do not sway at your hips. Maintain a strong rigid position. Do not rock the bar on your shoulders, do not take more of the weight on one leg than the other, and do not rotate your hips. Just stay rigid, with the weight distributed symmetrically. Also, keep your hips pushed back a bit in order to exaggerate slightly the natural curve in your lower spine. If you move your hips forward during the pause between reps, you will flatten the curve at the bottom of your spine and greatly weaken your back. But before you start a descent, make sure that your hips are back in line with your heels and the bar, and that there is no exaggerated lordosis. Never start a descent while leaning forward even slightly.

At the end of a set you must rack the bar, i.e., return the bar to its holders. While sliding your feet so that you always have both feet in contact with the floor, move forward until the bar is directly above the saddles or stands. Carefully check that you are not going to miss the weight holders with the bar. And be sure that your fingers are not lined up to be pinched between the bar and its holders. Then bend your legs and set the bar down.

The bar should be returned to its holders in a vertical motion. A common error is to stop short of the saddles or stands and lower the bar by leaning forward while keeping the legs straight. This is dangerous. It leads to reduced control over the bar, and excessive stress on your already tired lower back.

In power racks, and many squat racks, the saddles are attached to uprights that extend vertically. In those racks you can actually walk in and strike the barbell onto the uprights and then lower the bar. The posts will be your guide. But do not strike the uprights so hard that the bar bounces off; and keep the bar hard against the posts and watch out to be sure that you are not going to trap your fingers.

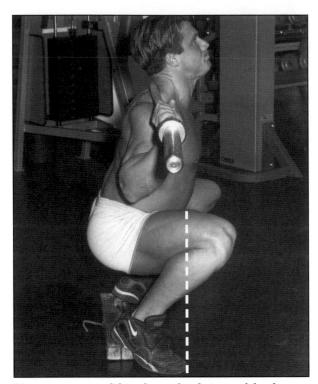

Never squat with a board, plate or block under your heels. Raising your heels produces a more upright torso, but at the price of increased leg flexion and greatly increased knee stress and wear and tear. Note how the knees have moved WAY in front of an imaginary vertical line drawn from the toes. For knee safety, the knees should NEVER move in front of this imaginary line, and preferably should be two or more inches BEHIND it. Do not elevate your heels! Also, the bar is too high here.

Other tips for the squat

Do not squat in a sweat-strewn shirt. Change your shirt before you squat, if need be. And never squat with a bare torso because it greatly reduces the stability of the bar on your back.

Before you get under the bar for a work set, chalk your hands and get someone to chalk the area on your shirt where the bar will rest. This will help the bar to stay in position during the set.

Protect your knees. *Do not* use a board, block or plate under your heels. Instead, improve your stance, and work to increase the flexibility of your Achilles tendons, hamstrings, thigh adductors and glutes. Then you will not need anything under your heels to maintain your balance.

Heel elevation increases forward travel of the knees, and exaggerates stress on the joints. *Never* should the knees travel forward of an imaginary vertical line drawn from the toes. Best to keep the knees two *or more* inches *behind* this line.

Progressively increasing your shoulder and pectoral flexibility will help you to hold the bar in position with less difficulty.

Practice, practice and practice again, with just a bare bar over your upper back, until you can get into your correct squatting stance *without* having to look down or fiddle around to get your feet in the right position. But after the first rep of a set, if you know your stance is not quite right, then adjust it but without looking down. If your stance is in a mess, return the bar to the saddles, rest a few minutes, and then restart the set properly.

Never turn your head while you are lifting or lowering the bar. If you do, the bar will tip slightly, your groove will be spoiled, and you could hurt yourself.

The orthodox breathing pattern when squatting is to catch your breath between reps and take a final inhalation just prior to the descent. The breath is briefly held until the ascent when it is forcefully exhaled.

Do not squat to a bench, box or chair as that would cause compression of your spine. To squat from a dead stop at your bottom position, squat inside a power rack with the pins appropriately positioned for you.

Consolidating the groove arising from a new stance and squatting technique takes time and patience. Start with a very light weight and practice on alternate days for as many sessions as it takes until you master the form and embed the groove. Then take *at least* two months to build your poundages back to their former best. Only *then* will you be able to work into new personal best poundages and start to build muscle. Your new and improved form will *increase* your squatting potential and *reduce* your chances of getting injured. But if you rush to build your poundages back, you will destroy the new form, and probably injure yourself.

As observed from the side view of your squat, get feedback from a training partner. Alternatively you could record yourself with a video camera. Watching yourself in a mirror is not good enough for analyzing your squatting technique.

Once you have mastered the technique you must still give 100% attention to ensure that you deliver perfect form during every rep you do. Never become casual or overconfident and think that you can deliver good form even if your focus is not 100%. Just a slight slip of concentration can lead to lowering the bar just slightly out of position, having one hand getting ahead of or in front of the other, or having one leg taking more load than the other. Any of these will ruin the groove, make the weight feel heavier, make your reps harder, cause frustration, and risk injury.

Do not squat while your lower back is still sore from an earlier workout or some heavy manual labor. Rest a day or few longer. And never deadlift or stiff-legged deadlift intensively before you squat. Do not fatigue your lower back and reduce its potential as a major stabilizer in the squat.

Using a lifting belt is optional for low-rep squats, but inhibiting in high-rep work because of the heavy breathing involved.

Spotting for the squat

As soon as the bar stalls, moves laterally, tips, or the squatter starts to twist to one side, then the spotter or spotters must act to prevent the rep deteriorating further.

If two spotters are involved, there must be excellent communication. If there is not excellent communication, one spotter could take one end before the other spotter grabs his end of the bar. If one spotter shouts "Take it!" then the other must respond even if he thinks the assistance could have been delayed a little.

If one spotter is involved, he should stand directly behind the lifter. Assistance is given by the spotter standing astride the lifter, grabbing the lifter around his chest, maintaining bent legs and an arched back, and applying upward pressure. This will work only if a little help is needed to get the trainee through the sticking point. It is no way of providing a lot of assistance when the lifter is exhausted and cannot even make it to the sticking point. But it is a quick way of injuring the *spotter* because he will end up leaning forward and heavily stressing his lower back.

If only one spotter is available, then you *must* have rack pins or safety bars in position to catch the bar if the combined efforts of you and your spotter cannot get the weight up. In fact, the single spotter should not even try to help you up if a lot of assistance is needed. Instead it would be much better if he helped you to lower the bar safely onto the rack pins or safety bars.

For maximum single attempts, three spotters—one at each end, and one in the center—is the ideal number. If you are squatting without any arrangement set to catch the bar, and are squatting for heavy and low reps, then three spotters are compulsory. In this situation all three spotters must act together. If one spotter calls, then all three must respond. You should never be squatting like this unless at a powerlifting contest, where competent spotters should be in attendance.

Multiple spotters are only there to take the bar off, if needed. Because more than one person is involved, symmetrical assistance cannot be guaranteed. Assisted reps should be avoided because there is a high chance of the squatter losing the groove and getting injured.

Even if the spotter does not need to assist during a rep, he should be very alert to help guide the bar back into the weight saddles after the final rep. At the end of a hard set of squats you will be very tired. Without a guiding pair of hands on the bar from a spotter you may miss getting the bar into the weight saddles.

Further detail on safe squatting

You must maintain a flat back during the descent and ascent of the squat, and hold your spine's natural curvatures between reps. Flexible hamstrings and glutes are crucial here. Tight hamstrings and glutes can lead to rounding of the lower back in the squat (and in the bent-legged deadlift).

A major problem in the squat occurs when the flat back position is lost at the bottom of the descent. For learning about your technique, *not* as part of a regular workout, squat side-on to a mirror with a very light weight over your back. Closely observe the shape of your lower spine as you descend, bottom out, and ascend. If you reach the point where your back rounds a little, i.e., the tail end of your spine moves forward, you have hugely increased the stress on your vertebrae, making injury almost certain when you squat intensively.

The orthodox recommendation is to squat down to parallel or a little below parallel. "Parallel" is the point at which your upper thighs are parallel to the floor. This is the "bottoming out" position. For most people this is a fine depth. But for others, especially those who get lower-back pain from the squat, the "to parallel" may mean losing the flat position of the spine. In addition, trainees who do not have robust knees may irritate those joints

by squatting to parallel. But generally speaking, the danger from deep squatting is to the lower back, not the knees.

In the squat, most cases of sore backs and knees are caused by faulty form. Just because you may be getting sore knees and back from the squat does not necessarily mean that the problems come from going too deep. Many people too quickly assume that the depth of the squat is the problem.

More specifically, the root of rounding your lower back may be tight hamstrings, adductors and glutes, and poor form. Cutting your depth of squatting is not the first-choice solution. Once you have flexible hamstrings, adductors and glutes, and better form, you may be able to squat deeply and safely. Another factor involved in lower back rounding is inadequate lumbar strength. With a stronger lower back—from focusing on stiff-legged deadlifts for a few months—you may be able to maintain a flat back at a depth that previously you would round your back.

If your form is as good as that advised by this book, which should mean that you are flexible enough, and your lower back *still* rounds before you reach the parallel position, only *then* should you consider reducing the depth to which you squat. Consider it any earlier and you may end up making a bad situation worse because you have not corrected the deep problems.

If you are a competitive powerlifter, not squatting to parallel is a major problem because, at meets, you have to descend to parallel. But unless you have a sound back and good back positioning for the squat, you are unlikely to be a competitive powerlifter.

Squatting to parallel or deeper is one of the touted "must do's" of weight training. A traditional maxim in some circles is, "If you ain't been squatting, you ain't been training. And if you ain't been squatting deep, you ain't been squatting."

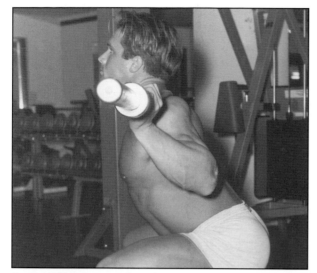 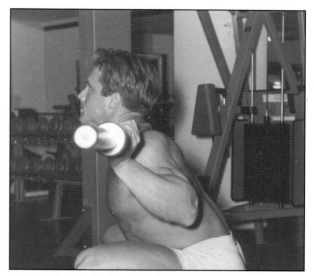

Left: Flat lower back. Right: Lower back having just started to round. The bar is positioned a little too high in both of these photographs.

The most critical "must do" of weight training is being able to train consistently and productively. Your first priority in training is to do no harm. It does not matter how deep someone else can squat productively. And it does not matter who recommends a deep squat. If it truly hurts you, and I am not talking about the desirable discomfort of a hard set of squats, the exercise is no good for *you*.

For some people, taking 2"-4" out of the squat's depth can remove a lot of stress from the lower back, and enable them to preserve a flat back throughout the squatting motion. For these people, this depth reduction spares the lower back to a large extent, and keeps the stress mostly on the thighs. While the overall training effect may not be as good as that from a deeper squat, it is better than not squatting at all, or squatting to a depth that will injure you.

To recap: If you have been experiencing problems with your lower back from squatting, first work on your flexibility and form. Squatting with good form will cure most people's former back and knee problems. But if you have been using good form like that urged in this book, and you still experience problems with your lower back, then reduce your squatting depth.

To determine by how much you may need to reduce the depth, you will need help from someone who watches you from the side. You cannot judge squatting depth and lower back position from the front. You also need a way of marking depth. It is no good someone just telling you, "There, your lower back has started to round." You need to know that specific point with reference to something you can use for determining your safe depth of squatting.

Using a power rack is perfect for this because you can set the pins at varying heights. Then, using one pin setting at a time, you can squat down to each. Of course you must use the same squat setup and form for each depth test. The only variable is your depth. As the bar touches the pins at each height setting, get feedback from a crouched observer who watches you from the side. Then stand, get your assistant to place the pins a little higher or lower as the case may be, and then squat down to that setting. Persist until you find the pin setting which, when you touch it with the bar, has your back just starting to round. Only use a very light weight on your back. But you do need some weight. Squatting without any weight will not duplicate your usual squatting mechanics. Find where your lower back just starts to round, and set your maximum depth at 2" above that point.

The more you shorten your squatting depth, the greater the poundages you will be capable of using. (Only reduce your squatting depth by the *minimum* needed in order to preserve a flat back at the bottom of the lift.) This increased poundage potential carries a risk of exchanging stress in one area of the spine for increased stress in another, or for increased knee irritation. You *must* build up your poundages in the reduced-depth squat *slowly*. Do not, for example, boost your squat poundage by 50 lbs at your first reduced-depth squat workout just because you know you can handle it. This is way too much of an increase. Add 10 lbs a week for three weeks, and then add 5 lbs a week. This will enable your back and knees to adapt to the increased loads it has to bear. If in doubt, build the weights up less quickly.

But do not misunderstand my advice. *If you can safely and productively squat to parallel or lower, then so you should.* The advice to reduce squatting depth is directed only at the minority of trainees who cannot safely squat to parallel even if their flexibility and form are in good order.

You need to find a way of monitoring your squatting depth so that you only go down to the depth that is safe for you. Do *not* sit down to a wooden box. This is an effective way of determining the depth you squat to if the box is the right height, but the stress on your spine from sitting on a box with a weight over your shoulders is huge, and dangerous. While you might argue that you can touch the box without sitting on it and the bar compressing you,

you only have to mess up one rep to seriously injure your spine. And squatting down to a cardboard box, though not having the potential of spine compression, has a serious problem. "Feeling" for the box can corrupt your form by exaggerating forward lean.

A much better way is to squat inside a power rack or between safety bars, or, as a final resort, between sturdy wooden boxes or crates (perhaps partially filled with sand for stability) set at a height so that the *plates* would touch the boxes if need be. The *secure* "catching" setup should be positioned so that when you are at the depth you have decided upon, you are an inch or two *above* actually setting the resistance down on the supports.

Knees coming in on the ascent is one of the most common symptoms of setup flaws in the squat. Insufficient toe flare is probably the most common flaw responsible for buckling of the legs. Tight adductors may also contribute. In such a case, stretch B on page 191 will help.

Squat to the predetermined distance *above* the safety supports. Do not squat all the way to the safety supports because, in this case, that would put you at or almost at the point where your lower back starts to round. Not only that, but rapping the supports will throw the bar out of the ideal groove. Only touch the supports if you get stuck on the ascent and are forced to set the bar down. Never try to make an ascent from this low position. Get out from under the bar, strip off the plates, return the bar to its saddles, and then reload it if you have not finished squatting for the day.

Once you are used to the groove and depth of squatting—from practicing with a very light weight—you should be able to squat almost automatically to an inch or two above the safety supports, especially if you squat in front of a mirror. But if you cannot avoid hitting the supports, change your style of squatting. Squat from the bottom, from off safety supports.

When doing pause or rack squats from the bottom, the height of the "catching" setup should be at the *exact* point of where you can safely descend to, i.e., 2" above the point where your lower back starts to round. The bar must be gently positioned on the supports at the bottom of each rep.

For rack squats from the bottom, a key point is that you cannot take a long pause in the bottom position while you are actually under the bar. You have two main performance options. First, you can descend and gently place the bar on the pins, very briefly pause to remove all momentum, and then immediately drive up. Take a longer pause while you are standing with the bar across your shoulders. Second, you can perform a series of rest-pause reps, or even singles. Lower the bar very carefully and place it on the pins. (Remember that a perfect descent is imperative or else you will be out of position for the ascent.) Then while keeping your feet and hands in position, stand up. Take the required pause between reps, then hold the final breath, tighten up your torso, descend, get in position under bar and immediately drive up.

I have repeatedly stressed the critical importance of keeping the stress from off the front of your feet while squatting. To see how important it is, stand side-on to a mirror. With just a bar on your shoulders, notice the difference made to your body alignment and squatting form from having the stress of the exercise felt through the front of your feet, and then the rear. Do a few reps with the stress felt through the front, and then a few with the stress felt over your heels and the pushing done through your heels. With the latter, your body will be a little more vertical while you are standing, the forward lean during the squat will not be as obvious, forward movement of your knees will be reduced, you will have more power potential, and the bar will trace a more vertical pathway.

To be sure you have the weight over your heels at the bottom of each rep ready for the ascent, you must have it over your heels during the descent. If you descended with the stress over the front of your feet you will not be able to shift it to the rear once you are at the bottom, at least not when you are using demanding weights.

On pages 184–186, in the section on video recordings, there is a description of how squatting form might evolve from poor technique into good technique.

Other alternatives to the squat

As well as the leg press, there is the Trap Bar deadlift—especially if done off a raised surface of 1" or 2"—and the modified straddle lift. The latter two exercises are described under *Deadlift*, and the leg press has its own section. All three provide very heavy work for the quadriceps and glutes, but with varying stress on the lower back.

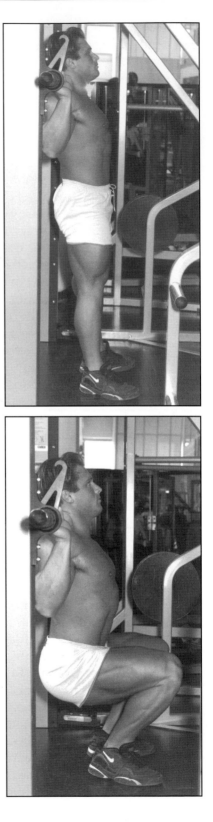

Do not squat in the Smith machine because the rigid vertical pathway corrupts natural squatting form. This is very hostile to the back and knees. See text.

The Smith machine

Smith machine squats give only an *illusion* of safety relative to the barbell squat. With the Smith machine the bar is locked into a fixed pathway so you do not have to be concerned with balance; and you do not have to take a barbell from stands, step back to perform your set, and step forward at the end of a set in order to return the bar to the stands. *But when you look further into the Smith machine squat, there are hidden perils.*

Do not squat in the Smith machine. Its use is loaded with dangerous compromises. Increase your flexibility (if you are not already supple) and learn to squat correctly with a barbell, as explained in detail in this book.

The Smith machine forces you to follow the bar path dictated by the machine, *but the bar path should be dictated by your body.*

If you put your feet forward in the Smith machine squat, to prevent your knees travelling in front of your feet at the bottom of the movement, you put your lower back at risk. When your feet are forward, you lose the natural inward curve/arch in your lower back because your hips are forward and away from their ideal position. Your hips may even move well in front of your shoulders, which produces severe rounding of the lower back. While you may think you are sparing your knees of a lot of stress, a back injury is around the corner.

But, putting your feet forward *does not* spare your knees. As you descend with your feet forward, there is *exaggerated* friction between your feet and the floor (to stop your feet slipping forward). This produces a shearing force in your knees that, internally, is trying to wrench open your knees.

If you bring your feet back so they are directly beneath your shoulders, all looks well *until* you go down in the squat. Your knees will travel forward in front of your toes when your thighs are parallel or near-

parallel to the floor, and the stress on your knees is hugely exaggerated.

The Smith machine has only been recommended three times in this book. The first was for the overhead lockout, which is a partial-range movement. Second, because the Smith machine has a bar that can be adjusted for height and which may be well knurled, it could be perfect for pullups—but this does not involve the machine's fixed bar pathway. The third recommendation was for the bench shrug— another short-range movement.

When used for full-range movements such as the squat, bench press, incline press, and overhead press, the correct exercise technique is corrupted by the rigid vertical bar pathway that the Smith machine forces upon you. This will set you up for chronic injuries. Free weights *used properly* give you the freedom needed to move through pathways that are natural to your body. Though the Smith machine gives the appearance of safety, because the need for control of the bar is reduced, the machine is a step backwards relative to free weights. It is a much overrated machine.

The calf raise is another possible exception to the general recommendation not to use the Smith machine. This is primarily because the calf raise uses a short range of motion. The Smith machine can substitute for the standing calf machine, but with two cautions. Any block you stand on must be stable and not tip during the calf raise, and your heels must not touch the floor during a set. If your heels hit the floor, your spine will be compressed between the resistance and the floor—see page 50 for more on this.

For Smith machine exercises it is essential that you have an alert spotter standing by. When you are exhausted at the end of a set you may be unable to put the latches in position in order to "rack" the bar, and thus may need assistance.

32

Stiff-legged deadlift

Main muscles worked
erectors, hamstrings, thigh adductors, glutes, lats, upper back, forearms

Capsule description
with your legs slightly bent, and arms straight, lift a bar from the floor

Introduction

The stiff-legged deadlift should not be done with completely locked out legs. The only time your legs should be straight is at the top of the movement. The slight bend in your legs helps to maintain a flat back, and reduces strain on your knees.

Safely done, this is a magnificent back, glute and rear-thigh exercise. But use poor form, an excessive range of motion, abuse low reps, overtrain, or try to lift a too-heavy weight, and you will hurt yourself. Learn to stiff-legged deadlift properly before you concern yourself with weight, and add weight slowly while maintaining perfect form.

Before you can stiff-legged deadlift with good form, you need to be flexible enough to adopt the necessary positioning. You especially need flexible Achilles tendons, hamstrings, thigh adductors, and glutes. Women who usually wear shoes with high heels are especially likely to have very tight Achilles tendons.

If you are inflexible, invest 4–6 weeks progressively and carefully increasing your flexibility before you start learning how to stiff-legged deadlift. The stiff-legged deadlift itself will help you to become more flexible, but you may not be able to adopt good form for a while. Thus you will practice bad habits that will have to be

"unlearned." This is why it is best to get flexible in the first place.

If you have had a serious back injury, do not stiff-legged deadlift without the consent of a sports-orientated chiropractor. If you have had any minor back injuries, still get a chiropractor's clearance.

Setup and positioning

The safety rule for this exercise is this: Keep your back flat. It is not necessary to stand on a box or bench and use an exaggerated range of motion. For many if not most people, the full-range stiff-legged deadlift from where the bar touches the feet is dangerous and must be avoided.

Doing the exercise from the floor with 45-lb or 20-kg plates on the bar provides a range of motion that is safer for most people. But even this range of motion will be excessive for some. Find the point at which your lower back rounds, and then set some "stops" to avoid exceeding that point. Not letting your torso descend to below parallel to the floor will be about right for most people. If need be, raise the plates or bar by just enough so that your back does not round at the bottom position. Get feedback from an observer who watches you from the side, to determine whether you need to raise the bar a little in order to keep your back from rounding.

Keep your legs slightly bent during most of the stiff-legged deadlift. Notice in this example how much the back rounds when the legs are kept straight at the bottom of the exercise.

These two photos do not show the required pulling back/retracting of the shoulders. Keep your shoulders pulled back.

The observer should crouch so that his eyes are level with your hips. Observing from above that height will give a distorted view of your back at the bottom of the exercise.

To raise the height of a resting straight bar, set it on pins placed at the appropriate height in a power rack, or set the barbell's plates on blocks, boards or plates placed on the floor. If you use a Trap Bar, and need to elevate its starting position, put plates, blocks or boards under the plates that are loaded on the bar. (A standard Trap Bar is too short to position on the pins of a standard power rack.)

You will still give the involved muscles lots of intensive work in this less-than-full-range motion. You may not even lose any growth stimulation for your erectors, rear thighs, lats and traps by not going deeper, but you will spare yourself a lot of stress on the intervertebral discs, ligaments and tendons in your lower back.

Use a hand spacing a little more than hip width, and a pronated grip if you use a straight bar. With a Trap Bar you must use a parallel grip and a spacing determined by the handles. In either case, always keep your arms straight—do not bend them.

With your hands in position on the bar, put your feet under it (if using a straight bar), and position your legs just inside your hands. Do not put your feet together because that will make balance harder to maintain. You do not want to risk losing your balance. If using a straight bar, your shins should be touching it. Keep your feet parallel to each other, or slightly flared.

Each foot must be exactly the same distance from the bar. If one foot is just slightly ahead or behind the other, relative to the bar, this will produce a slight twisting action. For symmetrical form you must have symmetrical foot positioning.

Performance

Keep your legs slightly bent throughout the exercise except during the top phase. Start at the bottom with your legs slightly bent, and maintain that degree of slight flexion until the bar is a little below the mid-thigh position. Then straighten your legs during the final phase of the ascent. Over the rest of the rep your legs must remain stiff in the slightly bent position. A common error is varying the degree of flexion during the middle and bottom parts of the exercise. This can be dangerous.

From the bottom position, smoothly and steadily lift the bar. No jerking, twisting, bouncing, or rapid acceleration. Lead with your head, and look forward or slightly up. Never look down during the course of the ascent. Keep your back flat. Keeping your head up as you pull the bar will help you to avoid rounding your back.

Keep the straight bar moving smoothly right next to your legs. Do not allow the bar to move out and away from you. This means that your arms cannot be vertical throughout the exercise when seen from the side. The only way to keep your arms vertical is to have the bar out in front of your legs during the early part of the lift. This is dangerous because it hugely increases the stress on your lower back. Keeping the bar next to your legs means that, during the bottom phase, your hands must be behind an imaginary vertical line dropped from your shoulders.

Over the final stage of the ascent, as your legs straighten, pay special attention to keeping your shoulders pulled back and your scapulae retracted. If your shoulders slump your back will round severely, stress on your back will be hugely increased, and you will set yourself up for a serious injury. Incline shrugs will develop the strength needed to keep your shoulders pulled back.

Never slump your shoulders. If you cannot complete a rep without your shoulders rounding even just a little, dump the weight (under control). *Do not try to get that rep.* End the set of your own volition before you get hurt. Keep a flat back.

Stand vertically at the top. Do not lean back. Hyperextension in *all* variations of the deadlift invites damage to the vertebrae because the stress is moved *away* from the load-bearing body of each vertebra and onto weaker structures. During the short pause at the top, keep your scapulae retracted, lower back arched a little, weight felt through your heels, and your shoulders, hips and ankles lined up vertically. Descend under control, taking 2–3 seconds for the complete descent. Start the descent by simultaneously leaning forward *and* bending at your knees. Once the bar is a little below the mid-thigh point, do not flex your legs any further. From that point down, your legs must be kept stiff but still slightly bent. The bar is then lowered only by further forward bending. But keep the straight bar grazing your legs. (A Trap Bar, however, should not touch your legs.) Do not round your shoulders as you descend. Look forward or upward, keep your shoulders pulled back, and your back flat. *Gently* touch the plates to the floor, or stop the descent just above the floor. Then immediately start the ascent. Do not relax at the bottom—keep all your muscles tight. Take 2–3 seconds for the ascent of each rep.

Pull and lower the bar in a symmetrical manner. (You can check this by performing the exercise in front of a mirror.) Do not take more stress on one side of your body than the other. And do not let one side of the bar move forward of the other.

Inhale at the top and hold the breath during the descent. Exhale on the ascent.

Other tips

If you are new to the exercise, start with no more than half your bodyweight, and add weight slowly—at most 10 lbs each week to begin with, dropping to no more than 5 lbs after a few weeks. Increase the intensity slowly. Later, as the sets become hard, reduce the size of the weekly increment.

When acclimatizing to the exercise, train it twice a week. Once you are training hard on it, once a week is enough. And perhaps once every ten days may be better.

***Trap Bar stiff-legged deadlift. The back
has rounded because of the increased
range of motion due to a wider grip
being necessary than on a straight bar.
For this trainee, the Trap Bar should be
raised so that his back does not round.***

Do not work this exercise to absolute
failure. Working to total failure pushes the
back structure too far and could cause
injury. Stop this exercise one rep short of
failure. Such a point, if really gotten to, is
still many reps farther into the set than
most trainees take it.

A Trap Bar can be used in this exercise,
which permits a parallel grip. Another big
benefit is that an imaginary straight line
connecting the ends of a Trap Bar can pass
through you. A straight bar can only travel
in front of your legs. With a straight barbell
the pathway is guided by the bar grazing
your legs. If the bar does not brush against
your legs then you will know that the bar
is in the *wrong* position. But with a Trap
Bar there is no brushing of metal against
your legs to guide you. Ensure that the
imaginary line joining the ends of a Trap
Bar is as far to the rear as you can
comfortably keep it. This will reduce the
shearing stress on your spine.

A Trap Bar necessitates a wider than
shoulder-width grip (unless you have huge
shoulders), because its handles are about
23" apart (varying slightly according to the
manufacturer). This increases the range of
motion relative to a closer grip on a
straight bar, when comparing bars loaded
with plates of the same diameter. If this
causes your back to round, elevate the bar
a little. Grip the Trap Bar's handles on their
centers. If one hand is off center, you will
likely produce torque and dangerous
asymmetrical distribution of stress. If both
hands are off center, the bar will tip.

Do not use straps. With specialized grip
work if need be for a few months, chalk,
and working up in poundages slowly, you
will be able to hold any weight you can
stiff-legged deadlift.

Full-range stiff-legged deadlift

I do not recommend the full-range stiff-
legged deadlift because of the high risk
attached to it. But if you insist on doing it,
at your own risk, the tips that follow will
reduce (but not eliminate) the danger.

In the full-range stiff-legged deadlift,
because your torso goes below parallel to
the floor, this can lead to a lot of back
rounding. How much curvature depends
on individual flexibility and body structure
(length of legs, arms and torso, and their
relative proportions).

The starting position of the full-range stiff-legged deadlift, in a power rack from off pins set just above the feet. Note the severe and dangerous degree of rounding of the back.

Do not do this exercise until you have the flexibility to touch your knuckles to your toes while keeping your knees *locked.* Until you have this flexibility, do stiff-legged deadlifts standing on the floor, using 45-lb or 35-lb plates on the bar.

Once you have the necessary flexibility, do the movement while standing on a sturdy bench or platform in a power rack. Position the rack pins so that the barbell, when placed on the pins, just touches your laces. Alternatively you could stand on a sturdy block or platform that is just the right height (about 5") so that a bar loaded with 45-lb plates and resting on the floor can be taken off your instep.

If you are taking the bar from off a bench rather than from off the pins of a power rack, and while stood on that bench, take the bar using a flat back and legs that are well bent. (The toes of your shoes should be touching the bar before you take it.) Then with the bar touching your instep right next to your shins, assume the stiff-legged deadlift starting position, with your legs only slightly bent.

The bottom position of the full-range stiff-legged deadlift is *not* where your fingers can touch the bench in front of your feet. It is where the bar touches your instep nearest to your shins.

While performing the full-range stiff-legged deadlift, be meticulously careful—keep the bar brushing your legs, and pull smoothly and symmetrically. Because of the exaggerated range of movement, the consequences of form faults are magnified.

But why do the full-range stiff-legged deadlift when the risks are so high, and the additional benefits minimal or nonexistent?

Partial stiff-legged deadlift

For most trainees, the best form of stiff-legged deadlifting is probably the partial version. Reduce the range of motion by raising the bar's starting position till it is a little below knee height. See page 118 for further information on this variation of the deadlift. When the quadriceps contribute to the exercise, it is a partial deadlift. When the quadriceps do not contribute, it is a partial *stiff-legged* deadlift.

Regularly review "Critical General Factors," which starts on page 17. *Those sixteen factors are of vital importance for all exercises.*

Never forget...

❑ *In order of priority, exercise technique comes before program design.*

❑ *If you want your training to be a terrific success, and not produce injuries, you must use excellent exercise form. There is no alternative.*

❑ *Good exercise technique is the exception in nearly all gyms of the world, not the rule. Do not expect to learn first-class exercise technique from a gym.*

❑ *Be patient. Most people who learn of improved form immediately want to apply it to their usual weights. Then because they cannot maintain the new form with those weights they immediately return to their old inferior form.*

❑ *To implement an overhaul of your exercise form, take a temporary break from full-bore training. Start a new training cycle, reduce all your poundages, practice the new form with light weights, and then gradually build the weights back. Be religiously uncompromising about using perfect form.*

33

Thick-bar hold

Main muscles worked
finger muscles (especially with a very thick bar), forearms

Capsule description
hold a thick bar next to your thighs while you stand with straight legs

Introduction

As well as being superb grip work, thick-bar holds are a lot of fun and a terrific way to end a workout. During thick-bar deadlifts, or other exercises where skill is a big factor, there is the risk of losing control of the bar and getting injured. But in thick-bar holds done as described here there is no danger. All you have to do is hold onto the bar until your grip is exhausted.

For best effect you must use a bar that is thicker than usual. A standard bar of an inch, or slightly thicker, will work your grip hard, but a thick bar will do a *much* better job. Use a 2", 2.5" or 3"-thick bar (see photograph on page 21), or mix up the bar you use from workout to workout, or cycle to cycle. The different thicknesses produce different effects. A small increase in diameter produces a big change in girth, and a big increase in difficulty of handling the bar. A 2"-thick bar has a circumference of 6.28", a 2.5"-thick bar has one of 7.86", and a 3"-thick bar has a girth of 9.43".

If there is no thick bar where you train, improvise to produce one. At the very minimum you could wrap something around a bar to mimic a thick bar. Then use the same modification each time you do the exercise. But it is not difficult or expensive to get a proper thick bar. A local metal worker could economically construct a thick bar or an attachment to "convert" a regular bar into a thick one. A length of strong 2" or 2.5"-diameter pipe a metal worker could cut for you would do a great job. A scaffolding pole will work well. But you may not be able to load plates on the pipe, depending on its thickness and the diameter of the holes in the plates you use. An example of how to solve this problem is to fix inside the pipe a 1"-thick bar for loading exercise plates on. Get the pipe and bar welded together, or have the pipe welded between the bar's inside collars.

If you train at home it will be easy to get your own thick bar or mock-up. If you train at a commercial or institutional gym you will need to persuade the management to buy a proper thick bar or get an improvisation made locally. It will be a terrific addition to the gym and will not be expensive unless it is a solid, chromed and knurled bar.

Setup and positioning

Load a thick bar on boxes, or set it on pins in a power rack, or across safety bars in a squat rack, so that you only have to pull it up a couple of inches before holding it. You will then only need to lower it a couple of inches once your grip has given out at the end of the hold. In effect, you hold the lockout of the deadlift.

In a power rack, getting into position for the thick-bar hold.

Select a duration for the holds. Between 30 and 60 seconds will probably suit most people. Settle on a *specific* number of seconds. Once you can hold the bar for that time, add a little weight next session.

You could use more than one duration, and alternate from workout to workout, or cycle to cycle. Or you could use more than one bar, and a different length of hold for each. When comparing timed holds of the same duration, the thicker the bar, the less weight that you will be able to support.

Performance

Start with clean and dry hands and bar, and apply plenty of chalk to your fingers, palms and the inside area of your thumbs and index fingers. Take a pronated grip on the bar a little wider than hip width, and keep the back of each hand in a straight line with its forearm. Then like in the partial deadlift, stand upright.

Keep your legs straight, shoulders retracted, back flat, and torso vertical or tilted forward slightly. The bar can be pressed against your thighs, but do not bend your legs or lean backwards. If you should bend your legs or lean backwards you will cheat by taking some of the weight on your thighs. In addition, leaning backwards is harmful for your spine.

During the second half of each timed hold, do not merely grasp the bar. *Crush it!* Just hanging onto the bar is not the way to get the most staying power out of your grip. Squeeze the bar as hard as you can. Then when your grip is close to failing, try to bend the bar. While you cannot possibly bend it, attempting to can extend the life of your grip. Shrugging your shoulders a little, and keeping your arms slightly bent, may also help you to get more "mileage" out of your grip.

Do not be concerned about when to breathe during thick-bar holds—just breathe as you need to.

Wrist roller training

Main muscles worked
forearms

Capsule description
with cord, attach a weight to a handle; roll the resistance up and down

Introduction

The wrist roller is a classic grip and forearm developer, though it is rarely performed in gyms today. Its equipment needs are simple. You can make yourself a wrist roller to use at home if where you train does not have one. When using a thick handle you do not need much weight, and you can even improvise for resistance if you do not have weight plates at home. Alternatively you could take your own wrist roller to the gym with you.

Setup and positioning

Make a wrist roller by getting a smooth wooden rod at least 18" long and, very importantly, between 2" and 2.5" in diameter. You could even use a length of pipe. While you could use a thinner rod, a thicker one will train your grip, hands and forearms much more effectively. Drill a vertical hole through the center and securely tie a piece of strong cord through the center hole. At least initially, try a cord about 40"–45" long. Securely attach a hook or carabiner to the dangling end of the cord. Then hook it onto the loading pin that holds the weight plates. Of course you could use some other loading system if you prefer. Just make sure it is secure.

Hold the handle with both hands, knuckles on top. Use a grip spacing that feels most comfortable for you. This exercise is usually done with a close grip. This is a necessity in most cases because wrist roller handles are usually on the short side. But with a handle at least 18" long you have the choice between a close or a medium-width grip.

Wrist roller training can be done with an underhand grip, but this is awkward and less effective than an overhand grip. If you want to try an underhand grip, use a shoulder-width one rather than a close grip. The description that follows concerns the knuckles-on-top pronated grip.

Do not keep your arms out straight in front of you. Done straight out in front, you may end up suffering from more fatigue in your shoulders than in your grip. The point is to train your lower arms to the fullest, so keep your arms hanging (with bent elbows) in the vertical plane, and focus on your grip and forearms.

Stand on a pair of boxes, benches or chairs. If you do the wrist rolling while standing on the floor, you will not have enough space in which to do the exercise well while keeping your arms hanging in the vertical plane. You would have hardly any range of movement.

Another problem with wrist rolling while standing on the floor comes from the resistance moving around at the bottom of the exercise. This puts your shins and feet at risk of injury. Make the exercise safe by standing on a couple of sturdy and stable boxes, benches or chairs. Space them so there is plenty of room for the resistance to move in as you do the exercise. Then even on the final rep of the exercise, when you are having a great wrestle to get the weight up, you will not risk hitting your legs or feet. Your legs and feet will be out of the way. Then you can concentrate on the exercise. Use small and medium-diameter plates so that there is less potential for the resistance striking whatever you stand on.

Wrist roller in use.

The taller the objects are which you stand on, and the shorter the loading pin that you employ, the longer the cord you can use without the weights hitting the floor at the bottom of each rep. Tailor the cord's length according to your own individual circumstances.

Put something on the floor to protect it in case the handle slips out of your hands and the resistance crashes to the floor.

Performance

Along with sheer holding strength, there are two actions involved in this exercise: wrist extension and wrist flexion. In extension, the knuckles are raised; and in flexion, the knuckles are lowered. A different set of muscles is involved in each action. Because your extension and flexion strengths are not the same, doing the exercise with the same weight for both actions means that you will need more reps for one action than the other, to produce a comparable degree of work. Alternatively, use more weight for the stronger action.

Focus on flexion first. With the cord extended and the weight hanging just above the floor, and using a pronated grip, roll the weight up by turning each hand alternately. Your knuckles on a given hand should move *downward* while that hand turns on the handle to roll the weight up a little. The cord will hang on the side of the handle nearest to your body. When the cord is fully rolled up, immediately unroll it by moving your wrists the other way, i.e., through extension. Do not rest at the top.

While the downward movement of the weight involves the extension muscles, that involvement is much less severe than that on the flexion muscles while raising the weight. Gravity helps you on the descent but hinders on the ascent. Do not rest at the bottom, when the cord is fully extended Keep the exercise moving until your grip and forearms are exhausted.

Rest at least a few minutes. Then repeat the exercise but this time reverse the movement. This is the second wrist rolling action. Start with the cord extended and the weight just above the floor. Use extension to raise the weight, and flexion to lower it. This means that the cord will hang on the far side of the handle.

Other tips for wrist rolling

The second wrist rolling action will suffer due to fatigue from the first action. Because of this you will probably want to rest longer than a few minutes between doing the two sets. If you do this exercise at home you can do the two actions at different times of the day. Or do the different actions on different days.

As far as weights and record keeping go, you have two options. First, use the same weight for both actions, and max out on reps in both cases and be content with a different rep count for each. The other option is to use more weight for the stronger action. Determine your strength difference between the two actions. Then you can target the same rep count for each action, but use a different weight for each. This assumes a consistent rest period between whenever you perform the two actions. If you vary the rest period, that will affect the strength difference and ruin record keeping consistency. Be consistent with how *and* when you do the two wrist rolling actions.

When rolling the cord around the handle, avoid getting your fingers caught in your clothing. Keep your shirt well tucked in your shorts, and the handle of the wrist roller a few inches away from your body or legs.

You may feel the tendency to favor your stronger hand, and move the handle more on each turn with that hand than the other. Avoid that. Make a deliberate effort to involve both hands equally, both on the ascent and descent of the exercise.

A little chalk on your hands may help, depending on the surface of the handle you use. Experiment to find how much works best for you.

Because the wrist roller with a thick handle does not have a big poundage potential, small discs are vital for applying progressive resistance gradually. A fixed-weight dumbbell could be suspended from the cord, but you will need to inch your way from one dumbbell size to the next. For example, do not make a single 5-lb jump from a 40-lb dumbbell to a 45-lb one. Instead, using small discs, progress a quarter or a half pound at a time by attaching progressively more weight to the 25-lb dumbbell, or the cord. Instead of a dumbbell and separate plates you could suspend just a number of plates.

Simpler wrist rolling

If you get a hollow pipe it can be used in a fixed position in a power rack, to enable greatly simplified wrist rolling. Page 32 shows lengths of pipe together with a rack pin. One length of pipe could be fitted over a rack pin and locked at a suitable height in a power rack. Then you could focus purely on grip work rather than divide your attention over grip work and technique while involving many other muscles.

Critical reminder
Photographs alone cannot explain good exercise technique. Please do not skip any of the accompanying text. Study it all very carefully.

Part 3
Critical additional issues

How to compose form checklists

When overhauling the form of an exercise you are familiar with, or when learning a new exercise, there are many points to remember. To begin with you will be unable to remember all of them. But with time you should be able to execute good form almost automatically, so long as you are serious and alert.

Use a checklist for each exercise to remind you of the key points that are not yet embedded in your mind. This will help to ensure that you do not forget any key points. Even an experienced trainee can develop bad habits and would benefit from composing a checklist to remind him of specific points to get right.

Write a checklist for each exercise that needs it, on a separate card for each. Use bold and clear writing. Review the relevant card prior to doing an exercise. Of course you do not read as you lift. Keep the checklist very brief. But each phrase or word will remind you of something to which you must pay special attention.

An example checklist

Here is an example of a checklist for the deadlift. For this illustration the points are explained in parentheses, but the details would not be on the actual checklist.

1. **Chalk** (*chalk your hands*)

2. **Feet** (*correct positioning of your feet*)

3. **Hips** (*hips in correct position—ankles, hips and shoulders in a vertical line*)

4. **Heels** (*weight felt over your heels*)

5. **Knees first** (*bend at knees before hips*)

6. **Slow descent**

7. **Straight arms** (*keep your arms straight both in the descent and ascent*)

8. **Heels** (*keep weight felt over your heels*)

9. **Shrug and drive** (*shrug, and then simultaneously push through your heels and pull with your back*)

10. **Scapulae** (*keep your shoulder blades crushed together*)

11. **Symmetrical descent** (*lower bar to floor symmetrically and under control*)

A spotter or training partner can be of tremendous value for giving you reminders of specific technique points. This can ensure that you do not break any of the points on your checklist. This applies to all rep counts, but perhaps especially to high-rep sets where concentration is particularly difficult to sustain. A sharp reminder from a spotter or training partner may be all that you need to keep your form bang on track. Not only will this keep your form tight, but it will help you to reach your rep target. Suppose, for example, you lose the right groove during a set of squats. This reduction of control will decrease your chances of making your rep target, but greatly increase the risk of injury.

As valuable as form checklists are, they are no substitute for serious study of the detailed technique descriptions given in this book. And even after you have studied all of this book you will need to review parts of it regularly. Review the technique of the exercises in each program you undertake, to be sure that you apply good form in its entirety to every exercise you use. No one can remember everything. Everyone will benefit from review work.

How to get more help

If practical, find an expert to give you hands-on help with your exercise form. This does not have to be on a regular basis to be useful. If you always train alone at home you will have no hands-on coaching unless you know someone who can help you out when needed. Either way, there are few truly expert trainers around.

Do not assume that anyone who claims to be a qualified "personal trainer" really knows what he is doing. Strings of letters that indicate certifications of various organizations, or degrees obtained, do not necessarily signify competence as a coach. Outrages are committed and stupidities are often babbled by holders of Ph.D. degrees, and by trainers who are "approved" by organizations.

There may be a chance that a trainer has competence in exercise form. Even physique title winners, though knowing little or nothing about program design for drug-free typical trainees, may have a good grasp of exercise technique.

To help determine whether someone can help you to improve your form, watch the trainer at work with a client, with this checklist in your mind:

❑ Is the form he teaches like that explained in this book?

❑ Does he remind his charge of key technique points before an exercise and in the course of it?

❑ Has he modified his client's exercise selection and form according to any limitations the trainee may have?

❑ Does he keep accurate records of weight and reps for each work set?

❑ Does he consult his client's training log before each set, to ensure that the correct weight is selected? And does he carefully load the bar?

❑ Is he supportive and respectful?

❑ Does he keep his charge's mind focused on the work at hand?

If he does not score positively on all these points, look elsewhere. If he scores well on these points but the deadlift, squat and some other major movements were not done in the workout you inspected, ask the trainer to demonstrate how he teaches those movements. Compare his instruction with what is described in this book. If there are more than just minor differences, then look elsewhere for hands-on help with your lifting technique.

Joining a local powerlifting club, or just attending occasionally, may help you. A savvy coach should be able to provide you with technique tips.

Once you know about good exercise technique, from studying this book, you can teach an observer what to look for. Then have him watch as you train, and provide feedback to help you to improve your form. But even better than that, you can use a video camera and actually record your own form. This can be an outstanding tool to use to improve your exercise form. Proper use of a video camera is described in detail later in this book.

How to fine-tune your form

The exercises in this book have been selected carefully, and technique has been described in extensive detail. The great majority of trainees will be able to use all of the exercises in this book safely and productively, providing that they are done *in the prescribed form.*

If you have carefully followed the technique instruction of this book, but all does not feel well in a specific exercise, then fine-tuning or modifying your technique may be needed. But if your form is in a mess, you need to start from the beginning and learn to practice good form. Mere fine-tuning is not what you would need. Your form would be in a mess if it was not like that described in this book.

Once you are using good technique as described in this book, you can fine-tune it, if necessary, so that you experience no undesirable post-workout reactions. But change only *one* variable at a time, to determine the effect of a single change.

If, however, fine-tuning or modifying does not prevent negative post-workout reaction from a specific exercise, then eliminate that exercise from your program. Always remember that for an exercise to do you good, it must not do you any harm.

Fine-tuning, example #1

Suppose you are doing warmups plus one all-out set of 20 reps in the leg press, and you get knee discomfort during the two days immediately after training. Rest until your knees feel fine, wait a further three days, and then train the exercise again.

At that next leg press workout, keep the weight, sets and reps exactly the same, and change one factor. As one example of a change, you could move your feet further up the foot board, unless you are already at the highest position. A second example

would be to alter the seat position, or depth of descent of the foot platform, depending on the machine used. This would reduce the range of motion. A third example of a change to try, assuming that the foot plate is adjustable, would be to alter its angle so that you can apply more force through your heels throughout each rep. Repeat the weights, sets and reps of the previous workout and see if the negative post-workout discomfort is eliminated. If it is, then continue as you are, and work on gradually increasing the poundage. If you still get post-workout joint discomfort, work further on the same change, or make a single change in a different area. If the first change helped a bit, keep it in. But if it made matters worse, drop it.

Leg pressing while wearing shoes with heels may significantly increase stress on your knees. Experiment with doing the exercise with bare feet. Compare the reaction you get in your knees, if any, to that you got at the previous workout while doing the movement with shoes on.

Assuming you have no glaring errors in setup and positioning, the biggest impact on knee reaction from leg pressing may come from locking out your legs. Compare locking out and not locking out.

Following warming up, perform a hard set of 20 reps. Use sufficient weight so that you must fully lock out (carefully) before each of the final 8 reps or so of the set, in order to get all 20 counts. If that causes a negative knee reaction the following day(s), wait till the soreness has gone away, and then wait a further three days. Then repeat the same leg press workout, in good controlled form, but *without* fully locking out your legs even once. This will mean that you will get fewer reps when using the same weight as in the locking-out style, but it will wipe out the musculature of your thighs and hips if you work intensively enough. Work to failure and then see if you get any knee soreness during the following days. If you do not, then you know that you should never fully lock out your legs when leg pressing.

Caution!

It is very important that you do not interpret the end of joint soreness as the signal that hard training is now safe for the joint(s) concerned. The absence of soreness does not mean that full recovery has been made. This is why I stressed that you wait until three days after when the joint soreness ended. Even that time period may not be enough in some cases, to ensure full recovery. If in doubt, take an extra day or two of rest. If you exercise the joint(s) hard before you have made a full recovery from the previous workout, then it is almost inevitable that joint soreness will reappear even if you use perfect form.

When good exercise form is being used, excessive training frequency is at the root of joint problems and injuries in general. Excessive training volume is also a major player. Training less often, and with less volume but more intensity, will not only improve the gains of most people, but will reduce injury problems.

Fine-tuning, example #2

As an example of a small exercise that may need to be individually modified, consider the curl. You may not be able to curl with a straight barbell without pain in your elbow attachments. But use dumbbells and then you may be able to curl intensively without elbow problems. Keep in mind, though, that many people suffer elbow problems in the barbell curl because they use a grip that is too narrow or too wide. The variable wrist positioning when using dumbbells is a great advantage in the curl.

If you are recovering from a shoulder or elbow injury, the barbell curl may be prohibited but the hammer curl (with thumbs up, using dumbbells) may produce no problems. This is not to say that the hammer curl works the biceps to the same degree as does the barbell curl. But if you cannot do a regular curl, the hammer version is a great alternative.

Video recordings— the acid test of good form

The study of good exercise technique is one thing, and vital in its own right. But being able to practice it yourself is another matter. Intelligent use of a video camera will help you to develop good exercise technique. If you train alone at home with no one to check your form, the video camera can be an even greater blessing than it is for those who train among others. While having your own video camera is the ideal, there are alternatives.

Most trainees, over a single year, will spend more on nonessential training-related items than the cost of a no-frills video camera. Not only that, but most of those expenses will yield no positive return. A video camera, used well, will teach you so much about how to improve your exercise technique. Consider a video camera an investment for your training longevity and success. Get your priorities sorted out so that you invest in a video camera *before* you ever spend on items that are, at best, of only marginal value. A video camera *is* that important.

While most people have the option to train in front of a mirror, this only offers a limited view for observing and monitoring exercise technique. While this is good enough for keeping a check on some relatively small exercises, assuming you know what is and is not good technique, it is woefully inadequate for most exercises, for reasons that include the following:

❑ You cannot carefully observe your form while training hard.

❑ Some exercises, e.g., the bench press, cannot be reflected in a mirror for easy viewing.

❑ Some exercises need to be seen from the side view, e.g., the squat and deadlift. While appropriate use of more than one mirror can let you see yourself from the side without having to turn your head much, that bears little comparison with a video recording from the side.

❑ A video recording is something you can keep and view repeatedly, if necessary, and use to compare with an earlier or later recording in order to monitor your form thoroughly.

The first few times you view video recordings of your exercise technique are likely to be eye openers. The lifting technique you think you use may not be what you actually use.

Using a video camera

For video recordings of your training to have the potential to teach you much, you first need to know what constitutes the details of good technique, and the errors to look out for. With that knowledge acquired from studying this book, record yourself from the side view of each exercise you do. To do this you will need to have someone operate the camera while you exercise. Alternatively you could mount the camera on a tripod and, for each exercise, set it at the appropriate height and position to record the full range of the exercise. Then before your next workout, analyze your form and find the flaws.

In a commercial, college or other public gym, time the recording for when the place is quiet; and preferably have someone operate the camera for you, to avoid the use of a tripod and having to set things up yourself. As a bonus, this assistance should reduce how conspicuous you feel. In a home-gym there should be fewer logistical obstacles to recording your exercise form.

Study the recordings and set about correcting form errors. Major errors will necessitate that you drop your poundages in the exercises concerned to little more than the bare bar. Learn the proper lifting technique, and then record and analyze your revised form to check that you really are delivering what you think you are delivering. Then if all is well, gradually build the weights back over a couple of months, or longer, with regular video taping done to ensure that the new form is being maintained.

If the errors are small, you will only need to reduce your poundages a little, and gradually build back the weights while maintaining proper technique.

When learning technique in major lifts, record yourself every workout for a few weeks. Then you can check that you are being consistent with the new form. Once the new grooves are embedded, then you may only need to tape yourself every few weeks. But if you want to record at least a single work set of each major exercise you do at every workout, and if this is practical, then do so. Some lifters video tape many of their workouts.

When focusing on a specific detail of an exercise, it is critical that the camera is positioned at the right height. For example, if you are aiming to determine whether you are reaching or breaking parallel in the squat, you must have the video camera positioned at knee height. If you have the camera at eye level while standing, you will not get a true picture of the precise position of your thighs at the bottom of the descent. To illustrate this, and while viewing from the side position, observe someone squatting while you are standing.

Then get down on your knees and observe the same squatter from the low position. You will see a small but noticeable difference between the two perceived depths. At powerlifting meets, squatting depth is observed from the low position, not while the judge is standing.

If you are trying to determine at what depth your lower back rounds in the squat, to discover the depth to which you should never descend with a heavy weight over your shoulders, you must have the camera set up at the height at about which the back rounding occurs.

There is another lesson here. If you squat in front of a mirror, what you may think is squatting to parallel may, in fact, be a couple of inches *below* parallel when seen from the side. Depth misjudgment in the squat may be responsible for your lower back rounding.

While plenty can go wrong in the small lifts, the larger exercises are much more complicated. They give far greater scope for errors, and much can be learned about the impact of relatively small adjustments in technique.

With very little weight on a bar, an unloaded bar, or a broomstick, make small adjustments in your technique, one at a time, and video tape yourself from a side view. Provide a commentary so that when you view the film you know what each adjustment is as it is made on the recording. Then you can accurately analyze your form and the impact of technique changes. Do not try to rely on memory alone for what adjustment was being made at a given moment in the recording.

Make a recording of the evolution of your form in the major exercises. This will provide you with a permanent reminder of what you used to do, the changes you made, and the excellent form you are now capable of using. Periodic viewing of the tape will keep you firmly on course for maintaining good technique, and perhaps make you wonder how you could have being doing things so poorly for so long.

An example of what to do

Here is an example of how you might go about composing a recording of the evolution of your squatting form. Do this sort of study for all your major exercises, and then you will go a long way to getting a tight grip on exercise technique.

First you need to acquire a good academic grasp of squatting technique from studying this book. Then, without making any adjustments to your squatting form, record just three reps done in your *exact* old style using your usual 12-rep poundage. Have the recording taken from the side view. When you examine the recording you may notice:

❏ The bar is placed too high on your shoulders.

❏ You bend at your hips before you bend at your knees.

❏ You go so low that your lower back rounds a little.

❏ Your knees come inward during the ascent. (It may be difficult to see this from the side view.)

❏ You have a tendency to topple forward a little.

❏ An imaginary vertical line dropped from the end of the bar during the descent falls in front of your feet.

If you have been squatting in a style anything like this, it is likely you were neither enjoying the exercise nor aching in the right areas of your body after a workout. If the squat was injuring you, and you were squatting in a form akin to that of the above scenario, then now you know why you were getting hurt.

Start to make form changes, providing commentary of what you are doing as you go along. Finding the best squatting form for you needs experimentation and a lot of practice. Because you will be illustrating form errors as well as improvements, only use a bare bar or a broomstick so that you do not hurt yourself.

Start by lowering the bar on your upper back so that it is positioned on the pad of muscle just above your shoulder blades. Your aim is to hold the bar as low as you can without losing stability during the course of a set. The lowered bar placement will move the stress from the weight a little to the rear relative to the old position. Record a few reps using the new bar positioning. You may need to widen your grip on the bar to accommodate the lowering of the bar on your upper back. It may feel awkward to begin with, but you will get used to it if you persist.

Now record the impact of stance variations, while keeping other variables constant. Do some reps with your heels spaced hip-width apart and feet parallel to each other. Then do some reps with the same heel spacing but toes flared. Try a flare of about 25° first and then about 45°, and compare. Then try other heel spacings (wider and narrower) *and* different degrees of toe flare. Notice how some setups cause you to lean forward more than do others, and that some make deep squatting much harder than do others. Settle on the heel placement and toe flare that feel the most comfortable, stable and powerful.

Stick your butt out in an exaggerated way while standing, and then squat. This will exaggerate your forward lean and increase the stress on your lower back. Record a few reps in that style and see the impact on your squatting form.

Next, while standing and with a normal inward curve/arch in your lower back, position your hips so that the bar, your hips and ankles all line up in a vertical or almost-vertical line. Holding that position, bend at your knees *first* and then, as you descend, you will automatically bend at your hips. Do a few reps in this fashion, and compare it with the butt-out style. You should see a significant difference in the degree to which you bend forward, and in the position of the bar relative to your feet.

> **When demonstrating very poor form, use little or no weight. If you have unusual sensitivity, and are in doubt as to your ability to tolerate very bad form even when using only a broomstick, then skip this activity or use a subject who can tolerate it.**

Getting your hips in the right position does *not* mean overdoing it so that your hips are forward of the straight line from ankles to bar. The latter is very dangerous for two reasons. First, you risk having the bar fall off you. Second, you will lose the natural inward curve in your lower back and hugely increase the stress on your lower back and risk of injury. *Do not* round your shoulders as you stand between reps. This too ruins the strong curves of the back, and is often used to compensate for the hips being too far forward. Record yourself on video tape and you will see that too much forward movement of the hips is as undesirable as too much rearward movement. Also record the effect on the shape of your spine of rounding your shoulders.

Next, record a few squats with the weight being felt through the front of your feet. In this style you should not be able to wiggle your toes either during or between reps, because the weight distribution is over the front of your feet, and your toes must be pressed hard against the floor to keep your balance. Then while standing and without moving the bar, shift the stress to over your heels. Do it so that you can wiggle your toes between and during reps. You can only do this because your toes are not pressed against the floor to maintain your balance. Record a few reps. While you should not wiggle your toes during a serious work set, it is okay to do so during this learning phase.

When viewing the recording, notice the difference to your body alignment (during and between reps) that the different stress distribution over your feet makes. While it may appear to be only a slight difference, slight changes can make a great impact on how an exercise acts on your body. Add up a few "slight differences" and you will produce a huge variation that can make the difference between destructive form and productive form.

Then, while keeping all other form pointers constant, compare the relative speed of your hips and shoulders during the first few inches of the ascent. Record some reps with your hips moving quicker than your shoulders. Then record some with your hips and shoulders rising at the same speed. Notice the difference in the relative stress on your lower back, and the path of the bar during the ascent.

If you have the bar too high on your shoulders, and if you start the descent by sticking out your butt, then you are going to exaggerate the harm from having your hips rising faster than your shoulders when coming out of the bottom position. Demonstrate and record this. Remember to use only a bare bar or a broomstick when illustrating very bad form.

Now put a few of the errors together, e.g., bar too high, stress felt through the front of your feet, butt out to start the descent, and feet parallel to each other. Record the impact made on your squatting form. Remember to provide commentary of what you are doing, for easy reference and explanation when you play the recording.

Record yourself squatting, *with perfect form*, to different depths. (Remember to have the camera operating from the same height as that of your lower back when at the bottom of a squat.) Squat in a power rack where you can set the pins at different heights, to determine depth of descent. Be sure you have some identification for each depth. Number or letter each pin hole so that you have reference points. Note in your commentary that you are, for example, "Squatting to pins set in holes number 29." Squat down to a series of different depths, and then examine the impact of the depth changes on your lower back. Determine the depth at which your back just starts to round a tad. Then the pin setting just above that point becomes your maximum safe squatting depth.

To finish the squat "evolution" video tape, after having studied what has already been recorded, load a barbell with half your usual 12-rep squatting poundage. Now do a series of relatively slow but as-good-as-you-can reps, to the right depth for you. Then compare your new form to the old style recorded prior to all your adjustments. If need be, fine-tune with a little wider foot spacing and a bit more toe flare, to discover even better positioning for you. There are many components of good squatting form, and you need to consider them all when working to discover your optimum technique.

When making an "evolution" recording for other exercises, keep in mind that the biggest exercises are the most complex, have the greatest possibilities for errors, and the largest potential for improvements in form. Take the video analysis very seriously and you will learn a great deal.

Obtaining access

Here are some of the ways to get access to a video camera:

❑ Buy your own. This is the ideal option. But you do not need a professional camera or one with a lot of features. All you need is a basic and reliable video camera. Such a camera is much more likely to be within your budget than one with many features that you would probably not use much if at all anyway. You do not have to restrict use of the video camera to your training. You may find many other useful and enjoyable ways to employ it. You should easily be able to get support for the investment from those you live with. Unlike a camera that takes photographs, there are no processing costs or delays for homemade video "productions." Once you have your own video camera, the running costs are minimal—just maintenance and a few video tapes. But if buying your own video camera is out of the question for the time being, there are other options.

❑ Perhaps you know someone nearby who owns a video camera—maybe a relative. Ask that person if you can borrow the camera. Initially you may need to borrow it quite often as you work on perfecting your exercise technique. Later on you will not need to use it as much. Then you will be using recordings only periodically, to check that you are maintaining good form. If the owner of the camera is not happy about letting you use it yourself, then try to persuade the owner to operate the camera, and probably settle for fewer recordings than you would prefer. You cannot expect very frequent visits from the owner of the video camera, but you should be able to work something out if you are persistent and persuasive.

❏ Rent a video camera when needed.

❏ Perhaps your employer has a video camera that employees are allowed to use out of working hours.

If you are determined to do what it takes, you should be able to make one of these suggestions work. If you rent a video camera, bear in mind that rent is "dead" money in the sense that once it has been paid, it is gone. Count up several rental fees and you will have a chunk of the price of getting your own no-frills video camera.

Form and the perceived difficulty of your reps

By recording all the work sets of a whole workout you can observe the influence of form on the perceived difficulty you feel during each rep. You will see that a rep done out of the correct groove will be more difficult to perform than a rep done in the correct groove.

Two reps done even slightly *out* of the right groove may fatigue you as much as three reps done *in* the right groove. This should ram home how critical good technique is. The need to get all your reps in the groove is crucial if you are to make all your target reps in a tough set. If you are doing very low reps, the loss of the right groove could cost you an entire set. This could possibly also cost you several months for rehabilitation following an injury. *The consistent use of good exercise technique is critical!*

Of course a rep that is "cheated" with excessive momentum may be out of the correct groove but will feel easier to perform. That is why people cheat—to make an exercise easier. But cheating greatly increases the risk of injury *and* reduces if not eliminates the stimulation of strength increase and growth. Cheating has no part to play in safe and productive exercise technique.

How to become flexible

As noted a number of times in this book, a flexible body is an essential requirement for proper performance of weight-training technique. It is also crucial for reducing the risk of injuries. Include a stretching routine in your exercise program, but do not be in a hurry to progress in flexibility. If you try to rush your progress, you will get hurt and then have to recover and start again. Take special care when you stretch.

Developing or maintaining a flexible body matters a lot. It should become a lifetime habit. The older you become, the more important flexibility work will be.

Basic guidelines

Never stretch when you are cold. Stretch in a warm room or after you have done some aerobic exercise that has broken you into a sweat. The warmer you are, the more supple you are likely to be before starting the stretches. Keep yourself covered and warm while you perform your stretching routine. Do not vigorously stretch before you weight train unless you want to risk irritating certain body structures in ways that will lead to an injury during the weights workout that follows.

When you stretch, watch out for flexibility imbalances between one side of your body and the other, and give more emphasis to your tighter side. While such imbalances may just reflect how you have used your body over the years, and can be easily corrected with regular stretching for a few weeks, they may indicate physical problems that need to be corrected. Your body may be compensating for a limitation in one area with a relative excess in another. If you have a substantial flexion imbalance between the two sides of your body, get the professional guidance of an expert in biomechanics and manipulative

therapy, e.g., a sports-trained chiropractor, or an osteopath with a weight-training background. This expert may find (and be able to fix) the structural problem that is causing the flexion imbalance. Flexion imbalances can lead to asymmetrical exercise technique which greatly increases torque on one side of the body relative to the other. This can seriously increase the risk of injury.

Doing your serious stretching *after* you have trained with weights or, perhaps better, immediately after an aerobic session, is recommended. By then you will be "oiled" and will develop flexibility more quickly, and experience less discomfort during the stretches. Also, stretching after a workout may help to reduce soreness from the workout. When you stretch at a time other than after a workout or aerobics session, it is ideal to get yourself warmed up first with 5–10 minutes on, for example, an exercise bike, stepper, or ski machine. Alternatively, use stair climbing, bench stepping or the like if you have no machinery available.

When you stretch at home and not immediately following an exercise session, do it in a warm room, take more time with the progressive holds you need in order to work into your demanding stretches, and time it late in the day rather than early. You will be more "pliable" then.

Sometimes it is necessary to stretch before you train with weights. If you feel that some muscles are tight, especially if on one side of your body only, or if related to an old injury, you need to work on them to remove the tightness. More warmup work for each exercise may or may not do the job of loosening up the tight muscles. If you do not get all your muscles equally loose and pliable on both sides of your body, you will promote asymmetrical exercise form and greatly increase the risk of injury. For example, assume that your right hamstring muscles are tighter than those on your left side. When you squat or deadlift, the less flexible right hamstrings may "lock up" while the left hamstrings keep stretching. You may then flex your legs more on your left side than right, causing you to distort your lifting form.

Before you work out—especially prior to squatting and deadlifting—check your major muscles for flexibility imbalances between the two sides of your body, and invest time in additional (but careful and progressive) warming up and stretching to rectify imbalances. If you are equally stiff on both sides of your body, though you will not set yourself up for asymmetrical form, you should still invest the time to get yourself loosened up to your normal state. Then maintain that flexibility by stretching between sets.

Never, ever force a stretch. Stretching is a dangerous type of exercise if done incorrectly. Not enough about caution has been written into books and courses on stretching. You need to work progressively, both within a given workout, and from week to week until you reach the flexibility that you will maintain. Never bounce while stretching, and avoid holding your breath. Breathe rhythmically. Do not place your joints in positions that are uncomfortable and a threat to the integrity of your body. Stretching is not a battle. Do it regularly and seriously, and the flexibility will come.

Here is an example of how to stretch. Suppose you can, when warm and ready, grab the soles of your feet while sat on the floor with your legs straight. If, while cold, you sit with straight legs and immediately grab your feet, you will probably hurt yourself. Never stretch like that. Do it the gradual and safe way. You should only feel *slight* discomfort as you stretch.

For this illustrative stretch, start by holding your ankles while keeping your knees *unlocked*. Then slowly straighten your knees until you feel the tension. Hold it until you feel the muscles slackening, and then relax into the stretch. Keep your head up and chest stuck out. Then move further into the stretch by straightening your legs more. Hold the stretch until you feel the muscles slackening once again, and relax into the stretch. Then go farther still into the stretch. With your legs fully locked out, hold your feet rather than your ankles.

That makes three progressive "reps" of the illustrative stretch. Unless a different procedure is described for a specific stretch that follows, do the minimum of three "reps" of 20–45 seconds for each stretch. Err on the side of being overcautious—do more rather than fewer progressive stretches before getting to your current limit stretch, and hold each for more seconds rather than fewer.

As you hold each "rep" of a stretch, so long as you hold it for long enough, you should feel the muscular tension diminish. But, depending on the stretch and the individual, you may need to hold a stretch for up to 45 seconds (and perhaps even longer) before you feel this slackening. The easing of tension is the signal to move further into the stretch, in order to make the muscle(s) feel tight again. If you do not feel the tension diminishing even after a "rep" of 45–60 seconds, let the stretch go and then slowly move into the next "rep."

You will not feel the same each day. Some days you will be tighter than on others, so do not expect to stretch equally well on consecutive days.

Do not try to become a contortionist. Do not plan to get ever more and more flexible. Once you are already very flexible, after a few months of regular use of a well-balanced program of stretches, you will not need to become more flexible. But you will need to keep stretching in order to maintain your flexibility.

Never force yourself to feel pain, but you must feel tension during each stretch. Never have anyone force you into a stretch. Never be in a hurry or you may end up rushing into an injury that may take weeks to recover from, and then you will have to start from scratch again. Haste makes waste in stretching as it does in weight training and many other endeavors in life.

Stretching is a pleasure, if done properly. It is good for both your mind and your body in general, so enjoy your stretching time.

If you feel you are overdoing the stretching and not getting good results, take a few days off, and then perhaps stretch less often than before. Like you can overtrain with the weights, you can overtrain on stretching. On the other hand, you may feel like doing more stretching. Whenever you feel tight during the day, carefully fit in an appropriate stretch, to limber yourself up and remove tension.

Finish each stretching session with some eye exercises. Your eyesight may benefit over the long term—mine has. Sit comfortably and move your eyes in a variety of directions: up and down, side to side, and clockwise and counterclockwise rotation. Perform several reps of each movement. Your eyes will quickly get tired to begin with. Over a few weeks, slowly build up the repetitions and ranges of movement. If doing the exercises with your eyes open is uncomfortable, do them with closed eyes. Finish by clenching and relaxing your eyes a few times.

All this eye work only takes a couple of minutes at most and will help to keep your eye muscles in good condition. Strong eye muscles are needed for good eyesight.

Rather than following a long routine of flexibility exercises to be performed daily, adopt a moderate schedule of stretches to be done alternate days. This is likely to have the best chance of being maintained. Maintained it has to be to yield the desired results. Here is a set of stretches that will give your body a thorough going over. They have been put together in a sequence that makes for smooth movement from one stretch to another. The muscles primarily involved in each stretch are noted.

Some stretches have you positioned on the floor. Be careful how you get up from lying on your back, or else you may irritate your lower back. Avoid sitting up with straight legs. Bend your legs and, with your knees held above your chest, roll off your back into a sitting position. As an alternative you could roll onto one side and then, using your arms for assistance, push into a sitting position.

A. *Glutes, back, obliques*

Lie on your back and, with your left leg bent, pull it onto your chest and over to the right side, using your arms. Hold and feel the tension in your glutes. Repeat with the other leg.

While still on your back, put your legs together, and your arms flat on the floor perpendicular to your torso, as if imitating a crucifix. Bend your right knee to a right angle, and bring it over towards the floor at the left of your left hip. Keep your right arm against the floor but take your left hand and pull your right knee towards the floor *and* a little towards your left shoulder, for a better stretch. Rotate at your hips and in your spine, but keep one arm and your head and shoulders in contact with the floor. Do not turn completely onto the side of your left hip or else you will lose the effect of the stretch in your glutes. Find the right position that produces a good stretch for your glutes. Repeat on the other side.

B. Groin and thigh adductors

Lie on your back, arms by your sides. Bend your knees while keeping your feet on the floor. Put the soles of your feet against each other, resting their outside edges on the floor. This makes your legs form a rhombus shape. Relax with your legs in this position.

Just let gravity gently pull your legs towards the floor. Hold for a minute or so, straighten your legs, adopt the stretch again, and gravity will pull on a more supple body.

To progress in flexibility, gradually work from week to week to bring your heels closer to your hips. You can also rest your hands on your thighs and very gently apply downward pressure.

This is a relaxing stretch and you may want to end each session with it rather than do it early on; or you may want to do it at the beginning and end.

c. Spine

Lie on your front with your arms together and outstretched. Let your body sag. Pull your arms back so that your hands are alongside your head. Then raise your head and shoulders sufficiently so that you can rest your forearms on the floor with your elbow joints at right angles. Hold this for 20 seconds or so, then return to the floor; relax for a few seconds and then repeat and hold for a little longer. Then relax.

Next, while still on your front, put your hands alongside your chest or, if you prefer, next to your shoulders, depending on your current level of flexibility. Then slowly push yourself up so that your back arches and your arms straighten. Do not force anything. Push up and lift your head and shoulders as far as is comfortable. Relax your pelvis and legs so that your lower back sags. Hold only for a few seconds to begin with and then return to being flat on the floor. Do several reps. Over a few sessions, build up the duration of how long you hold the sag, the degree of sag, and the number of reps. Work into this one very carefully and progressively.

This can be a great therapy tool when you have back discomfort. It can also contribute to preventing back pain in the first place by helping to maintain a natural degree of lordosis (inward curvature of the lower back). Doing this stretch on a daily basis can help to maintain the curves of your spine, which tend to flatten with age.

D. *Hip flexors*

Put your right knee on the floor. Then place your left foot flat on the floor in front of you, with your left leg bent at about a right angle. Your right knee, hip and shoulder should be in a vertical line. Then move your hips straight forward until you feel the stretch at the front of your right hip. Repeat on the other side.

E. **Rear thighs**

Instead of a doorway you can use a power rack for this stretch. By shuffling a little you can adjust the position of your torso and vary the tension on your rear thighs.

F. **Quadriceps**

Please see the text for important caveats.

Rest your right foot on a bench, table or back of a chair, depending on your flexibility. Keep both legs straight. Without rounding your back to give an illusion of flexibility, lean forward. Hold your right leg as far down as is comfortable. Keep your head up and chest stuck out during the stretch. Repeat for the left leg. Start with a low bench if necessary, and add to the height as you progress.

This stretch, like the variation where you sit on the floor with straight legs and pull on your ankles or feet, tends to create an illusion of flexibility in the hamstrings by developing flexibility in the spine.

To be sure you do a proper job of stretching your rear thighs, lie on your back in a doorway. Find the position on the floor so that you can raise one leg and, keeping it straight, place it, or its heel, against the wall next to the door jamb.

Stand with your left hand braced on a fixed object. Lift your left foot behind you, bending your leg at the knee. With your *right* hand, grab your *left* ankle. Keep your torso vertical or near vertical.

Keep a good angle between your calves and hamstrings. *The illustration on the previous page has too close an angle. To keep the angle much more open, don't keep the thigh vertical, and don't pull the foot up vertically.* Keep the foot lower, and pull the knee mostly *to the rear* to produce the stretch. Both the knee and the foot should go mostly *rearward*, not vertically. Don't jam your calves against your hamstrings. Repeat on the other side.

If you pursue extreme flexibility here you will stretch your knee ligaments. The stretch is only for the quadriceps, *not* the knees. Do not try to stretch ligaments.

Avoid pulling your *right* ankle with your *right* hand, or *left* ankle with your *left* hand. The stretch done that way forces the knee to move in an unnatural angle.

Do not perform this stretch while lying face down because that style reduces the angle between the calves and hamstrings, and increases compression on the knees.

G. *Spine, back, neck, shoulders*

Sit sideways on a chair that has no arms, or, as in the illustration, on an adjustable bench that you can set at a high incline to simulate a chair.

Keeping your feet planted on the floor, and your backside on the seat, rotate your torso and grab the back of the chair or bench with both hands—one at each side. Turn your shoulders and head as much as you comfortably can, keep your torso vertical, and hold. Now reposition yourself and rotate to the other side. Work into the movement slowly and carefully, pulling enough to feel the stretch.

H. *Neck*

Sit with good posture, i.e., no slouching, and no protruding of your neck and head. Retract your head while keeping your chin tucked in and down a little. While maintaining this position, gently rotate your head to one side as far as comfortable, and then to the other side. Assist the rotation by gently pulling on your head. Carefully do this a few times and your neck should feel more supple and less troubled with stress.

I. Legs and lower back

Do several slow, almost-all-the-way-down squats with no weight. This will give your knees a full-range of motion, and may help to keep them in good condition. A full range of motion for the knees here is desirable, but *avoid compression* at the bottom.

Go down only to a little *above* where your hamstrings would fully fold over your calves—avoid full contact. And your knees should not travel forward of your toes. Keep your weight on your heels.

The illustration above shows too much forward travel of the knees, and compression of the knees. The model should not have gone down quite so far. Proceed especially carefully if your knees are easily

irritated. If necessary, keep your hands on the floor when at the bottom position. This will take some of your bodyweight off your knees as you work into the stretch over the first week or few.

If, despite being very cautious and progressive, this stretch *still* causes a negative reaction, *do not persist with it*. What can help most people may hinder others.

J. Shoulders and chest

Stand, upright, with your toes about 3" away from a doorway. Place your hands flat against the wall or wooden frame around the edges of the doorway. Your palms should face forward and your upper arms should be parallel to the floor. The elbow joint is maintained at an angle determined by the width of the doorway and the length of your arms. This is about a right angle for a typical doorway and an average-size person. *Very* gently and slowly, lean forward, feeling the stretch in your shoulders and pectorals. Take great care—do not overstretch and hurt yourself. Do not try to push your shoulders forward. Rather, as your torso leans forward, your shoulders will move forward too.

To progress in flexibility, step back a little from the doorway, but maintain your arm placement. Then there will be more tension in your shoulders when you lean forward. Do this very carefully, finding your way into the "groove" of the stretch.

K. Ankles and calves

Stand on the bottom step of a staircase, or some similar elevation. Put the ball of your right foot on the edge of the step so that the rest of your foot is off the step. Take your weight on your right foot. Slowly let your heel descend so that your calf and Achilles tendon are gently stretched. Ease into the stretch; do not force anything. Repeat with your other foot. Flexible ankles

are vital for knee-friendly squatting that does not involve a board, block, plate or any other form of heel elevation.

L. Post-workout spine stretch

After each workout, and especially after deadlifting and squatting, gently stretch your spine to help keep it in good order.

Hang from an overhead bar with a shoulder-width grip, and relax your lower body so that it gently pulls on your spine to relieve pressure from your vertebrae. Though *not* illustrated, bend your legs a little, and then raise your knees a few inches, for a better stretch as you hang.

If you have shoulder or elbow problems, be very careful here because the hanging could aggravate the joint problems. Avoid relaxing your shoulders. Keep them tight. Raise your knees to your waist and slowly rotate at your hips to stretch your spine from other angles.

If you have the equipment available that enables you to invert yourself, then use it as an alternative to the overhead bar.

A simple alternative is to lie on the floor and place two or more firm cushions under your hips and lower back. Find the height of support, and the precise position of it, to produce the best effect.

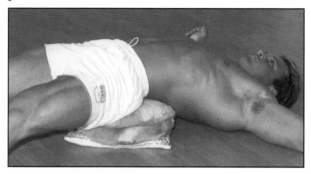

Relax and feel the tension drain out of your lower and middle back. This is a gentle and relaxing stretch that you can hold for several minutes. But be careful how you get out of the stretch. Do not perform a situp. Roll onto one of your sides, off the support, and then get up.

As well as one of these spine stretches, do *Stretch C* after each workout.

M. *Shoulders, arms and chest*

Once you are familiar with *Stretch J*, consider adding an additional shoulder stretch—dislocates. This will help with the flexibility needed to hold a barbell fairly low on your traps when squatting.

With a very wide grip, and straight arms, hold a towel or broomstick in front of your thighs. Grip the towel or stick with your thumbs and first fingers. Keep your arms straight and bring the towel or bar over your head and then behind you as far as you comfortably can.

Letting your palms face outwards during the course of the stretch should make it more comfortable. The wider the grip is during these dislocates, the easier the stretching. To progress in flexibility, gradually decrease the distance between your hands. But take your time with this stretch; do not force it.

Implementing the routine

This stretching routine, with three "reps" for each stretch, can be completed in 25–40 minutes, depending on how long you hold each "rep." Do not see it as a burden on your time. See it as an injury-proofing and enjoyable supplement to your training program. Flexibility is only one of the benefits of a good stretching routine.

Done on alternate days, a stretching routine makes little demands on your time, and it is not physically stressful. If you prefer, divide the routine into two equal parts, and alternate them, thus stretching daily. Assuming that you watch some TV most days, do your stretching during some of that time. Then you will not have to cut out anything to fit in the stretching. But even if you had to cut out something to make time, that would be part of the vital discipline needed to stick to a long-term and serious exercise program.

Done *properly*, stretching makes you feel good and you will be reluctant to miss any sessions. This especially applies as you get older; and at any age if you have or have had a back problem.

After a few weeks you may want to do more than the minimal number of stretches given here. Any book on yoga postures will supply lots of stretches. Once you are familiar with the stretching routine and principles of this book, compose a number of balanced routines. The routines could then be rotated so that no three consecutive days of stretching are the same.

Never bemoan a blessing

Never bemoan the discipline that must accompany serious training using perfect form. Never bemoan the discipline needed to follow a flexibility program. Never bemoan the discipline that must be applied to your diet and other components of recovery. To have the opportunity to apply all of this discipline is a great blessing—appreciate it and make the absolute most of it because it will not last forever.

Important extra information

The following eight pages provide information not included in the first edition.

The ball squat

The ball squat is an alternative to the barbell squat, though it would need to be combined with a form of deadlifting in order to work the lower back thoroughly too. Here is an excerpt from the article "Experiments in the Gym: The Squat" by Bill Piche, in HARDGAINER issue #57:

Matt Brzycki, strength coach at Princeton University, told me about ball squats after he trained in the Penn State football weight room with Penn State strength coach John Thomas. The first time I performed ball squats, I knew they were a winner. The following days after performing ball squats my knees and lower back felt great and my legs were really blasted.

To perform ball squats, a smooth unobstructed wall is needed. You stand up straight and put a medium-size, pliable ball behind your lower back against the wall. By "pliable," I mean such that you can easily depress your fingers into the ball. The ball should be approximately 26 inches in circumference. A basketball is probably too big, unless it is severely deflated. A deflated soccer ball would be better.

Your feet should be placed to duplicate the position used to perform the barbell squat, especially the amount of forward movement of your knees in the bottom position. Slowly lower your hips until the tops of the thighs are in line with where your hip joint bends. Pause briefly in the bottom position and slowly return to the starting position. Most of your bodyweight should be centered on your heels.

Do not lean too hard on the ball; it is not a crutch. The ball travels along the

Bill Piche demonstrating the top position of the ball squat, with 390 lbs. The other photograph shows the required equipment.
Photos courtesy of Bill Piche

groove between the erectors during the squatting motion. It does not travel very far up and down the groove in the back. If you lean too hard on the ball with your feet too far in front of you, the movement can turn into a hack squat. Do not bounce in the bottom position. The knees should not lock or "snap" when returning to the starting position.

You can add resistance by holding dumbbells or by adding weight around your waist using a belt. I started using ball squats in my leg routine as a "finisher." However, the movement felt so good that I decided to use it as my primary leg exercise because, unlike regular squats, ball squats removed the stress on my lower back.

I use a leather dip belt to add weight. I found that when I out-gained my dumbbells and started using 45-pound plates, my range-of-motion was hindered. I built wooden platforms to stand on when performing the movement, so that the weights would not hit the floor. Another problem I encountered was the chain tearing into my inner thighs. A couple of old towels underneath the chain solved this problem.

You may find your breathing awkward at first because there is no pressure on your torso like with regular squats. Avoid the temptation to speed up the positive part of the movement. Ball squats are also well suited for performing very slow reps. After all these years, my legs have never been bigger and my lower back has never felt better.

The Tru-Squat

The following is a slightly revised version of the Tru-Squat section in BEYOND BRAWN.

In summer 1997 I bought a Tru-Squat (from Southern Xercise, see page 209) and with it was able to return to intensive squatting. (Instead of the leg press and stiff-legged deadlift as my core leg and back exercises, I moved to the Tru-Squat, and stiff-legged

deadlift from knee height.) The Tru-Squat is a machine that mimics the barbell squat but with some major differences and improvements. In fact, even some outstanding barbell squatters believe the Tru-Squat to be superior to the barbell squat. There is *no comparison* with the Smith machine squat. The latter puts the lower back and knees at great risk. If used properly the Tru-Squat spares the knees and lower back but while working the involved musculature to the hilt.

Here are the Tru-Squat's major differences and improvements relative to the barbell squat:

a. The resistance is applied through shoulder pads, akin to a standing calf machine. This is a far less uncomfortable way to bear weight than from a barbell. Additionally, there is no contact stress on the vertebrae.

b. The back is supported.

c. During the descent there is no forward lean of the torso. The torso and hips actually move rearward during the descent. Despite the lack of forward lean there is still heavy involvement of the musculature of the lower back.

d. There is reduced forward travel of the knees relative to a barbell squat, reducing stress on the knees.

e. There is an adjustable depth control.

f. The user can squat to failure in total safety, *without* spotters.

g. The leverages of the machine reduce, by approximately 40%, the resistance needed to produce the same degree of muscular work as in the barbell squat. This reduces compressive forces, and

The Tru-Squat demonstrated by Mike Schmeider at Iron Island Gym. The stance used by Mike is closer than what works safely for me.
    Photo courtesy of Dr. Ken E. Leistner

makes loading and unloading plates easier because you need fewer plates.

h. Breathing between reps is much less restricted than it is with the barbell squat.

i. Once you have discovered the best setup for you, the guided pathway removes all concerns with balance. When the reps become very hard you can focus on effort and not be distracted by matters of form.

j. As a bonus, the Tru-Squat is an excellent calf machine—with the addition of a

block for elevating the balls of the feet, if desired—and shrug machine.

I can use the Tru-Squat without back or knee problems, and I can safely descend to the parallel position. My lower back is not put at risk at this depth, though it is in the barbell squat.

Though a costly machine, it does not take up a great deal of space, and enables people who cannot squat safely with a barbell to be able to obtain the potential great benefits of the squat. Without it I would never have squatted again.

Performance tips for the Tru-Squat
a. Prior to use, the Tru-Squat needs to be adjusted according to the height of the user. The heights accommodated range from 5-0 to 7-0. But the height settings

can only be approximate. For example, if you have legs a little longer than the norm for your height, try the height setting immediately *under* your actual height. This will slightly alter the pathway your torso moves through, and reduce the forward travel of your knees. This may put you in a better position than you would be if you were at the setting that directly matches your height. Experimentation is needed to fine-tune the machine to best suit you. This should simultaneously include adjustments of stance, to discover the optimum setup for you. For example, if you are 5-9, and set the machine at the 5-9 height, you may feel that you want to put your feet forward excessively. But if you set the machine at the 5-7 height, you may find that you are placed in a more efficient squatting groove, and no longer want to move your feet forward. Or you may want to use the 5-7 setting and a *very slight* forward movement of your feet relative to where your feet would be if you had stood with your legs perfectly vertical.

b. With the resistance on your shoulders, stand directly upright, like you would with a barbell squat. (Do not elevate your heels.) You may, however, find that moving your feet an inch or two forward puts you in a better position for squatting. Experiment! But do not move your feet forward by more than about 2–3 inches. Find the foot spacing and flare that best suit you by following the same guidelines as for the barbell squat—see the section on the barbell squat in this book. "Dock" the resistance and use tape to mark the foot platform in such a way that you can easily adopt your optimum foot placement in every set you perform.

c. Your lower back should not be pressed flat against the back board because this would weaken your back. The natural arch of your lower back should be preserved but *not* exaggerated. If the machine's belt is fixed tightly around the belt line it will flatten the arch of your lower back. The belt should be as low as possible without hampering flexion at your hips. Then your buttocks can be kept against the back support, and your lower back be free to adopt its natural arch. *Lumbar support is strongly recommended.* A small rolled-up towel tied to the back board (e.g., by using a scarf), and placed in the hollow of your lower back, will suffice.

d. Before being used as a calf machine, the height setting should be adjusted to the individual's height *plus* the height of the block used, to make getting in position easy.

e. While the Tru-Squat can be used for the calf machine shrug, I no longer recommend this exercise—see page 143.

While using the Tru-Squat I found that wearing knee supports (made of fabric, available from pharmacies) helps my knees. I *do not* use tight supports because they are crutches that can mask serious joint problems. The ones I use are sufficiently loose that they slip down when I walk, but stay in position for a set of squats. If I do not use the loose supports I experience a slight ache in my knees for a couple of days after training. The reason why the supports help probably lies in the temperature increase around my knees caused by the fabric.

The big little things

What may appear to be just a few minor personal things—whether of exercise form, workout design, or nutrition—can add up to a major factor affecting the effectiveness of your training program.

For example, when I squat, my feet are not perfectly lined up with each other. My right foot is almost half an inch in front of my left. This is where my feet naturally fall. If I pull my right foot back so that it is perfectly lined up with my left foot, my form is skewed when I squat; I rotate slightly—like a corkscrew—and I get a negative reaction in my knees. The explanation for this asymmetrical foot positioning is probably due to my scoliosis, and one leg being longer than the other.

As I mentioned in the previous section, I squat using the Tru-Squat machine. This is simply because I cannot squat safely with a barbell, or bent-legged deadlift either. I am left with the Tru-Squat or leg press. The Tru-Squat is by far the pick of the two.

I had a chiropractor visit my home gym to observe my form as I squat. He compared the effect on my overall form of the perfectly lined up foot position, and my "natural" asymmetrical position. He agreed that I should stick with what feels best. This is an example of an aspect of form that might be "wrong" on paper, but is right in practice for me.

For the sake of my knees I have to use a stance that puts my feet on the perimetral frame of the foot platform. The platform should be a little wider, to accommodate a wider stance than the designer of the Tru-Squat had anticipated squatters would use.

I was talking recently with a reader who was considering adding the bent-legged deadlift to his program. I pointed out that I am unable to bent-legged deadlift safely, but that I can stiff-legged deadlift safely, and prefer to perform it with a reduced range of motion—from knee height. He pointed out that he had had excellent experiences with the same movement. He also noted that he could

barbell squat safely and intensively, and that he liked the squat a lot. With the squat in the primary slot, and with the partial stiff-legged deadlift being a proven safe assistance exercise for him, why should he even consider incorporating an exercise that might be a positive addition, but which also might be a negative addition? Why not just stick with what has been proven to be successful?

If he could not squat well, then for sure he should give the bent-legged deadlift prime focus, especially the Trap Bar version, but why push his luck when he has got his thighs covered with the squat?

No book or article can teach you the personal "idiosyncrasies" you may have. They are things you come across only through experience. You have to combine intelligence, common sense and intuition, and go with what feels right and works best for you. This does not mean you should try any whim or fancy. It means sticking with a sensible program, and with any unique "customizing" that has proven to suit you. So long as it is safe, stick with what works best for you, even if you are doing something that runs contrary to what is supposedly the "best" way.

In the heat of a workout

During a summer 1998 workout I was performing warmup sets on my Tru-Squat machine. I was using my usual stance, with not-quite 20 inches between the insides of my heels, and toes well flared. I have this stance marked on the platform, for consistency of reproduction. Because this is quite a wide stance for someone of my height (5-9), and it means that my feet are bang on the perimetral frame of the machine's platform, I got this notion that I should narrow my stance a little. Caught up in the excitement of a workout, I acted. I brought my heels in, narrowing my stance by about three inches. This placed my feet inside the frame of the platform. The 20 reps went perfectly, and even felt a tad less demanding than the previous week's. I even had half a kilo more iron on the weight carriage. My knees felt fine, and I was delighted.

The next day my knees started aching, and my satisfaction from the previous day turned into annoyance at my having changed a stance that was working well. I suffered several days of real discomfort.

It was not until ten days later that my knees felt back to normal. I usually squat once every seventh day. This time I waited sixteen days. Then I returned to my usual stance, with a further half kilo on the bar. The set went well and I suffered no delayed-onset soreness. Seven days later I squatted again, with a further half kilo of added weight, and again it went well with no delayed-onset soreness.

On hindsight, to adjust one's squat stance by three inches and continue to use one's best working poundage, is foolish even if there is no history of knee problems. But for someone with my knee track record, such a substantial adjustment was madness. In the heat of the workout while gearing up for the 20-rep squat, I was oblivious to the foolishness.

Whenever you make adjustments to your form, no matter how minor they may appear, do it in an incremental and progressive way, and never while using your working weights. The more of a history of physical problems and injuries you have, the more careful you need to be. I paid the price with a period of discomfort, and one missed squatting session. I could have paid a much heavier price.

One of the rules I would not even think of tinkering with, is heel elevation. To ensure that I have zero elevation of my heels, I only squat bare foot. This is practical because I train in my own home gym. If I was training in a public gym I would wear shoes with zero heel elevation. Elevating the heels, even through the heel of a shoe, increases the stress on my knees to intolerable levels.

I could still try a closer stance, and do it progressively, but I am not going to bother. What I am doing is working well, so why tinker with it? The greed for "the more" is ever present; so watch out for it in your own training! Slow and steady progress is the target. If that is happening, then stick with it for a period of a year or two, and then you will see substantial progress. Try to hasten the progress, and though you might succeed, the more likely result will be that you disrupt the slow but steady progress. The greed to speed things up too often ends in killing progress, and producing injury. Especially watch out for training too often, adding weight too quickly, including unnecessary exercises, and adding bodyweight too fast. But the irony is that the "slow and steady" approach is the fast way over the long term. It is sure, safe and practical. And that is what sensible training is all about.

A "miracle"

For at least fifteen years, my left shoulder has been nearly an inch higher than the right. I never thought much of it. Over recent years, since discovering in 1992 that I suffer from "borderline serious" scoliosis, I thought that the shoulder tilt was a side effect of my unusually curved spine. The shoulder tilt was very noticeable, and a T-shirt always looked to have been pulled over to one side.

In 1998, HARDGAINER author Mike Thompson paid a visit to Nicosia, along with a friend. Kevin, a dentist with an interest in healing skills, had learned some techniques from a chiropractor he had seen at work. Kevin noticed I had a hip tilt—one hip higher than the other. Because my hips were tilted laterally, so were my shoulders.

Kevin had me lay face down on the veranda table, and performed a minute or two of work on my lower back and the area at the base of my sternum. What he did, I learned afterwards, was to normalize the nerve flow to balance the musculature of my body, as well as normalize my "chi." (Chi is the vital life force in the body that is regulated by, for example, acupuncture.)

After the minute or two of work, and absolutely no forceful noise-making adjustments, I stood up and looked at the reflection on one of the veranda glass doors. I was stunned! For the first time I could remember, my shoulders were horizontal. For the few days following the correction I gazed in a bathroom mirror in utter amazement at my properly lined up shoulders. The reflection of the bathroom tiles provides a "grid" I used to check my shoulder alignment. Nearly a year later, my shoulders were still perfectly aligned, and I had had no further work on my hips. And since the day of adjustment, T-shirts have laid on my shoulders symmetrically.

I trained a few days after the adjustment, and was shocked to discover I had "lost" so much strength. I had cut the poundages back to about 85%, but 85% for the usual reps felt harder than my previous week's 100% weights. Not only that, but I experienced post-workout pain in my knees. I was depressed, and regretted Kevin's work.

Though the corrective adjustments seemed so minor, the effect on my body was major. My body went into shock and was inhibiting my strength. My body had major neuromuscular adjustments and realignment to make. New "grooves" had to be adjusted to for each exercise. And slightly changed stresses in joints, especially my knees, had to be adapted to. Over about 6–8 weeks my strength came back, and the knee problems faded away. Then I was back to normal, but with properly aligned hips and shoulders, less pronounced scoliosis and, I believe, a better potential for sustained gains and a reduced probability of degenerative changes to my spine as the years go by. I am very happy that Mike and Kevin paid their visit.

If you have tilted hips—especially noticeable if the tilt is a lateral one—and/or shoulders that are tilted, seek a chiropractor for possible correction. Chiropractors, however, vary in their competence and areas of special interests, and only some are trained in the normalizing of chi. You may need to hunt around to find a really good one. A good chiropractor is a miracle worker!

Clearing up mixed messages

I never recommend that anyone trains in an explosive way (unless he is a highly skilled Olympic-style weightlifter), or uses high-risk exercises, or goes to muscular failure at the expense of good form.

I know, however, that some people train in a very risky manner on a regular basis, and do so relatively safely. *But they are the exceptions.* More important is the fact that most people who persist with explosive training, high-risk movements, and form liberties are racked with injuries.

I would never touch the odd-object lifting that some people encourage. And neither would I ever consider doing any explosive lifting even with barbells or dumbbells. My body has limitations due to my having used explosive lifting and loose form in the past. I am living proof of what happens if you abuse exercise. Had I not abused exercise so much in the past I would be able to use a wider range of exercises now than I actually can, but even then I would still not use high-risk exercises.

There are exceptions to every rule, but those exceptions should not be presented as role models for the rest of us. I tried to copy such role models, and paid a heavy price.

I am not keen on singles or very low reps, and never use them myself; but I know they can be safe for some people so long as perfect form is used, and absolute limit weights are not used very often.

Not performing presses behind neck, barbell rows, rock-bottom squats, stiff-legged deadlifts from an elevated surface, cleans, jerks, snatches, odd-object lifts, or any type of explosive exercise, does not mean that the individual concerned is less of a training devotee than someone who can do those exercises. And not being willing to go to muscular failure at the expense of safe exercise form does not indicate a wimpish character.

The most sensible approach is to train safely for the *long term*. For nearly everyone that means avoidance of all explosive lifting, sloppy form and high-risk exercises. The conservative way is the best way.

Many coaches are naturally more robust than are typical trainees, *because those coaches are not typical hard gainers.*

Because they can get way with various liberties, they usually apply the same approach to their training charges. But I am a typical hard gainer, so I know the score for hard gainers.

A surprising number of coaches give excellent advice in their writings and lectures regarding the use of controlled exercise form and the avoidance of explosive movements, but then in practice they allow great liberties with form and rep speed. I have witnessed this glaring contradiction both in person and on video recordings, and have been shocked. Watch out for this contradiction, and be sure to follow the recommendations for controlled exercise form and rep speed.

Some coaches, however, suffer from serious injuries as the result of their years of training bravado, and are now shadows of their former selves. They have learned the hard way of the perils of taking training liberties. Do not learn by the same route!

But what if you do get injured?

Before I gave exercise technique the pivotal priority it merits, I took many liberties in my training. As a result I paid a heavy price in terms of injuries, just like countless others have. The recovery from serious injuries taught me two major things—the importance of not getting injured in the first place, and how to speed up the recovery period should an injury be sustained. Like so many other people, I wasted years of my training life because I did not apply the techniques and know-how that are needed for speedy recovery. What I learned in order to produce a near miracle in recovery is detailed in Chapter 18 of BEYOND BRAWN—*"How a training nightmare was silenced." The healing technique described there is little known in the training world. In fact, hardly anyone seems to have heard about it, and as a result countless people are suffering unnecessarily from slow- or even apparently impossible-to-heal injuries. That chapter has proven to be one of the most influential in* BEYOND BRAWN, *and undoubtedly can help you to recover from injury as quickly as possible.*

Take charge!

Having arrived at the end of this book you can now master one of the most pivotal aspects of successful training—exercise technique. But a wealth of helpful information counts for nothing unless you act on it. Make it real by your own conscientious, disciplined, committed and so-very-serious application. *Take charge!*

You have a book to refer to again and again to ensure that you consistently deliver the good exercise form needed to maximize your training gains. And you have made a connection with me that I want to cement. This can help ensure that you never go off the rails of effective training.

While this book is thorough on technique, it provides no information on program design. Even excellent exercise technique will not deliver the results you want unless it is combined with a good training program. See pages 211–212 for details of how I can assist you with program design. If you are serious about making the most of your bodybuilding and strength potential, keeping in touch with me is in your best interest. It will spare you from wasting your time and money on inferior or even useless training strategies.

I wish you much training success, and look forward to hearing from you.

Your input, please

All books have room for improvement. Please provide some feedback to help improve this book in a future edition. Let me know of any typos and errors that you may find, and feel free to make any suggestions on how to improve the book.

Stuart McRobert
CS Publishing Ltd.
P.O. Box 20390
CY-2151 Nicosia
Cyprus

e-mail: cspubltd@spidernet.com.cy

Action, not words!
Put what you learn from this book into disciplined practice. Please do not just study this book, learn how to train with excellent exercise technique, but then not actually apply the mass of learning. Life is too short to waste a moment more. Let go of the unproductive ways— time is pressing!

Physique analysis

The bodybuilding world in particular is notorious for exaggerating measurements. Here is a fiction-free analysis of the bodybuilder used to illustrate this book. Though Constantinos Demetriou is a large and lean man, most of his girths are smaller than those *claimed* by many bodybuilders who are really about the same size as Con.

Unless noted otherwise, all muscular girths were relaxed when measured, and taken at the largest circumferences. They were taken on February 4, 1996, at the end of the period over which the photographs were taken for this book. But Constantinos was not "ripped" at the time because he was three weeks away from peaking for a bodybuilding contest.

Wrist, elbow, knee and ankle girths were taken at their smallest circumferences, with the surrounding musculature relaxed.

Neck: 18"
Shoulder girth: 54"
Shoulder width: 23"
Chest: 47½"
Waist (contracted): 34½"
Hips: 39"
Upper thigh: 25½"
Lower thigh (5" above center of knee): 22½"
Calf: 17"
Upper arm: 17" (hanging), 18" (flexed)
Forearm (arm straight, hand clenched): 14½"
Wrist (hand side of bony prominence): 7½"
Hand (tip of middle finger, to wrist): 7¾"
Elbow: 12¾"
Ankle: 10"
Knee: 15"
Height: 5' 10½"
Bodyweight: 229 lbs (104 kgs)

I took all the girths myself and verify them as being true and accurate.
— Stuart McRobert

Biographical sketch

Con was born in Sydney, Australia, in 1972. He grew up on his father's farm at Orchard Hills, one hour's drive west of Sydney. A very gifted athlete, he reached state level in New South Wales in athletics, swimming, cross-country running, and gymnastics.

He took up bodybuilding in 1988, age 16, and discovered an exceptional natural talent for it. After only nine months of training he won the 1989 Teenage Mr. Australia. In 1992, and 50 lbs heavier, he won the Junior Mr. Australia title. Then just three years later he won the heavyweight division and overall Mr. Australia title.

Resources

In alphabetical order here is a limited list of suppliers and manufacturers of the training equipment recommended in this book.

Bars and plates

1. IronMind® Enterprises, Inc., P.O. Box 1228, Nevada City, CA 95959, USA (916-265-6725)
2. Watson Gym Equipment, Unit 8, Washington Road, West Wiltshire Trading Estate, Westbury, Wiltshire BA13 4JP, England (01373 859617)
3. York® Barbell Company, Box 1707, York, PA 17405, USA (717-767-6481)

Cambered bar

1. IronMind® Enterprises, Inc., P.O. Box 1228, Nevada City, CA 95959, USA (916-265-6725)
2. Watson Gym Equipment, Unit 8, Washington Road, West Wiltshire Trading Estate, Westbury, Wiltshire BA13 4JP, England (01373 859617)

General heavy-duty equipment

1. Custom Weightrooms, 2851 Barber Rd., Hastings, MI 49058, USA (616-945-3388)
2. IronMind® Enterprises, Inc., P.O. Box 1228, Nevada City, CA 95959, USA (916-265-6725)
3. Johnny Gibson Gym Equipment Co., 11 South Sixth Ave., Tucson, AZ 85701, USA (520-622-1275)
4. Watson Gym Equipment, Unit 8, Washington Road, West Wiltshire Trading Estate, Westbury, Wiltshire BA13 4JP, England (01373 859617)

Little discs

1. PDA, 104 Bangor Street, Mauldin, SC, 29662, USA (864-963-5640)

2. Watson Gym Equipment, Unit 8, Washington Road, West Wiltshire Trading Estate, Westbury, Wiltshire BA13 4JP, England (01373 859617)

Magnetic little discs

PlateMates®, Benoit Built, Inc., 12 Factory Cove Road, Boothbay Harbor, ME 04538, USA (207-633-5912, 800-877-3322)

Shrug bar (trap bar alternative)

1. PDA, 104 Bangor Street, Mauldin, SC, 29662, USA (864-963-5640)
2. Watson Gym Equipment, Unit 8, Washington Road, West Wiltshire Trading Estate, Westbury, Wiltshire BA13 4JP, England (01373 859617)

See page 27 for a note about trap and shrug bars.

Thick bars

1. IronMind® Enterprises, Inc., P.O. Box 1228, Nevada City, CA 95959, USA (916-265-6725)
2. Watson Gym Equipment, Unit 8, Washington Road, West Wiltshire Trading Estate, Westbury, Wiltshire BA13 4JP, England (01373 859617)

Tru-Squat

Southern Xercise, Inc., P.O. Box 412, Cleveland, TN 37364, USA (423-476-8999, 800-348-4907)

Contact the companies you are interested in, and request their catalogs. Some suppliers only send catalogs to inquirers from the same country in which they are based.

A local metal worker can be a great ally. Even one who has no experience of making exercise gear can economically produce simple pieces made to your specifications.

HARDgainer

the path to physical excellence

bastion of no-nonsense drug-free training

FREE magazine!

Published by Stuart McRobert since 1989, HARDGAINER is probably the most instruction-dense, drug-free, bull-free and hype-free training magazine on the market today, providing more practical and result-producing advice for drug-free bodybuilders and strength trainees than is available in any other magazine. It's crammed with practical advice and nuggets of wisdom to lead you to training success.

Here's some of what to expect from HARDGAINER. You'll get the undiluted truth—no exaggerated claims filled with puffery. What we say may not always sit easily with you. But you can count on one thing—it will be frank and down-to-earth. As the title implies, we speak to hard-gaining typical individuals—people like you. But average potential doesn't have to mean average achievements. In fact, an impressive physique and a terrific level of strength are well within your reach. The key is in the right approach. That's what HARDGAINER is about.

A 12-month/6-issue subscription costs US $29.95 (or UK £18.95), and a 24-month/12-issue subscription costs US $54.95 (or UK £34.95).

You don't have to take our word for HARDGAINER being probably the most instruction-dense, practical, drug-free, bull-free and hype-free training magazine on the market. Write in and we'll send you a FREE sample copy of the magazine, with no strings attached.

HARDGAINER is a subscription-only magazine. You won't find it at newsstands. *So write in today, and grab yourself a free growing experience!*

Please send me a free sample copy of HARDGAINER.

Name _____

Address _____

_____

Code/zip and country _____

CS Publishing Ltd., P.O. Box 20390, CY-2151 Nicosia, Cyprus

This book's three companion texts...

This book is part two of the series of four interrelated texts that make up **The Muscle & Might Master Method.** While each book can stand alone as an excellent instructional tool in its own right, *together* they provide the most complete and *responsible* package of instruction for achieving physique and strength goals. The four interrelated books are ...

1. **BEYOND BRAWN**
2. **THE INSIDER'S TELL-ALL HANDBOOK ON WEIGHT-TRAINING TECHNIQUE**
3. **THE MUSCLE & MIGHT TRAINING TRACKER**
4. **FURTHER BRAWN**

No Drugs, No Hype, No Bull & No Irresponsible or Impractical Training Routines. Instead, *AN HONEST APPROACH TO YOUR TRAINING*

Stuart McRobert's Muscle & Might Master Method is a series of interrelated instructional materials. You can use each component part separately—but to get the most out of your training, use them all together as an integrated whole. Though Stuart didn't "invent" the various parts of The Master Method, he put them together into a cohesive, interrelated, detailed and easy-to-learn whole.

The Master Method is a responsible and individualistic approach, not a "one size fits all" one. For busy people of average genetic endowment, who are serious about their training but have a life outside of the gym, there really isn't any other choice. And there's no risk—our publications are BACKED BY AN UNCONDITIONAL MONEY-BACK GUARANTEE.

The core of The Master Method: *BEYOND BRAWN*

Published in 1998, this encyclopedia contains the essential core of The Master Method. It will put you on the road to your bodybuilding and strength-training revolution. *BEYOND BRAWN: The Insider's Encyclopedia on How to Build Muscle & Might* is 496 pages crammed with information about every facet of bodybuilding, and weight training in general.

If you don't think that *BEYOND BRAWN* is the most practical, detailed, relevant and helpful book of its kind, return it for a no-questions-asked refund.

BEYOND BRAWN is essential for anyone who is serious about effective and long-term training to improve physique, strength and health. It will provide a lifetime of valuable help, no matter whether you're just beginning training or have been working out for years, whether you're male or female, young or not-so-young, in great shape or finally ready to get rid of the flab and build a terrific physique.

"This book has my highest endorsement—it is without a doubt the very best book on strength training I have ever read."
– Kevin R. Fontaine, Ph.D., Johns Hopkins University School of Medicine

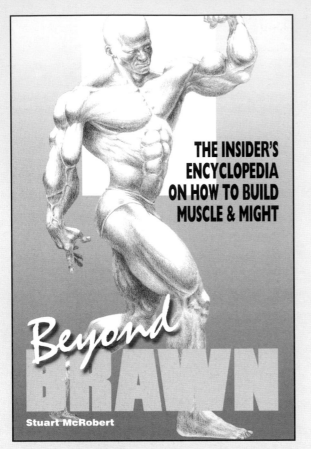

496 pages
22 chapters
21-page index

BEYOND BRAWN
is available in both
softcover and deluxe
hardcover editions.

McRobert is direct, frank and on the mark. He's not ashamed to discuss tough issues, such as his own crippling injuries in the early 90s—and how he overcame them. The lessons you can learn from that section of the book alone, to ensure you never have to suffer like Stuart did, are worth *many* times the price of *BEYOND BRAWN*.

"*BEYOND BRAWN is the book we all wish we had years ago. It is an absolute MUST READ.*"
– Richard A. Winett, Ph.D., Publisher, MASTER TRAINER

"*BEYOND BRAWN is the definitive Encyclopedia on Bodybuilding—a superb book that is truly very special.*"
– Bill Piche, triple bodyweight deadlifter in drug-free competition

"*BEYOND BRAWN is the greatest book ever written on how to train with weights. And it is the greatest book ever written on how TO LAST while training with weights. It is the greatest—period!*"
– Dick Conner, 25-year-plus proprietor of The Pit

"*BEYOND BRAWN...provides real-life insight along with amazingly in-depth solutions to the great many problems and obstacles which dog trainees of all levels of experience...I recommend it unreservedly.*"
– Mike Thompson, a drug-free training veteran for over 35 years

"*BEYOND BRAWN is the most comprehensive, helpful and honest book on natural strength training today.*"
– Bob Whelan, M.S., M.S., C.S.C.S., President, Whelan Strength Training

Unlike most other training books, BEYOND BRAWN acknowledges your individuality, and teaches you precisely how to train yourself. Become your own *expert* personal trainer! Building a terrific drug-free physique is simpler than you may think. This 496-page encyclopedia will show you how.

How to track your training progress

BEYOND BRAWN is best used with its two companion volumes—*THE INSIDER'S TELL-ALL HANDBOOK ON WEIGHT-TRAINING TECHNIQUE* and *THE MUSCLE & MIGHT TRAINING TRACKER*.

    THE MUSCLE & MIGHT TRAINING TRACKER is a 136-page workbook which contains everything you need in order to track your progress, day by day, month by month, and year by year. The systematic organization and focus upon achieving goals that an intelligently designed training journal enforces, will help you to improve your physique steadily and consistently. As simple as it is to use a training log, do not underestimate the critical role this can play in helping you to maximize your training productivity.

The Muscle & Might Training Tracker

Stuart McRobert

One training log will track your bodybuilding and strength-training progress for at least 24 months—that's a cost of just $1.00 per month. And this log is built for the job it's designed to do. *This is no ordinary training diary.*

    The log pages cover not only the specifics of your weight training routines—what exercises, how long you performed them, and a comment area to note your performance and any issues you need to address—but also nutrition, sleep and body composition.

1. This book lets you track your progress for at least two years

2. Big pages provide plenty of room for entering data

3. Robust paper provides the strength to withstand heavy use

4. Spiral binding enables book to open flat for easy use

5. Design enables you to track your training AND recovery

USE THIS TRAINING LOG TO GET IN CHARGE OF YOUR PROGRESS

Most trainees are aware that they should record their workouts in a permanent way, but few actually do it. Even those trainees who keep some sort of training log usually fail to exploit its full potential benefits. This is one of the major reasons why most trainees get minimal results from their training. *This book will make your data keeping easy.*

Further BRAWN

OVER 230
QUESTIONS
& ANSWERS ON
HOW TO BUILD
MUSCLE & MIGHT

Stuart McRobert

320 pages . . . answers to over 230 questions

FURTHER BRAWN **is available in both softcover and deluxe hardcover editions.**

Through our other books we tried to provide all the information needed to achieve lifelong bodybuilding and strength-training success. But over time we found there were questions that had slipped through unanswered. That's when we decided we had an obligation to address those questions, fill in the gaps, provide further information and wisdom, and in turn reinforce trainees' understanding of what it takes to hit the success target.

Many of your unanswered questions are answered in *FURTHER BRAWN* even if you've read our other books.

Index

An illustrated item is identified by the suffix *illus* and usually has text related to it on the same page. Two types of cross-references are used in this index. The *see* references refer you to the specific key words or phrases under which you can find the required information. The *see also* references are used where *additional* information can be found in another entry or subentry. *Resources* have not been indexed.

How to train hard but with discipline

You may find visualizations helpful. Try the following and see if they help. The essence of training well is to work hard, without rushing, and while holding good form. Good form means perfect technique *plus* a controlled rep tempo. Executing this demands great discipline. It is not about just banging out reps to failure.

With the bar loaded for a work set, switch onto training mode. Switch off from your life. "Become" your training. *Nothing else matters now.* Visualize huge muscles and power to spare to complete your set.

Perform the set one rep at a time. Look no further than the current rep. Do not rush. *Use perfect exercise form.*

When the discomfort intensifies, dissociate yourself from it. Imagine you are watching yourself on film. Push on. Do not rush. *Use perfect exercise form.*

Regroup your thoughts during the brief pause between reps. Remind yourself of how much you want a stronger and better physique. Keep the reps coming. Do not rush. *Use perfect exercise form.*

To be able to train hard is a privilege. Remind yourself of this during the between-rep pauses. Think of people less privileged than you—those in nursing homes, and those in graves. Resolve not to quit before you are spent. Forge on. *Use perfect exercise form.*

As the set nears completion, and you are at your hilt, visualize a vivid life-or-death situation where if you fail to make the rep, you die. Then squeeze out a rep or few more. *But use perfect exercise form.*

Training hard is no excuse for getting sloppy with exercise form. *In fact, the harder you train the more important that good form is.* Remember, intensity *together* with disciplined good form is what successful training is about, not just banging out reps to failure.

visit us online at www.hardgainer.com